John A. Broadus

A LIVING LEGACY

EDITED BY
DAVID S. DOCKERY
AND ROGER D. DUKE

STUDIES IN BAPTIST LIFE AND THOUGHT
MICHAEL A. G. HAYKIN, SERIES EDITOR

NASHVILLE, TENNESSEE

John A. Broadus: A Living Legacy
Copyright © 2008 by David S. Dockery and Roger D. Duke

Published by B & H Publishing Group
Nashville, Tennessee

ISBN: 978–0–8054–4738–5

Dewey Decimal Classification: 286.092
Subject Heading: BROADUS, JOHN A. \
BAPTISTS—BIOGRAPHY

Printed in the United States of America

1 2 3 4 5 6 7 8 9 10 11 12 • 16 15 14 13 12 11 10 09 08
VP

In Memoriam

John Albert Broadus
1827–1895

He has set for us an example (Titus 2:7) . . .
As Preacher, Teacher, Scholar,
Churchman, and Denominational Statesman

Contents

Contents

List of Contributors

Craig Christina, Pastor, First Baptist Church, Jackson, Tennessee

David S. Dockery, President, Union University, Jackson, Tennessee

Roger D. Duke, Assistant Professor of Religion and Communication, Baptist College of Health Sciences, Memphis, Tennessee and Adjunct Assistant Professor of Christian Studies, Union University

A. James Fuller, Associate Professor of History, University of Indianapolis, Indianapolis, Indiana

Timothy George, Founding Dean, Beeson Divinity School, Samford University, Birmingham, Alabama

Beecher Johnson, Pastor, Emmanuel Baptist Church, Raleigh, North Carolina

Richard Melick, Professor of New Testament and Director, Ph.D. Program, Golden Gate Baptist Theological Seminary, Mill Valley, California

Thomas J. Nettles, Professor of Historical Theology, The Southern Baptist Theological Seminary, Louisville, Kentucky

Mark M. Overstreet, Vice President and Assistant Professor of Communication and Leadership, Criswell College, Dallas, Texas

James Patterson, Professor of Christian Studies, Associate Dean, School of Christian Studies, Union University, Jackson, Tennessee

Series Preface

This new series of studies on the history of Baptists, our life together, and our thought, is vital reading for anyone who loves the truths for which Baptists have lived and died. Given the many significant changes that the world is undergoing in our day, Baptists are being tempted to divorce themselves from their theological and spiritual roots. Behind this series is the conviction that such would be suicidal and that the volumes in this series will provide a way for Baptists to learn from the past how to live faithfully for God in the present.

One of the great gifts that God has given the Southern Baptists is their seminary in Louisville, Kentucky. John Albert Broadus, the second president of the seminary, was one of the four men who constituted its founding faculty and who proved to be a tower of strength to the seminary throughout the school's first four decades. On the verge of the sesquicentennial of the school's founding, it is only right to reflect afresh on the significance of the life and ministry of this profound and passionate preacher-scholar. This superb collection of studies, rooted as they are in solid scholarship and love for the body of churches that Broadus faithfully served, provides Southern Baptists—and all interested in Baptist life in nineteenth-century

America—with the resources for such a reflection. May these studies ultimately lead to rejoicing over what God's grace can do in and through the life of a redeemed sinner.

Michael A. G. Haykin

Professor of Church History and Biblical Spirituality,
The Southern Baptist Theological Seminary,
Louisville, Kentucky, and

Research Professor of Irish Baptist College,
Constituent College of Queen's University
Belfast, Northern Ireland

Preface

A new work on the life and legacy of John Albert Broadus (1827–1895) is long overdue. Shortly after his death, his son-in-law, A. T. Robertson, considered by many to be the finest scholar in Southern Baptist history, compiled a tribute to Broadus, *The Life and Letters of John A. Broadus* (American Baptist Publication Society, 1901). Robertson also wrote an important piece on "Broadus as Scholar and Preacher" (1923). Apart from the works of Broadus, himself, Robertson has provided the best window for us to get a glimpse of Broadus. About Broadus, Robertson said, "No man has ever stirred my nature as Broadus did in the classroom and the pulpit."

Over the last century a variety of articles have appeared in the *Review and Expositor*, among other places, on the multifaceted contributions of Broadus. Former Southern Seminary president, W. H. Whitsitt, and W. J. McGlothlin, former president of Furman University, contributed biographical articles in 1907 and in 1930. Articles reflecting on the history of Southern Seminary, which appeared in 1985, included discussion about Broadus and New Testament studies by J. Estill Jones, and Broadus and preaching by James Cox. Walter Elwell's collection of *Bible Interpreters of the Twentieth Century: A Selection of Evangelical Voices* (Baker, 1999) included an important chapter on Broadus as a transitional figure from the nineteenth to twentieth centuries.

Southern Baptists often know of John A. Broadus as one of the founding faculty members and the second president of The Southern Baptist Theological Seminary. Pastors and preachers know of Broadus through his classic work, *A Treatise on the Preparation and Delivery of Sermons* (1870). New Testament expositors and scholars have long looked to the *Commentary on the Gospel of Matthew* in the American Commentary Series (1886) as a premier example of faithful biblical interpretation. The volume that you hold in your hand introduces us to Broadus in all of those areas and more. Broadus serves as a model for us today as author, teacher, preacher, scholar, seminary leader, and denominational statesman.

A Living Legacy approaches the study of Broadus as one "mighty in the Scriptures," for he has long been recognized as such by preachers and New Testament scholars alike. This work also takes a look at Southern Baptists' premier nineteenth-century scholar from the vantage point of churchman, institution builder, and denominational statesman. Some of the chapters dealing with the various aspects of Broadus's life and work tend to overlap. We have chosen, as editors, to allow such overlap to stand so that each chapter can be read on its own. Though we want to encourage readers to read all the chapters, we believe that readers can greatly profit from the book without necessarily reading it sequentially from beginning to end.

The time is right to revisit Broadus as we approach the 150th anniversary of the founding of The Southern Baptist Theological Seminary. Moreover, as Southern Baptists seek to reestablish a new consensus to move forward in the twenty-first century, Broadus is an example of balance, careful thinking, biblical faithfulness, and denominational statesmanship (Titus 2:7). We trust that in God's good providence a new generation will both learn from and about Broadus.

We are grateful for the guidance of Ray Clendenen, Terry Wilder, and the staff of B&H Publishing Group throughout this project. Cindy Meredith has offered much help for this work, and we express our deep appreciation to her, as well as to Melanie Rickman. We want to acknowledge the love, support, and encouragement provided by our families. We thank God for them. For the contributors who have joined us in this project, we are most grateful. We are thankful for their spirit of cooperation and their excitement about the book. Together we present this volume with the hope and prayer that God will use John A. Broadus once again as a model in so many areas for Southern Baptists and Evangelicals as we serve in the twenty-first century. We offer this work to the glory of God, for the advancement of the gospel, and for the building up of the church of Jesus Christ.

Soli Deo Gloria,
David S. Dockery
Roger D. Duke

Chapter I

Introduction to
John A. Broadus:
A Living Legacy

Timothy George

U ntil quite recently, John Albert Broadus (1827–1895), one of the most formative shapers of American Christianity in the nineteenth century, has been relegated to the realm of affectionate obscurity. His name is known to historians as a pioneer in theological education, a popular Baptist preacher, and a biblical scholar of note. He was also the second president of the first Baptist seminary in the South of which he was a founding faculty member. But such facts alone do not capture the heart of the man. Sadly, an entire century of several generations that "knew not John" has come and gone. Nearly 115 years after his death, it is time to revisit the legacy of John Albert Broadus, a titanic figure in the history of the evangelical church and a prince of the pulpit who, in his own day, "girdled the globe with his influence."[1]

---

[1] A statement by F. H. Kerfoot at a memorial service for Broadus held in Washington in connection with a meeting of the Southern Baptist Convention. Quoted, A. T. Robertson, *Life and Letters of John Albert Broadus* (Philadelphia: American Baptist Publication Society, 1901), 438.

1

I myself first discovered the brooding presence of John Albert Broadus in 1979 when I moved to Louisville to teach at The Southern Baptist Theological Seminary. Occasionally one of the older professors would mention Broadus in a chapel sermon or hallway conversation. Some of them had studied under teachers who had known Broadus personally. In those days the portraits of all the seminary presidents were mounted in a sitting area known as Broadus Lounge. All of the portraits were impressive, of course—Boyce the cavalier, Whitsitt the scholar, Mullins the visionary, Sampey the stalwart, Fuller the churchman, McCall the administrator—but Broadus's portrait was somehow different. There was something pensive, wistful about the likeness it portrayed. One was drawn to Broadus— his gentle eyes, his humble demeanor, his noble bearing, his spiritual depth, his kindly countenance. Near his portrait was a plaque inscribed with the famous words Broadus had uttered in 1865 when it seemed that the Seminary would not be able to go on after its collapse at the end of the Civil War: "Suppose we quietly agree that the Seminary may die, but we'll die first."[2]

During my ten years on the faculty at Louisville, I would often take my students to Cave Hill Cemetery. Here, secluded in a beautiful glen, was a special burial plot where Broadus was laid to rest next to his friend James Petigru Boyce, near the graves of John R. Sampey, Basil Manly Jr., A. T. Robertson, and other great leaders of the school. Sometimes I would give lectures around the tombstones reminding the students of the admonition inscribed on the tomb of Governor William Bradford (1588–1657) at Plymouth, Massachusetts: *qua patres difficillime adepti sunt nolite turpiter relinquere,* "What our forefathers with so much difficulty secured, do not basely relinquish." The students sometimes referred jokingly to these "séances" in the graveyard, as such field trips were called, but they always came away with a deeper appreciation for the great saints buried there and the debt we owed to them all.

---

[2] John A. Broadus, *Memoir of James Petigru Boyce, DD., LL.D.* (New York: A. C. Armstrong and Son, 1893), 200.

But who was John A. Broadus? He was born on January 24, 1827, in Culpepper County, Virginia, some two weeks after Boyce, his future life partner in theological education, was born in Charleston, South Carolina. Unlike the latter, Broadus did not come from a wealthy family of grandees but rather from one of moderate means. Yet the Broaduses of Virginia were well-known for their integrity and great usefulness in public and religious life. His father, Major Edmund Broadus, had served in the Virginia legislature, and his great-uncle, Andrew Broaddus (spelled with two *d*'s) was a noted evangelist and orator of his day. Converted at a revival meeting, John A. Broadus was baptized at age 16 and called to preach several years later under the ministry of A. M. Poindexter.

In 1850 Broadus was called to be the pastor of the Charlottesville Baptist Church, one of the largest Baptist congregations in Virginia at this time. He also began to teach that year at his alma mater, the University of Virginia. During the next decade, Broadus became widely known throughout the Old Dominion and beyond both as a preacher and a scholar. In 1851 Broadus was invited to preach on a special occasion at the First Baptist Church of Richmond. One person who heard his sermon that day described the effect of his preaching: "No gush, no attempt at mannerism or display of learning: it was the pure gospel in simple, earnest, well-chosen diction and impressively delivered." This same person later said about Broadus that "he never allowed his reputation to outrun his ability or his merit."[3] William E. Hatcher, who would become a famous pastor himself, was a student at Richmond College when he first heard Broadus preach in 1857. His sermons were marked, Hatcher said, by "refined piety and the emotion of the Holy Spirit."[4] Clearly there was something both winsome and compelling about Broadus the preacher. It is not surprising that Broadus became such a popular preacher among the Confederate soldiers during the Civil War. Stonewall Jackson invited

---

[3] *Life and Letters*, 92.
[4] Ibid., 147.

him to address his troops in northern Virginia, and on one occasion Broadus preached to more than 5,000 men in the army of Robert E. Lee.

Andover Theological Seminary was established in 1807, the first such institution in America. Baptists entered the field of advanced theological education with the founding of Newton Theological Institute in 1825. Ten years later Basil Manly Sr. issued the first serious call for the establishment of a similar institution among Baptists in the South. This idea was debated vigorously among Baptist leaders in the South leading up to the opening of The Southern Baptist Theological Seminary in 1859. Broadus himself did not at first think well of the idea and published an article expressing his dissent in the *Religious Herald*. However, his developing friendship with James P. Boyce, together with the assignment he was given to develop a curricular plan for the new school, won out over his earlier objections. When Broadus was asked to join Boyce and two others on the seminary's first faculty, he faced a great dilemma. Perhaps the most difficult decision of Broadus's career was to leave his flourishing pastoral work in Charlottesville, and his teaching responsibilities at the University of Virginia that he loved so much, to accept the call to the fledgling new school in South Carolina. After much prayer and wavering, however, the decision was made and Broadus wrote to Boyce—*iacta est alea*, "The die is cast." In this commitment John Albert Broadus had found his life's work.

Broadus was a convinced Baptist and wrote prolifically on behalf of Baptist distinctives such as believers' baptism, religious liberty, and congregational polity. But he did so with a generous spirit and a breadth of wisdom not often found in the denominational apologetics of the era. As a young man in Virginia, Broadus married the daughter of a Methodist teacher and preached his first sermon in a Presbyterian pulpit. More than any other Southern Baptist leader of the nineteenth century, Broadus's appeal extended beyond the bounds of his own region and denomination. Brooks E. Holifield was right to include Broadus in his study of "the gentlemen theologians" who shaped the orthodox Southern religious mind in the decades leading up to the Civil War. But Broadus was also a luminal figure who bridged the polarities of North and South, rural and urban, elite culture and popular religion in the emerging evangelical consensus of the late nineteenth century. Broadus and Henry Drummond shared the same platform at D. L. Moody's Northfield Conference, and his correspondents included the likes of Philip Schaff, B. F. Westcott, and John R. Mott. The invitation Broadus received to deliver the influential Lyman Beecher Lectures on Preaching at Yale Divinity School in 1889 is a mark of the national stature he had attained in his mature years.

Broadus is rightly remembered as a master of the pulpit and a great teacher of homiletics. His enduring classic, *A Treatise on the Preparation and Delivery of Sermons*, which originated in lectures he gave to one blind student, has been a guide to generations of aspiring preachers and still remains in print! His facility with classical languages prepared him to write a major commentary on the Gospel of Matthew and to serve as an editor of the homilies of John Chrysostom in the Nicene and Post-Nicene Fathers series.

Still, Broadus's high scholarly attainments did nothing to diminish his passion for communicating the content of the Christian faith to all of God's people, including the children of the church. He was a great fan of Charles Haddon Spurgeon, whom he heard preach on several occasions. Like the great London pastor, he supported the use of catechisms in the religious instruction of children. When the Baptist Sunday School Board (now LifeWay Christian Resources) was organized in 1891, the first publication projected was *A Catechism of Bible Teaching* by John A. Broadus. Several years ago while I was serving as the interim pastor of a Baptist congregation in Birmingham, one of the elderly members in the church presented me with a first-edition copy of Broadus's catechism. It was worn with age and torn along the edges from many years of storage in her attic trunk. Her grandmother, she said, had used this catechism to acquaint her with the rudiments of the Christian faith many years before. We began a series of lessons in basic Christian doctrine organized around the questions and answers of Broadus's classic document. More than 100 years after Broadus's catechism first appeared in 1892, the clarity and power of its simple yet profound presentation of the gospel were still bearing fruit among the people of God called Baptists.

The time is long overdue for a modern critical biography of John Albert Broadus. The essays in this volume do not meet that need, nor do they cover in a comprehensive way every important aspect of Broadus's life and work. However, they do present fresh perspectives and new interpretations of one of the most important figures in Southern Baptist history. David S. Dockery, president of Union University and coeditor of this volume with Roger D. Duke, opens the volume with an overview of the lives of Broadus and his son-in-law, A. T. Robertson. Robertson is the greatest New Testament scholar Southern Baptists have ever produced, and his famous mega-grammar of New Testament Greek is a legendary volume in its own right. Dockery argues that the legacies of Broadus and Robertson should be seen as together constituting a discrete tradition of biblical scholarship in the service of the church. Some of the fruits of this tradition may be glimpsed in the pulpit work of the expositional preachers Herschel H. Hobbs and W. A. Criswell. Both were students of Robertson, and both served as major leaders among Southern Baptists in the second half of the twentieth century.

A. James Fuller is a careful historian of American Christianity who has earlier written a distinguished biography of Basil Manly Sr. In his chapter, "'The Way to Learn to Preach Is to Preach': John A. Broadus's Early Career and Influence," Fuller shows us how Broadus's early training and experience as a young preacher in Virginia shaped his later career and ministry. Broadus's conversion and call to the ministry were confirmed through his preaching experiences in various settings: at protracted meetings, in concerts of prayer, and his extemporaneous speaking to slaves and later to soldiers during the Civil War. These experiences, together with his superb academic training at the University of Virginia, laid the foundation for Broadus's future greatness.

Roger D. Duke, coeditor with David S. Dockery of this volume, presents a textured study of Broadus as a classicist and exemplar of rhetoric in the work of preaching. Using Broadus's *A Treatise on the Preparation and Delivery of Sermons* as the basis of his analysis, Duke shows how Broadus knew the categories of classical rhetoric (invention, arrangement, elocution, delivery, and memory) and intentionally adapted this paradigm for the task of proclamation. Of special interest here is the discussion of Broadus as an extemporaneous preacher, an approach which, as V. S. Stanfield once observed, made "each person in the audience feel that he was talking directly to him." In Duke's analysis Broadus comes across as a masterful communicator with great persuasive ability yet one who never allowed substance to be seduced by style.

In "New Wine in Broadus Wine Skins?" Rick Melick, a theological educator and New Testament scholar of note himself, poses the question, "How would Broadus fare in today's world of biblical scholarship?" Working primarily from Broadus's noted commentary on Matthew in An American Commentary on the New Testament, as well as his classic textbook on homiletics, Melick looks carefully at Broadus's use of the original languages of Scripture, his understanding of the authority of the biblical text, as well as his engagement with issues of textual criticism, biblical introduction, and exegesis. Melick also reviews how Broadus used rules of interpretation (hermeneutics) in his exposition of the Bible. Broadus emerges here as a prescient scholar of Scripture, often anticipating future trends and developments in biblical studies while ever resisting trajectories of destructive biblical criticism.

Craig C. Christina, who embodies the Broadus tradition as a pastor and scholar of preaching, explores the critical role Broadus played in the establishment of Southern Seminary. At every crisis the Seminary faced in its early history, he was indispensable in helping the struggling institution to overcome difficulties and establish firm foundations for the future. Christina traces Broadus's role in that formative period of the Seminary's life—from the debacle of the Civil War, through the financial panic of 1873, amidst the rigors of Reconstruction, through the difficult relocation from Greenville to Louisville, in the turmoil of the Toy Controversy, and the grief occasioned by the death of Boyce.

Boyce assumed the title of president only during his final year. Until then he was officially the chairman of the faculty. though Broadus became the Seminary's second "president" upon the death of Boyce, in many ways he continued to function more as the leader of a team than a company executive. Though clearly recognized by everyone as *primus inter pares*, he fostered a strong sense of collegiality and served as a personal mentor to the younger men on the faculty. Inscribed on the tomb of Boyce at Cave Hill Cemetery are Broadus's words of endearment to his "best and dearest friend" and this expression of his hopes for the future of the Seminary to which he, no less than Boyce, had devoted his life: "And may the men be always ready, as the years come and go, to carry on, with widening reach and heightened power, the work we sought to do, and did begin!"[5]

Mark M. Overstreet's chapter on Broadus's "lost" Yale lectures recounts his discovery of 193 pages of Broadus's handwritten notes, which fills an important gap in our knowledge about the 1889 Lyman Beecher Lectures on Preaching. Heretofore, Broadus's talks at Yale had been known from religious periodicals and summaries provided by reporters in the press of the day. Overstreet analyzes his contribution to homiletics by reviewing the recently discovered notes in light of the preaching program set forth in *A Treatise on the Preparation and Delivery of Sermons*. The content of Broadus's Beecher Lectures reveals a practical theologian at work dealing with the kinds of issues faced by every preacher every Sunday in the pulpit. Overstreet concludes

---

[5] Broadus, *Memoirs of Boyce*, 371.

that Broadus's performance in Marquand Chapel shows how the principles he had set forth with such clarity some twenty years earlier in the first edition of his classic homiletics textbook were confirmed and reinforced on this occasion.

Tom J. Nettles begins his discussion of *A Treatise on the Preparation and Delivery of Sermons* by recounting how Broadus was recently misused as the butt of an anecdote in a popular book on preaching. However, a careful reading of Broadus's discussion of preaching, not to say an honest review of his life and labors, would easily give the lie to anyone who claimed that such a great Scripture scholar and master of the pulpit would deliberately twist a text of the Bible in the way claimed. On the other hand, Nettles shows us a portrait of Broadus the preacher as he really was—ever concerned to be faithful to the text, aware of the special needs of the audience addressed, and mindful of the holy task assumed as a herald of God's good news. Nettles does a superb job of placing Broadus's great book in the context of his times, examining contemporary reviews, and also the continuing appeal this volume continues to have in the field of homiletics. Nettles also points out the close connection Broadus made between the character of the preacher and the message he proclaimed. Broadus himself emphasized the co-inherence of both in the closing words of his book:

> Nor must we e'er forget the power of character and life to reinforce speech. What a preacher is goes far to determine the effect of what he says. There is a saying of Augustine, *cuius vita fulgor, eius verba tonitrua*—if a man's life be lightning, his words are thunders.

Beecher L. Johnson takes an in-depth look at what might be called today Broadus's preaching style in his chapter, "How to Preach Marketable Messages without Selling out the Savior: Broadus on the Role of Sensationalism in Preaching." Johnson defines sensational preaching as "using any means to gain the ear of, or have an effect on, the audience that does not honor the sacred nature of God and the things of God or ensure singular focus on the spiritual and theological message of God in the text." It is not difficult to find numerous examples of sensational preaching defined as such in the evangelical church of today. Broadus, however, regarded such techniques as a form of peddling the gospel, and he had no sympathy for them. It is one thing to have one's "fancy charmed" by a sermon and quite another to be moved by the Spirit in response to the clear delineation of gospel truth. At the same time, while Broadus repudiated anything that smacked of gimmickry or showmanship in the pulpit, he never used this principle as an excuse for preaching dull, boring sermons. While I hope every chapter of this book will be read and digested carefully, this one should be made required reading for every course in homiletics!

James Patterson is a distinguished historian and professor of Christian studies at Union University. In his concluding chapter to this volume, "Broadus's Living Legacy," Patterson provides a good summary of the themes presented in the earlier essays. He shows how Broadus casts a long shadow across Southern Baptist life in his roles as theological educator, denominational statesman, biblical scholar, and advocate of faithful expository preaching. Patterson also develops a theme not fully explored in earlier essays but one with continuing relevance today: Broadus as defender of biblical orthodoxy. While always embracing a humble and irenic spirit, Broadus was well aware of the spiritual and theological erosion inherent in liberal theology. While still a pastor in Charlottesville, Broadus had baptized Crawford Howell Toy and later befriended and encouraged the younger scholar as a junior member of the faculty. Yet Broadus stood solidly with Boyce when Toy's acceptance of destructive biblical criticism forced his departure from the Seminary. Patterson also rightly presents Broadus as standing squarely within the Reformed tradition, embracing the kind of missions-minded evangelical Calvinism of Andrew Fuller, William Carey, and Charles H. Spurgeon. Broadus avoided the extremes of hyper-Calvinism on the one hand and a pelagianizing decisionism on the other. He thus remains a good model for Baptists today who seek in faithfulness to Scripture to stress both divine sovereignty and human responsibility in proclaiming the glories of God's grace.

When John Albert Broadus died in 1895, tributes came streaming in from around the world. One of those who spoke at his funeral was P. S. Henson of Chicago who, as a young man, had first heard the great preacher in Virginia many years before. The words Henson offered in Louisville's Walnut Street Baptist Church that day still ring true today:

> He is gone, but his light is not out. There are stars so far away that if they were blotted out they would still shine on for a hundred years. So will Broadus continue to shine. He will live in your hearts and in other hearts all over the world. When Moses died the people wept, and well they might, for there was but one Moses. But lo! Joshua comes, and the walls of Jericho fall down, and the Promised Land becomes the heritage of God's people. Elijah is taken up, but his mantle falls on Elisha. So God's work goes on.[6]

---

[6] *Life and Letters*, 436.

Chapter II

Mighty in the Scriptures:
John A. Broadus and His Influence
on A. T. Robertson and
Southern Baptist Life

David S. Dockery

One of the most influential streams of thought impacting and influencing Baptist theology for the last 140 years developed from the life and work of John A. Broadus and his son-in-law, A. T. Robertson. From these two giants, brilliant in every way and mighty in the Scriptures, came a devotion to biblical exegesis, expositional preaching, and church-focused theology. Throughout the twentieth century this tradition shaped seminary and college classrooms in Baptist life but moreover influenced hundreds of pulpits across the land. We will begin this chapter with a look at the life and work of John A. Broadus.

Life and Work

John Albert Broadus was born January 24, 1827, in Culpepper County, Virginia. When he died on March 16, 1895, he was regarded as one of North America's most capable Christian scholars of the nineteenth century and certainly one of the world's greatest preachers. Almost three decades after Broadus's death, his greatest student, A. T. Robertson, reflected:

> The world has never seemed the same to me since Broadus passed on. For ten years I was enthralled by the witchery of his matchless personality. For three years I was his student. For seven years I was his assistant and colleague and for part of the last year an inmate of his home. It was my sacred and sad privilege to see the passing of this prince in Israel. No man has ever stirred my nature as Broadus did in the classroom and in the pulpit. It has been my fortune to hear Beecher and Phillips Brooks, Maclaren, Joseph Parker and Spurgeon, John Hall and Moody, John Clifford and David Lloyd George. At his best and in a congenial atmosphere Broadus was the equal of any man that I have ever heard.[1]

It comes as little surprise then that Robertson's first major publication was a tribute to the mentor whom he so greatly loved. *The Life and Letters of John A. Broadus* was first published in 1901. Robertson's esteem for the late Broadus and enthusiasm for the work were reflected in the length of the original manuscript. Robertson's original proposal was over one thousand pages in length! His high personal regard and appreciation for Broadus were clearly demonstrated in the content of *Life and Letters*. Evidence for this can be seen in Robertson's conclusion that his friend and mentor was "one of the finest fruits of modern Christianity."[2]

The Early Years

The Broadus family was of Welsh extraction (the name was formerly spelled Broadhurst) and had long been rooted in the soil of the Old Dominion. They were a farming family, but

---

[1] A. T. Robertson, "Broadus as Scholar and Preacher," *The Minister and His Greek New Testament* (1923; Nashville: Broadman, reprint 1977), 118.

[2] A. T. Robertson, *Life and Letters of John A. Broadus* (Philadelphia: American Baptist Publication Society, 1901), x.

several of Broadus's ancestors had devoted time to teaching and several had become ministers of the gospel, some of them having attained great distinction and power. The family had deep spiritual roots and were almost unanimously members of the country Baptist churches of Virginia.

His father, Major Edmund Broadus, was a man of high character, ability, and independence of judgment that expressed itself in a variety of ways. Not only was he a farmer and major in the Culpepper County militia, Broadus was also a miller, a teacher, a leader of the Whig party of the State, and a member of the Virginia legislature for eighteen years. He was gifted with strong common sense and keen insight into the character and motives of people. Above all he was a deeply spiritual man, an ardent Baptist, and a strong leader in his church and local association. His life and work demonstrated it was indeed possible to be invested in the public square of his day as an active Christian.

The significant accomplishments of John A. Broadus can in many ways be traced to the marvelous model and paternal love and wisdom provided by his father. The presence of social, political, and religious leaders in the Broadus home greatly influenced John. Major Broadus had offered much support to Thomas Jefferson in the development of the University of Virginia, with which his famous son was to be so long and so intimately associated. Broadus's mother was a woman of godly character and a competence that admirably prepared her to be the wife of her notable husband and the mother of her remarkable children.

John Broadus was educated in the private subscription schools of Culpepper County. His schooling was completed at the Black Hill Boarding School under the capable tutelage of his uncle, Albert G. Simms. Young John went from this classroom well prepared for his formative years at the University of Virginia.

While he was still at his uncle's school, a lengthy revival meeting was conducted at the Mt. Poney Church by Rev.

Charles Lewis and Rev. Barnett Grimsley. Broadus was converted at this revival. While under conviction and feeling unable to take hold of the promises of God, a friend quoted to him from John's Gospel: "All that the Father giveth me shall come to me. And him that cometh to me I will in no wise cast out." His friend inquired, "Can you take hold of this, John?" Somehow the work of the Spirit dawned in his life by the use of this passage and the gift of regeneration came to young Broadus at that moment. His close friend, James G. Field, wrote:

> I knew him quite intimately from 1842 to 1847. We were youths of about the same age, he going to school to his uncle, Albert G. Simms, and I living in the store of Thomas Hill & Son, at Culpepper. Our fathers had been opposing candidates for the legislature. In May, 1843, at a protracted meeting conducted by Elder Charles Lewis with the Mt. Poney Church, at Culpepper, we both professed conversion . . . and were baptized by Rev. Cumberland George. . . . He did not remain in the Mt. Poney Church very long, but took his letter and joined New Salem, the church where his father and family had their membership.[3]

University of Virginia Years

Following the advice of his teachers and pastors, Broadus began the study of Greek when he entered the University of Virginia in 1846. This eager and dedicated student was endowed with great and rich gifts of mind as well as heart, which he never allowed to substitute for intense and persistent study. Broadus was a toiler, the apostle of hard work throughout life, which he had learned in the farm country of Virginia. It was said of Broadus later in his life that if genius is the ability and willingness to do hard work, he was a genius. This diligent work ethic followed him all his days. Professor F. H. Smith of the University of Virginia observed that while a student at the

---

[3] Ibid., 33–34.

University, Broadus "cultivated a great power of application and grew to have a great ability to work, and was not ashamed that others should know it." Professor Smith continued, "The wonderful result of this steady, methodical industry was that in later years he could do unheard of things in the briefest time. His disciplined faculties were so under his will that the result, while natural, was surprising."[4]

While at the University of Virginia, he continued to mature in his Christian faith. For Broadus, conversion was closely related to the call to service, which meant he was involved in seeking to bring others to Christian belief. This practice had begun a few months after his conversion and continued throughout his lifetime. Robertson relates an early evangelistic effort that Broadus frequently shared with his students in later days:

> In a meeting a few months after John's conversion, the preacher urged all Christians at the close of the service to move about and talk to the unconverted. John looked anxiously around to see if there was anybody present he could talk to about his soul's salvation. He had never done anything of the kind before. Finally he saw a man . . . named Sandy. He thought he might venture to speak to him . . . and Sandy was converted.[5]

After Broadus went away to school, he would often return home where he would be met by Sandy who would run across the street to meet him and say: "Howdy, John! thankee, John. Howdy, John, thankee, John." In later years, as Broadus would retell the story, he would add: "And if I ever reach the heavenly home and walk the golden streets, I know the first person to meet me will be Sandy, coming and saying again: 'Howdy, John! thankee, John.'"[6]

Another formative event characterizing the university years is noteworthy. In a note to a fellow student, he once wrote this line in Greek: "*hen se hysterei* (one thing thou lackest)." This

---

[4] W. J. McGlothlin, "John Albert Broadus," *Review and Expositor* 27 (April 1930): 147.
[5] Robertson, *Life and Letters*, 35.
[6] Ibid.

simultaneous compliment and delicate admonition bore fruit in the conversion of Broadus's fellow student. Broadus frequently looked for these ordinary contacts and relationships in life to communicate the truths of the gospel.

These events and others like them provided the context that confirmed his call to ministry. It was not unexpected that a Broadus should consider ministry as a possible life work. His uncle was a notable preacher who took special interest in his gifted nephew. Many other members of the Broadus family (sometimes spelled Broaddus, as well as Broadhurst) had been ministers.

Broadus had manifested serious interest in Christian service since the time of his conversion. He regularly attended church services on Sunday as well as Wednesday and Saturday. His work in the Sunday school encouraged him to think that he was called to preach. He struggled with the call to preach, thinking he was not qualified because he could not speak well in public. But in 1846, the same year he entered the university, Broadus surrendered to the ministry; never again for one moment did he think of wavering.

The years at the University of Virginia had a profound influence on Broadus. Particularly was he influenced by two professors: Gessner Harrison, professor of Greek, and W. H. McGuffey, professor of moral philosophy. Though he initially struggled with the high demands of the University of Virginia curriculum, he was regarded as the leading scholar of the institution by the time he graduated with the A.M. degree in 1850. Following graduation, he set for himself a broad self-study course in Old and New Testament, church history, and theology. On August 12 of that same year, he was ordained to the full work of the ministry in the New Salem Church that he had joined soon after his conversion. If all of this were not enough for one year, he also (in 1850) married the daughter of Gessner Harrison, his great teacher, professor, and friend.

Numerous opportunities for teaching and preaching came to him. Such invitations followed him the rest of his life. It is doubtful if any Baptist anywhere during that period of time had more invitations both by churches and institutions of higher education than Broadus. Yet he held few positions over his lifetime. His first pastorate began in September 1851 at Charlottesville, Virginia, which enabled him simultaneously to accept the invitation from his *alma mater* to serve as assistant professor of Latin and Greek. Thus he was able at once to combine his dual loves of preaching and teaching.

Broadus served the church for eight years. After two years in the classroom, the university prevailed upon him to become their chaplain. During this time there was much discussion, especially in the South Carolina area, concerning the need for a Southern Baptist seminary.

The Southern Baptist Theological Seminary Years

Broadus himself had not attended a seminary. His university education provided him an outstanding background in the classical languages and philosophy, but his theological preparation, like so many other Baptist preachers in the South, came about through self-study. The freestanding theological seminary was a distinctively American idea and was by this time becoming recognized in the American educational system. Newton Theological Institute had been in operation in the North since 1825, but there was no Baptist seminary in the South. The vision for this seminary largely came through the work of James Petigru Boyce. While Boyce is generally credited with the founding of The Southern Baptist Theological Seminary, he could not have built such an institution without Basil Manly Jr. and especially John A. Broadus. In 1856 Broadus was appointed by the Southern Baptist Convention to serve on a feasibility study committee to prepare a plan for the new seminary. This work was the introduction for Broadus of what was to be his life's work. When Broadus and Manly were asked to join the original seminary faculty, both responded reciprocally to one another, "I'll go if you will go." Still Broadus wrestled with leaving the Charlottesville pastorate and his beloved Virginia homeland.

When the time came for him to respond to the invitation from the Seminary, he could not for a year tear himself away from his first love, and when he did decide to go to the new seminary in Greenville, South Carolina, it brought great sorrow both to him and to the church.

Even though Manly and Boyce had been educated in northern seminaries, it was Broadus, the one who had not attended seminary, who was given the assignment to organize the plan of instruction. Not surprisingly the new proposal was based largely on a University of Virginia model, one based on the English Bible, with freedom for the students in their selection of course work. It was a creative proposal that was fifty years ahead of other advances in theological education in North America. The plan emphasized scholarship for the able students with something worthwhile for all. The seminary opened its doors in Greenville, South Carolina, in 1859 with twenty-six students. During the Civil War years, however, the new institution was forced to suspend its course of study.[7]

At the request of Stonewall Jackson, Broadus was asked to become a preacher to the Army of Northern Virginia. Writing to an associate of Broadus, J. William Jones, Jackson said of Broadus, "Write to him by all means and beg him to come. Tell him that he never had a better opportunity for preaching the gospel than he would have right now in these camps."[8] During the years of the Civil War, Broadus became a chaplain in Lee's army.

The seminary reopened following the war in the fall of 1865. At this time Broadus began his famous commentary on *The Gospel of Matthew* in the *American Commentary*. He labored for 20 years on the project that was ultimately published in 1886.

---

[7] The story of the providential founding of The Southern Baptist Theological Seminary and the details of Broadus's significant role in the founding as I have described can be found in William Mueller, *A History of The Southern Baptist Theological Seminary* (Nashville: Broadman, 1959); and Roy L. Honeycutt, "Heritage Creating Hope: The Pilgrimage of The Southern Baptist Theological Seminary," *Review and Expositor* 81 (Fall 1984): 367–91.

[8] Robertson, *Life and Letters,* 197.

When the seminary began classes after the Civil War, Broadus had only one student in his homiletics class, and this student was blind. Therefore Broadus taught him by lectures that were later published in 1870. For decades it was the most widely used book on homiletics in the world. This volume, *On the Preparation and Delivery of Sermons,* is still employed today over 125 years later in some settings. Without question it was Broadus's most famous work.[9] The publication of the volume evidenced God's providential oversight. Here was a book that came about through lectures to one blind student in a small, at that time almost anonymous, institution in Greenville, South Carolina.

In this influential volume Broadus fleshed out the ideals of preaching he had formed over the past two decades. These ideas had been shaped by his study of the great masters of the art of preaching throughout the history of the church. By the time of the book's publication, Broadus was already known all over the country as a preacher of rare ability and power. The book expressed what Broadus preached about preaching.[10]

When the seminary faced seemingly insurmountable financial obstacles in the mid-1870s a decision was made to move the institution to Louisville, Kentucky. Broadus, too, moved to Louisville, his home until his death in 1895. The move was successful largely due to Boyce's courageous vision and Broadus's unrelenting will and their common trust in God. Broadus challenged his colleagues not to give up their efforts in behalf of the struggling seminary, uttering his famous words, "The seminary may die, but let us die first."

Although Broadus was offered pastorates in several prominent churches as well as the presidency of Brown University and Crozer Theological Seminary, all of which offered significantly greater salaries, he chose to remain in his faculty position at the seminary. In 1889 Broadus was elected president of The

---

[9] See R. Albert Mohler, "Classic Texts Deserve Valued Spot in the Preacher's Bookshelf," *Preaching* (March–April 1989): 33–34.

[10] James W. Cox, "On the Preparation and Delivery of Sermons: A Book Review," *Review and Expositor* 81 (Fall 1984): 464–66; idem., "The Pulpit and Southern," *Review and Expositor* 82 (Winter 1985): 77–78.

Southern Baptist Theological Seminary following the death of James P. Boyce. In the same year Broadus was invited to deliver the prestigious Lyman Beecher lectures on preaching at Yale University. Unfortunately the lectures were never written down, and their contents can only be reconstructed from newspaper articles from *The Examiner* and *The Christian Inquirer*. Broadus never took notes with him into the pulpit and did not like for his messages to be transcribed.[11]

Broadus's fame and influence continued to spread. He delivered prestigious lectureships around the country including a presentation on "Textual Criticism of the New Testament" at Newton Theological Institute and on "Jesus of Nazareth" at Johns Hopkins University.

The added responsibility of presidential leadership and the death of Boyce had a considerable impact on Broadus. A. T. Robertson observed that after 1889 Broadus never regained the buoyancy of life he had once had. In his final year as president, Broadus's health continued to grow weaker. Yet his standing as a national Baptist leader continued to build the seminary both financially and in terms of national and international recognition. The great Baptist leader, preacher, and scholar died on March 16, 1895. On that day the *Louisville Courier–Journal* reported, "There is no man in the United States whose passing would cause more widespread sorrow than that of Doctor Broadus."[12]

Broadus had no greater impact than his influence on his prize student and son-in-law, A. T. Robertson. A special bond was

---

[11] See Steve Reagles, "The Century after the 1889 Yale Lectures: A Reflection on Broadus's Homiletical Thought," *Preaching* (November–December 1989): 32–36; also see A. T. Robertson, "Broadus the Preacher," *Methodist Quarterly Review* 69 (April 1920): 152. E. C. Dargan, Broadus's successor in teaching homiletics at Southern Seminary, attempted to incorporate portions of the Yale lectures in a revised edition of *On the Preparation and Delivery of Sermons.*

[12] Most of the material in this section can be found in Robertson, *Life and Letters.* The concluding quote is from *Life and Letters,* 431. Also see Bernard R. DeRemer, "The Life of John Albert Broadus," *Christianity Today* (April 13, 1962): 22–23; E. Y. Mullins, "One Hundred Years: A Retrospect," *Review and Expositor* 24 (April 1927): 129–31; and Claude W. Duke, "Memorial Address of Dr. John A. Broadus," *Review and Expositor* 24 (April 1927): 167–76.

formed between them, especially during Robertson's years on the Southern faculty. Robertson affectionately called Broadus his "truest earthly friend." Broadus thought of Robertson as his greatest discovery and modeled for the young professor two disciplines for which Robertson became equally, if not more, famous: New Testament interpretation and preaching. The model of Broadus's approach to the New Testament later bore fruit in the method of interpretation used by Robertson in his mammoth *Greek Grammar.*

Broadus modeled for Robertson an interpretive method that took into account the recent developments in critical scholarship while still remaining true to the authority of Holy Scripture. Robertson's intimate acquaintance with Broadus's work, as seen in the critical textual notes he contributed to Broadus's *Harmony of the Gospels,* reveals his continuity with, and addition to, the Broadus legacy. One of the finest compliments Robertson ever received was from J. H. Farmer, of McMaster University, who observed, "Professor Robertson has worthily maintained the Broadus tradition."[13] Robertson's *Greek Grammar* and *Word Pictures* clearly reflect the impact of Broadus upon the prolific professor.[14]

Archibald Thomas Robertson (1863–1934)

Archibald Thomas Robertson taught at The Southern Baptist Theological Seminary for more than 45 years (1888–1934). Robertson, who was born on November 6, 1863, to John and Ella Martin Robertson in Chatham, Virginia, was the greatest biblical scholar in the history of the Southern Baptist Convention. He died on Monday evening, September 24, 1934, at six o'clock at his home on Rainbow Drive near the Seminary campus. Characteristically, Dr. Robertson at his death was

---

[13] See Everett Gill, *A. T. Robertson: A Biography* (New York: MacMillan, 1943), 198.

[14] See David S. Dockery, comp., *The Best of A. T. Robertson* (Nashville: Broadman & Holman, 1996).

writing another book on the New Testament for Harper and Brothers.[15]

Robertson began a teaching career at Southern Seminary in 1888, which did not end until his death 46 years later. His role as professor impacted the lives of hundreds, multiplying his scholarship and ministry through Baptist pulpits around the country and even around the world. Without question Robertson's teaching ministry was characterized by excellence and demanding rigor. Yet his writing career, which extended even to the day of his death, set Robertson apart as the greatest biblical scholar in Baptist history.

Both his teaching and writing ministry can only be understood and interpreted in light of Robertson's genuine evangelical piety and churchmanship. A churchman of the highest order, Robertson's scholarly pursuits were always in the service of the church, primarily for the preacher. He thought of himself first and foremost as a preacher. When asked which of the three kinds of service was the highest, preaching, teaching, or writing, Robertson replied: "Preaching! Yes, preaching is the greatest work in the world. The element in the other two that makes them worthwhile is the preaching that they contain."[16]

The Early Years

In 1875 the Robertson family moved from Virginia to Cool Spring, North Carolina, when young Archibald was 12 years old. For the next four years Robertson attended Boone Preparatory School, Statesville, North Carolina. From 1879 to 1885, he attended Wake Forest College, combining some high school subjects with the college core curriculum to earn the M.A. degree.

The Robertson family had little money. In fact, they, like other farmers, struggled desperately to make ends meet during the 1870s and 1880s. Yet during this time young Archie

---

[15] In fact it was Robertson's expanded translation of the New Testament. See Everett Gill, *A. T. Robertson: A Biography* (New York: Macmillan, 1943).

[16] Frank H. Leavell, "Archibald Thomas Robertson: An Interview for Students," *The Baptist Student* X (May 1932): 3.

used to say, "I learned to work, to work hard, and to keep on working."[17]

When the Robertsons arrived in their new North Carolina town, there was no Baptist church. For three Sundays of the month they attended the Presbyterian church, and the other Sunday they attended Baptist services at the Court House conducted by Rev. J. B. Boone. Pastor Boone was strongly attracted to the Robertson family. He sensed the interest that young Archie had in spiritual matters. Boone became a veritable Paul to this young Timothy. As the area grew and more Baptists came into the area, a church was formed. Baptisms were held in a pond at the edge of town, the first in the history of that strong Presbyterian center. Archie heard a neighbor say that she had seen the likes of a baptism before, but her husband had never seen the like, so she was going to let him go.

In March 1876, during a revival meeting led by Rev. F. M. Jordan, Archie "felt a change of heart." He was baptized along with his brother Eugenc and two older sisters. Baptism by immersion was so new and strange that Archie was mocked by his Presbyterian playmates when he was baptized.

Mr. Boone prepared the equivalent of a college preparatory curriculum for young people not able to attend school. The plan focused on Archie Robertson, who was given free tuition. Archie began his studies in 1878 with courses in Latin, arithmetic, geography, and grammar. The school desk always had to be set aside when plowing and farm duties took priority. Boone's plan enabled Robertson to fulfill his educational longing and his passionate desire to prepare to serve the Lord. Archie's older brother, Martin, made great personal sacrifices that allowed Archie to pursue work with Boone, as well as eventual studies at Wake Forest College.

On his sixteenth birthday, November 6, 1879, Archie enrolled at Wake Forest, having borrowed ten dollars from a friend to purchase the train ticket. He arrived with two dollars in his pocket. Though he entered two months late in November

---

[17] Gill, *A. T. Robertson,* 28.

1879, instead of September 1, he caught up with his classmates through his diligent effort. One of his former fellow students made this illuminating observation that Archie, though arriving late that first year, soon led his class in Greek because of his "meticulous observation and a marvelous memory." These same great gifts served him well throughout his years of brilliant scholarship.

When Robertson entered Wake Forest, he had a serious impediment in his speech. He spent many hours alone, reading aloud and reciting choice selections of literature, which he memorized for that purpose. He enrolled in a special course to help eliminate this self-conscious problem. Eventually by learning to breathe differently, the matter was corrected. He later joined and participated in the Evzelian Literary Society to improve his reasoning and speaking abilities. Robertson's mentors at Wake Forest included William Louis Poteat (languages), Charles Elisha Taylor (Latin), and William B. Royal (Greek). Robertson placed first or second in his class in French, Latin, and Greek, making grades of 95 to 100 in every course. He was coeditor of the renowned college paper, *The Wake Forest Student,* called by *The Cleveland New Era* "the best college magazine published in this country."[18]

Surprising as it may seem, it was in Greek, not French or Latin, where Robertson won the second place medal. What was then a keen disappointment became the motivating force for him in later years to excel in New Testament scholarship. His second place finish was used as a stepping-stone to higher achievement in forthcoming years. His six years at Wake Forest may well have been the most important of his entire career.

Robertson entered Wake Forest poorly prepared at the age of 16. He graduated in June 1885 as an accomplished student and budding scholar. Though offered a professorship at his alma mater, Robertson turned his efforts toward his calling to preach and headed for further training at The Southern Baptist Theological Seminary in Louisville, Kentucky.

---

[18] Ibid., 42.

The Southern Seminary Years

At age 16 Robertson was licensed to preach. During that same year he preached his first sermon in a black church in North Carolina. His journey to Southern Seminary was the next step on his lifelong pursuit of the "call to preach."

The seminary had been in its new home city eight years when Archibald T. Robertson entered as a new student in 1885. As yet the struggling institution had no home of its own. The Waverly Hotel served as dormitory while the lecture rooms were up two flights of steps in the library hall on Fourth Avenue, an arrangement that continued until 1888.

Robertson worked hard his first two years taking senior Greek, textual criticism, and patristic Greek, all courses normally taken in one's final year. He also found numerous opportunities to preach both in Louisville during the school session and back in the mountains of North Carolina during vacation periods. He also served the homeless in a downtown mission called the California Mission.

During the early days of the 1888 school year, D. L. Moody held a six-week campaign in Louisville. Robertson wrote in his diary of an encouraging opportunity he had in soul-winning. It was his privilege to lead a self-identified universalist from West Virginia to the Lord. Robertson was spiritually moved by that experience and the powerful preaching of Moody. Though Robertson was concerned about Moody's poor grammar and use of the English language, he nevertheless observed that, "He [Moody] has a grip on the Bible, human nature, and God." He commented that Moody's exposition of the Holy Spirit was "the most enrapturing and heaven-inspired discourse" he had ever heard.[19]

---

[19] Ibid., 57. In Robertson's journal he noted that one advantage of seminary life in Louisville was the added opportunity to hear great preachers and lecturers who would come to the city. In addition to Moody, he particularly mentioned Sam Jones, Henry Ward Beecher, Edward Judson, Joseph Cook, Will Carleton, Justin McCarthy, P. S. Henson, George W. Lorimer, Phillips Brooks, Joseph Parker, Arthur O'Conner, Sir Thomas Grattan Esmond, DeWitt Talmage, Francis Murphy, J. William Jones, and James G. Blaine.

As he neared the end of his student days, he recalled that on his fifteenth birthday his mother told him that she would still be prouder of him after 15 more years. Yet he wondered whether the Lord would fulfill his mother's prophecy. The answer came on April 7, 1888, when the faculty invited Robertson to become an assistant to John A. Broadus in Greek and homiletics. With this invitation Robertson's life course was set: he was to be a man of the Book and a teacher of preachers rather than a pastor. So it was that Archie Robertson, the student, found himself at age 25 at his desk, addressed as Professor Robertson, and affectionately as "Doctor Bob." His career as professor began October 1, 1888, and continued for the next 46 years.

He joined the esteemed faculty of what was becoming the most significant seminary in the land. Those men with whom he had studied—Broadus, James P. Boyce, William Whitsitt, Basil Manly Jr.—now became his colleagues. Upon joining the faculty, John R. Sampey observed that Robertson was clearly the foremost student of his period in the seminary. As he began his new work, the young professor remarked: "I am sure I do not know how to teach, but I am equally determined, by the grace of God to learn how."[20] Nothing Robertson ever penned opened up for us his person as these words that described his humility, his determination, and his dependence on the grace of God.

It was certainly the grace and providence of God that gave Robertson the opportunity to spend the first year of his professorate at the house of Southern Seminary's founding president, James P. Boyce. Unfortunately Boyce would pass away by the end of the year. Still, the opportunity to spend his first year as a faculty member living with Boyce, and Boyce's successor in the department of theology, F. H. Kerfoot, instilled within Robertson a love for the seminary where he would spend the rest of his academic career. Not unlike Boyce, Robertson threw himself wholeheartedly into every enterprise in which he was involved. In addition to his duties as a seminary professor, Robertson also

---

[20] Gill, *A. T. Robertson*, 65.

became pastor of the Newcastle Baptist Church in Newcastle, Kentucky. His eagerness to fulfill the role of both teacher and preacher, however, soon placed Robertson's well-being in jeopardy. The aggressive schedule of preaching and teaching eventually caught up with the young professor and threw him into states of deep melancholy.[21] Realizing his limitations, Robertson gave up his pastoral work at Newcastle. Nevertheless, Robertson saw his whole life as service to his God, stating, "After all, what is a man's life worth if it be not given to God, and his kindred and mankind?"[22]

There was no doubt that Robertson, however, was on the rise as an academician. The surrounding faculty admired his ability and motivation. Although already an original thinker and scholar, Robertson himself would have pointed to those same faculty members as the formative influences on his illustrative career. A. T. Robertson was gaining a solid reputation as a New Testament scholar in the already substantive Southern Seminary tradition. In particular, Robertson formed a special relationship with the famous Southern Baptist New Testament scholar, preacher, and cofounder of Southern Seminary, John A. Broadus, whom, as we have noted, he affectionately called his "truest earthly friend." Later Broadus's daughter Ella would become his beloved wife, and so Robertson truly became regarded as part of the Broadus family. Broadus himself thought of Robertson as his greatest discovery and modeled for the young professor two disciplines for which Robertson later became famous: New Testament interpretation and preaching. The model of Broadus's approach to the New Testament later bore fruit in the interpretative method of Robertson in his mammoth Greek grammar. Broadus modeled for Robertson an interpretive method that took into account the recent developments in critical scholarship while still remaining true to the authority of Holy Scripture. Robertson's intimate acquaintance with Broadus's work, as seen in the critical textual notes he contrib-

---

[21] Ibid., 67.
[22] Ibid.

uted to Broadus's *Harmony of the Gospels,* reveals his continuity with, and addition to, the Broadus legacy. One of the highest compliments Robertson ever received was from J. H. Farmer, of McMaster University, who observed, "Professor Robertson has worthily maintained the Broadus tradition."[23] Robertson's *Greek Grammar* and *Word Pictures* clearly reflect the imprint of Broadus upon the young professor.

However, Robertson was not one merely to be a student of the masters; he became a master himself. He would become regarded as the greatest New Testament scholar ever to teach at Southern Seminary and one of the greatest in the history of New Testament interpretation. Robertson's ardent dedication to study continually sharpened his keen mind, and he could always be found at his desk, between classes, pouring over his latest writing projects and research. Roberston's output of scholarly writings was exceptional. Edgar McKnight has observed that between the years 1914 and the year of his death in 1934, there were only two years in which Robertson did not have volumes published.[24] In addition, his scholarly contributions transcended his primary field of expertise in New Testament and included works of theology, preaching, history, and denominational analysis. Robertson also became a frequent contributor to numerous Baptist state papers in the South, the Seminary's *Review and Expositor,* as well as Northern Baptist periodicals such as *The Baptist* and *The Watchman Examiner.* In all of these, Robertson dealt faithfully with the weighty, fundamental theological issues confronting Baptists at the dawn of the twentieth century. While Robertson never penned a major work in theology, he nevertheless addressed the major theological issue of the day consistent with historic orthodoxy.

Robertson also carefully blended level-headed, genuine scholarship with a passion for the seminary classroom. Students found his courses extremely demanding but never boring. His

---

[23] Ibid., 198.
[24] Edgar McKnight, "A Baptist Scholar," Founder's Day Address, The Southern Baptist Theological Seminary, February 4, 1986, 6.

keen wit and dry humor were among the most notable aspects of his teaching style, and the daily recitations he required in class always kept his students awake. William Mueller recounts a situation in which a student sought to come to blows with Robertson over something the professor had said in class and asked "Doctor Bob" to take off his coat and defend himself. Robertson wisely replied, "All right, all right, but let us first kneel down and pray!"[25] Even in the most difficult situations, Robertson was there, pointing his students to Christ.

The professor also played a critical role during one of the most turbulent times in the history of Southern Baptists' mother seminary: the Whitsitt controversy. Along with his fellow faculty, Robertson stood behind the president, William Whitsitt, in the heated theological and historical debate over Landmarkism. Robertson realized that Whitsitt's historical investigations and evaluations of Baptist successionism were not unfaithful to sound Baptist theology and a proud heritage. Robertson and his fellow faculty prided themselves on the "theological soundness" of Southern Seminary and urged caution in dealing with the issue at hand.[26] Their concern primarily was for a "faithful preaching of a pure gospel," coupled with sound scholarship.[27]

Robertson cared deeply for his students and the seminary and the high calling of training ministers for the gospel ministry. Perhaps the greatest testament to this fact is that Robertson was teaching on the day on which he grew gravely ill, was taken home, and later died of a severe stroke. One student remarked that even before his death, students began to develop a historical consciousness concerning the import of their professor's work in the field of New Testament interpretation.[28] In spite of his established international reputation as a well-published scholar and theologian, the end of A. T. Robertson's life found him

---

[25] William A. Mueller, *A History of the Southern Baptist Theological Seminary, 1859–1959* (Nashville: Broadman, 1959), 124.

[26] See the Southern Seminary faculty's letter to their fellow Southern Baptists in Mueller, *A History,* 162–64.

[27] Ibid., 164.

[28] McKnight, "A Baptist Scholar," 3.

where he was preeminently dedicated and well remembered: the halls and classrooms of Southern Seminary.

Mighty in the Scriptures: Their Theological Influence

John Broadus: Exegesis, Exposition, and Pastoral Theology

John Broadus, along with James P. Boyce and Basil Manly Jr., shaped the Southern Baptist theological tradition. The combination of the names of Broadus and Manly were joined together to provide the name for the book publishing arm of the Baptist Sunday School Board: Broad(us) Man(ly) Press. Their theological commitments can best be seen in *The Abstract of Principles* (1859), which from the founding of the seminary has served as the guiding confession of faith.

The theological tradition reflected in the *Abstract* is in line with historic orthodoxy at every point. The soteriology can be called moderately Calvinistic and the ecclesiology Baptistic. Broadus's work was carried forth in a manner faithful to this tradition.

Many things shape a successful scholar-theologian. Obviously Broadus was blessed by divine enablement and multigiftedness. On the human level such a person is a complex force. The natural endowment must be there to begin with, and there must be tireless energy and much preparation. Many persons are gifted but are not successful as scholars or preachers. Broadus excelled because of his strong work ethic, the focus of his work, the subject matter explored, the drive for excellence, and his rigorous pursuit to handle the material accurately.

His first major work was *A Treatise on the Preparation and Delivery of Sermons* (1870). Broadus was not the first to address the subject of preaching, but the incredible success of the book can be traced to Broadus's marvelous ability to communicate complex material in a popular way. He presented similar material in a more challenging and scholarly treatise in

31

the publication of his five lectures on *The History of Preaching* given at Newton in 1876.

The volume that best exemplifies his first-rate scholarship was his 20-year effort on the *Gospel of Matthew.* While not as well-known as *A Treatise on the Preparation and Delivery of Sermons,* this volume in the American Commentary is generally considered the greatest of all his works. Just as there were significant volumes on preaching prior to Broadus's 1870 publication, so there were hundreds of works on the Gospel of Matthew prior to the work by Broadus. Yet for more than a century, it has clearly remained the most important published volume in the American Commentary series, and one of the truly scholarly volumes on the first Gospel.

Three other works on the Gospels are worthy of note. Shortly after the publication of the Matthew commentary, he penned a brief work on *Jesus of Nazareth,* which was the revision of lectures given at Johns Hopkins. In 1893 he completed the famous *A Harmony of the Gospels,* which had several revisions and editions over the years by A. T. Robertson. His *Commentary on the Gospel of Mark* was published posthumously in 1905.

He contemplated several other works on New Testament themes, which were never published. When the issue concerning biblical authority and the use of historical criticism became a major issue on the Southern Seminary campus in 1879, Broadus addressed the subject by defending the full truthfulness of the Bible in *Three Questions as to the Bible* (1883) and the *Paramount and Permanent Authority of the Bible* (1887).

Following the death of his beloved colaborer, Broadus authored *The Memoirs of James P. Boyce,* published in 1893. With every publication Broadus sought to do good, to edify his readers, to expand their knowledge, and to build up the church of Jesus Christ. The sentence that concludes the preface to *The History of Preaching* may be taken as the motto and prayer of all his writings: "God grant that the little volume may be of some real use!" Each work reflects his commitment to careful scholarship, industrious research, accuracy of knowledge, and conscientious thought in his communication. Whatever he did was worth, in his favorite phrase, "working at." His works have retained their place over the years because his work was not the effusions of mere ambition to be a published author.

Those who heard him said he was even a better preacher than writer. Here he combined his scholarly commitment to New Testament exegesis, evident in his commentaries, with his masterful understanding of the art and history of preaching. The skillful, yet simple, touch of a master was evident by all who heard him proclaim the message of God's Word. At this point it will be helpful to examine Broadus's views on biblical inspiration and his approach to biblical interpretation.

To have an accurate understanding of Broadus's exegetical method and his important and distinctive contributions to biblical exposition in the evangelical tradition, we need to examine his view on the inspiration of the Bible. The issue had become a major issue on the campus of Southern Seminary in the 1870s and 1880s as the faculty attempted to respond to their departed colleague, C. H. Toy, who resigned over his acceptance of historical-critical conclusions. The major treatise was produced by Basil Manly Jr., titled *The Bible Doctrine of Inspiration* (1888). The key to understanding Manly and Broadus is to recognize their common opposition and response to Toy. Both disagreed with Toy's doctrine of Scripture and its practical implications.[29] Manly affirmed plenary inspiration and carefully refuted any theory of mechanical dictation. Broadus also refuted any theory of mechanical dictation but was cautious in theorizing as to verbal inspiration.[30] Both clearly affirmed every aspect of Scripture as infallible truth and divine authority. In *Three Questions as to the Bible,* he answered "completely" to the question "To what extent ought we regard the sacred writings of the Old and New Testaments as inspired?" His work, *The Paramount and Permanent Authority of the Bible,* took seriously the human authorship

---

[29] For an account of the Toy controversy see Mueller, *History of The Southern Baptist Theological Seminary.*

[30] See John A. Broadus, *Commentary on the Gospel of Matthew* (Philadelphia: American Baptist Publication Society, 1886), 58.

of the Bible as well as its divine origin. He contended for the complete truthfulness of Holy Scripture in a manner reflective of other great Christian leaders of the nineteenth century like Boyce, Manly, J. L. Dagg, and Alvah Hovey, yet with an independence and creativity characteristic of all of his work.[31] Perhaps most telling are words expressed to a group of young seminarians in a New Testament class he addressed for the last time a few days before his death. He communicated that his earnest desire for them was they be "mighty in the scriptures."[32]

Broadus attributed the doctrinal unity among Baptists and other evangelicals during the nineteenth century to their emphasis on the authority of the Bible in matters of faith and practice.[33] In *The Paramount and Permanent Authority of the Bible,* he wrote:

> Now, I address myself to people who believe that the Bible is the Word of God; not merely that it contains the Word of God, which wise persons may disentangle from other things in the book, but that it is the Word of God.

He continued:

> It is entirely possible that we may have no creed or system of theology, no professors or even preachers, nor even newspaper writers, nor writers of tracts, that can always interpret the Bible with infallible success. But our persuasion is that the real meaning of the Bible is true.[34]

These statements reflect an explicit affirmation from Broadus that the Bible, apart from human interpretation, has objective meaning and value.

---

[31] See David S. Dockery, *Christian Scripture: An Evangelical Perspective on Inspiration, Authority and Interpretation* (Nashville: Broadman & Holman, 1995), 177–99.

[32] Robertson, *Life and Letters,* 430.

[33] Broadus, *Paramount and Permanent Authority of the Bible,* 1–2.

[34] Ibid., 3.

While Broadus was at the forefront of American biblical scholarship in the nineteenth century and was a pacesetter in certain areas, it is interesting to hear him say that with all the progress of the nineteenth century, "it does not follow that this century is superior to all previous centuries in thinking, for in some respects our age has not time to be wiser."[35] Thus we see that his careful and wise scholarship remained faithful to the authority of Holy Scripture as the only and sufficient revelation of God. As such he stated that "a 'progressive orthodoxy' that forsakes or adds to the teaching of Christ becomes heterodoxy."[36] His words for his time are equally applicable for contemporary readers in his discussion about current archaeological, philosophical, and scientific debates. "The great principle, in all such inquiries," he claimed, "is that while it is lawful to reinvestigate the Scripture in the light of current opinion and feeling, it is not lawful to put anything as authority above God's Word."[37]

Broadus unhesitatingly defended the trustworthiness and authority of the Bible but was cautious in asserting a definition of inspiration. In *Three Questions as to the Bible,* he wrote, "But whatever these (biblical) writers meant to say, or whatever we learn from subsequent revelation that God meant to say through their words, though not by themselves fully understood, that we hold to be true, thoroughly true, not only in substance but in statement."[38] In conclusion, Broadus summarized, "Even today I know of no discrepancies in the Bible which impair its credibility."[39] These foundational commitments served to undergird his painstaking and evenhanded exegesis that characterized his lifework.

In the preface to his *Commentary on the Gospel of Matthew,* Broadus thoroughly discussed textual matters, various

---

[35] Ibid., 5.
[36] Ibid., 8.
[37] Ibid., 13.
[38] John A. Broadus, *Three Questions as to the Bible* (Philadelphia: American Baptist Publication Society, 1883), 9.
[39] Ibid., 34.

viewpoints, evaluations, comparisons, and conclusions. For example he observed:

> The general contributions to textual criticism made by Westcott and Hort are invaluable, and most of their judgments as to particular passages seem to me correct. But in a number of cases I have felt bound to dissent, and to give the reasons as fully and strongly as the character and limits of this work allowed.[40]

The commentary offered insights on Greek grammar and syntax, with copious footnotes. Yet the direct word by word, phrase by phrase exposition makes the work useful for the Sunday school teacher, as well as pastors and scholars.

Broadus did not sidestep the tough questions impacting the veracity and accuracy of the biblical text. He addressed seeming contradictions and errors simply and directly, reflecting his convictional trust in the Bible's truthfulness.[41] After wrestling to determine the historical meaning of the text, Broadus practiced the steps outlined in *Three Questions* with his "homiletical and practical" comments, wedding exacting exegesis with solid application. By focusing on the practical aspects as well, Broadus brilliantly combined his two specialties showing that biblical interpretation and theology must ultimately be done in the service of the church.

His theological conclusions throughout the commentary evidence his Reformed convictions, reflecting the Philadelphia/ Charleston confessional traditions that gave birth to Southern Seminary. For example, he contended for the virgin birth (see 1:21), affirmed that Jesus claimed that he was the Messiah (see 13:10–17), and expounded the need for divine initiative for God to make himself known to depraved men and women (see 22:14).

Overall, Broadus's work on Matthew is a model commentary and in many ways ushered in a new era of commentary

---

[40] *Gospel of Matthew*, x–ix.

[41] E.g., the manner he dealt with the variations in the genealogies in Matthew and Luke; see *Gospel of Matthew*, 6–7.

writing within evangelical scholarship.[42] Significant advances included the incorporation of historical, textual, and grammatical research that was being advocated during his lifetime. He demonstrated an awareness and conservative openness to European critical scholarship, but he was not willing unreservedly to subject Holy Scripture to the antisupernatural biases of much of the German critical approaches. His work included grammatical, exegetical, theological, and practical comments, thus making it valuable to a wide readership.

His commentary work was not the only place Broadus made original contributions. In *A Harmony of the Gospels,* Robertson commented:

> Dr. Broadus was the first one to depart from the traditional division of the ministry of Christ by the Passovers rather than the natural unfolding of the ministry itself. . . . Dr. Broadus's work is the ripe fruit of a lifetime of rich study and reflection by one of the rarest teachers of the New Testament that any age or country has ever seen.[43]

Broadus's firm theological foundation and level-headed explorations allowed him to employ the best of European critical scholarship without embracing the conclusions. His

---

[42] The publication of The New American Commentary series (projected 40 volumes) in 1991 is in many ways a tribute to the legacy of John A. Broadus. In the preface of each volume the editors have penned these words:

In one sense *The New American Commentary* is not new, for it represents the continuation of a heritage rich in biblical and theological exposition. The title of this forty-volume set points to the continuity of this series with an important commentary project published at the end of the nineteenth century called *An American Commentary,* edited by Alvah Hovey. The older series included, among other significant contributions, the outstanding volume on Matthew by John A. Broadus, from whom the publisher of the new series, Broadman Press, partly derives its name. Broadman Press is named for John A. Broadus (Broad) and Basil Manly Jr. (Man).

See The New American Commentary, David S. Dockery and E. Ray Clendenen, general editors (Nashville: Broadman, 1991–).

[43] See the preface of A. T. Robertson, *A Harmony of the Gospels in the Revised Version* (New York: Doran, 1903); also the comments by Martin Marty, *Pilgrims in Their Own Land* (New York: Penguin, 1984), 304.

openness has been misinterpreted by some. For example, Finke and Starke claim "Broadus was extremely impressed with the application of critical methods to biblical studies that was going on in European universities, especially in Germany."[44]

Yet the comments from J. M. Carter's notes on Broadus's lectures on New Testament Introduction are informative.[45] While Broadus was certainly open to new advances, his interpretive method could not be considered progressive. He rejected notions that the Gospel of John was in conflict with the other Gospels, despite recent critical objections. He clearly held to a Johannine authorship of the Fourth Gospel. Throughout his lectures on the four Gospels, he affirmed the supernatural origin of the Gospels and the author's eyewitness accounts.

A. T. Robertson: Theologian and Statesman

Robertson's work and influence was not limited to the confines of the seminary life and the academic enterprise. Robertson gave himself to the larger work of Baptist denominational life, and especially the concerns of Baptists around the world. Robertson originally suggested the concept for what would later become the Baptist World Congress. In 1905, a year after his suggestion in *The Baptist Argus*, the Baptist World Alliance convened in London, a meeting in which Robertson took part. In addition, he contributed to the life and thought of the Southern Baptist Convention and especially its churches. Robertson had a passion for the centrality of preaching in the church and could regularly be found in pulpits throughout Kentucky preaching on weekends and ministering the

---

[44] Roger Finke and Rodney Starke, *The Churching of America, 1776–1990—Winners and Losers in Our Religious Economy* (New Brunswick, NJ: Rutgers University Press, 1992), 1790; also A. H. Newman, *A History of Baptist Churches in the United States* (New York: Scribners and Sons, 1915), 1518.

[45] These unpublished notes are housed in the James P. Boyce Library on the campus of The Southern Baptist Theological seminary. I am indebted to Greg Thornbury for his research help at this point in particular and for his help with other aspects of this chapter.

Word. Robertson wanted to model for his students a careful, expositional approach to preaching the Bible. Like Broadus, he wanted his students to be "mighty in the Scriptures." On one occasion Robertson wryly observed, "The greatest proof that the Bible is inspired is that it has withstood so much bad preaching." Roberston's biographer, Everett Gill recounts that when interpreting the Scripture passage, "a savor of life unto life or of death unto death," the professor asserted, "Preaching . . . is the most dangerous thing in the world."[46] Above all, Robertson's life and ministry had the edification and growth of the church of Jesus Christ in mind. He once remarked to his students, "God pity the poor preacher who has to hunt for something to preach—and the people who have to listen." The wise scholar had a heartbeat for God's people. As William Mueller has observed: "The great New Testament Scholar seemed happiest when he stood before a congregation pointing men and women to the Lord Jesus Christ as their only Master and Savior."[47]

Roberston's influence was also felt throughout the North during the contentious Fundamentalist-Modernist debates in the Northern Baptist Convention. It was not uncommon for the reader of such papers as the *Watchman-Examiner* and *The Baptist* to find articles and essays with Robertson defending the supernatural nature of the Christian truth claim and supporting the affirmation of the "fundamentals" of Christianity. Much like his colleague, President E.Y. Mullins, Robertson was a man in demand, one whose opinion Baptists would heed. Robertson proved to be a steady voice in unsteady times, a trustworthy scholar for all Baptists, both North and South.

As a theologian, Robertson did not hesitate to state his convictions. Robertson's confidence in the historical reliability and complete truthfulness of Scripture can be clearly seen in Robertson's view of biblical inspiration. While Robertson certainly believed that Christian scholars should avail themselves

---

[46] Gill, *A. T. Robertson,* 184.

[47] Mueller, *A History,* 206.

of the most accurate historical data and interpretation, he simultaneously believed that all such human speculations must fall under the authority of the divine disclosure of the Scriptures. Robertson declares concerning the historical reliability of the Gospel of Luke in reference to the divinity and virgin birth of Jesus: "It remains that the whole truth about Jesus lies in the interpretation given by Luke in the opening chapters of his Gospel. The view of Luke the physician holds the field today in the full glare of modern science and historical research."[48]

Thus, Robertson was convinced of the veracity of Scripture in light of the findings of modern historical methodology. As such, he was willing to use the best possible historical tools and research in demonstrating the full truthfulness of the Scriptures. Robertson felt that the tools of critical methodology, if cautiously used in reverence for the authority of Scripture, could aid the interpreter in understanding the biblical text. Consequently, Robertson's openness to the proper use of critical tools in interpreting Scriptures should not be viewed as an antithetical position to that of Robertson's forebearers such as John A. Broadus and Basil Manly Jr., but rather as a contemporary exposition of that same tradition.

As such, Robertson became a standard in Southern Baptist circles by which New Testament scholarship and biblical fidelity would later be judged. Upon the occasion of his death, one of his students remarked that if all the buildings of the seminary were blown down and Professor Robertson alone were left standing "the seminary would have been more real than it was with him gone."[49] He was part of the impetus that brought Southern Baptist life and scholarship to the forefront of the theological world. In many ways Robertson's reputation has yet to be paralleled. His legacy to his colleagues, students, and

---

[48] A. T. Robertson, "Is the Virgin Birth Credible Today?" *The Watchman-Examiner* (November 18, 1920): 1168.

[49] Gill, *A. T. Robertson,* 239.

Southern Seminary was, in the word of his successor Hershey Davis, "inestimable."

Epochs in the Life of Jesus showed a fundamental concern of Robertson's: expounding and retelling the stories of the New Testament. In the light of the work of liberal scholars, like Albert Schweitzer, who were seeking to give their position on the historical Jesus, Robertson saw the need to write his own biography of the life of Christ. In place of Schweitzer's assertion that the titles of Jesus are mere "historical parables," Robertson clearly confesses him as the Messiah, the Son of God. In place of the confused identity with which "The Quest for the Historical Jesus" had sought to depict Jesus, Robertson reveals the unified witness of the Gospel material: that Jesus is in fact Lord and Savior. In *The Christ of the Logia,* we see evidence of Robertson's careful mixture of both a conservative approach to biblical exegesis—utilizing critical method and a reverence and commitment to the Scripture's confession of the person and work of Christ. Robertson clearly confesses the unity of the Synoptic Gospels' witness to Jesus as both Savior and Lord.

In the article, "The Bible as Authority," Robertson asserted that the Bible is actually the Word of God, and "since there is no ultimate authority in the spiritual realm outside of God," the Bible has the authority to command obedience, action, and belief. In this essay Christ is revealed as the interpretive principle for all of Scripture. Robertson concluded that critical study of the Bible must be supplemented by the guidance of the Holy Spirit in its interpretation, stating, "The Bible must be studied by the scientific historical method, but also with an enlightened soul in touch with the Spirit of God." What is more, Robertson affirmed the historic Baptist principle that Scripture must be interpreted in light of Scripture and that the Bible can be plainly understood, on its own terms, and in its own words. The Bible, he felt, has stood against so much criticism, unbelief, and misinterpretation, so as to demonstrate through those facts alone that it must be the Word of God.

Robertson's work, "The Relative Authority of Scripture and Reason," was originally an address delivered before the Tenth meeting of the Baptist Congress in May 1892. For several days he had listened to theologians such as William Newton Clarke stand before the assembly and cast aspersions upon the infallibility and nature of the Bible. Robertson was so disappointed with the tone and spirit of some of the speakers from the platform that he decided to answer their toughest questions and advance a few theses of his own, which resulted in one of the greatest treasures of the Robertson literary corpus. Here is Robertson at his best: thinking on his feet, responding to critics, and defending the faith. In a similar vein he addressed the issue of the validity and importance of the supernatural conception of Jesus Christ in "Is the Virgin Birth Still Credible Today?" Robertson's answer to that question is a resounding "yes" as it appeared during the height of the Fundamentalist-Modernist controversy among Northern Baptists in the early 1920s. But Robertson's approach is not an uncritical literalism that hides away when the facts are presented. Rather, it embraces all of the truth God has shown us in the natural order as further evidence of his powerful ability to accomplish his providential purposes. As such, Robertson declared with his Baptist predecessors that the Scripture "has God for its author, salvation for its end, and truth, without any mixture of error for its matter."

Robertson converted his mastery of Greek into theological applications for the believer in "The Greek Article and the Deity of Christ" and "Grammar and Preaching." In the former Robertson refutes the questionable exegesis that has supplied false evidence for all those who seek to deny the deity of Jesus Christ by claiming a loophole in the grammatical construct of the first chapter of the Gospel of John. In "Grammar and Preaching" Robertson again weds the practicality of knowledge of Greek grammar with sound exegetical preaching that is faithful to the text as God's Word.

Conclusion

John A. Broadus and A. T. Robertson unhesitatingly affirmed and faithfully expounded what can be called Baptist distinctives. Robertson was once reported to have said, "Give a man an open Bible, an open mind, a conscience in good working order, and he will have a hard time to keep from being a Baptist." This commitment was carried forward in the lives and labors of both Robertson and Broadus.

Robertson was honored to carry forth the Broadus tradition, which today we may call the Broadus-Robertson tradition. They faithfully taught the Bible in the spirit and conviction of the Baptist heritage, while advancing Baptist scholarship into the twentieth century, and placing it on a solid but contemporary footing. We now have the privilege and responsibility to carry forth this tradition in a faithful way into the twenty-first century, a generation who will handle accurately the Word of God (2 Tim. 2:15).

The legacy of their work is not only in their writings but in the lives of those whom they taught, best exemplified in pulpit giants like H. H. Hobbs and W. A. Criswell and echoing throughout Southern Baptist life. Their commitment to exegetical theology, however, was simultaneously a strength and a weakness. They upheld the authority of Scripture, but both were cautious at best in developing a systematic approach to theology, even though Broadus appealed to the importance of systematic theology in *On the Preparation and Delivery of Sermons.* This approach advanced biblical theology but failed to advance a coherent Baptist theology. In a similar way that E. Y. Mullins' theology developed and reshaped the consistent Calvinism of J. P. Boyce, so Broadus to some degree and Robertson even more, moved to a more Amyraldian type of soteriology.

The strengths of the Broadus-Robertson tradition were New Testament theology and preaching. They stood faithfully on the truthfulness of Holy Scripture. Their works on the Gospels stand to this day as standard bearers. They recognized the pitfalls in harmonizing the Gospels if by doing so the unique emphasis of each Gospel would be lost. They warned that the Gospels are not a mere mass to be artificially reconstructed, for each Gospel is a living and independent whole. Yet they saw the value of providing an overall look at the life of Christ as a way to reconcile apparent discrepancies in the Gospels.

In conclusion, we must recognize in their works the pervasive tone of solemn reverence for Scripture and an abiding and deep spirituality. Their thoroughgoing scholarship and devotional spirit is a worthy model of imitation for Baptists in the twenty-first century. John A. Broadus and A. T. Robertson practiced what they taught their students, for indeed they were men "mighty in the Scriptures."[50]

---

[50] Portions of this work previously appeared in David S. Dockery, "John A. Broadus" in *Evangelical Biblical Interpreters,* ed. Walter A. Elwell (Grand Rapids: Baker, 1999) and David S. Dockery, ed. and comp., *The Best of A. T. Robertson* (Nashville: Broadman & Holman, 1999); as well as the "Broadus-Robertson Tradition" in *Theologians of the Baptist Tradition,* ed. Timothy George and David S. Dockery (Nashville: Broadman & Holman, 2001).

Chapter III

"The Way to Learn to Preach Is to Preach":
John A. Broadus's Early Career and Influences

A. James Fuller

J ohn A. Broadus read the letter from his college friend, J. R. Scott, and found it filled with advice. In February 1851, Scott, working as a Baptist minister in Maine, could not resist passing along words of encouragement to his fellow preacher laboring as a teacher in Virginia: "I should think . . . that you have abundant opportunities in the way of preaching. I hope you avail yourself of them. . . . Dr. Sharp once told me—*the way to learn to preach is to preach*." Having already received the call to preach and having been guided by several older ministers, Broadus took his friend's advice to heart and soon earned his reputation as one of the best preachers in the South.[1]

Scott based his insights on his familiarity with Broadus's personality and inclinations. "I know you too well to fear [that] you will [not] read and study, nor be content with low and superficial attainments." He recognized his friend was an intellectual:

---

[1] J. R. Scott to John A. Broadus, 25 February 1851, John Albert Broadus Papers, James P. Boyce Centennial Library, The Southern Baptist Theological Seminary, Louisville, Kentucky. Dr. Daniel Sharp long served as a pastor in Boston, Massachusetts, and was well-known for his support of Baptist education.

"Your tendencies are scholastic." Just a few months before, Scott had replied to Broadus's request for advice on a course of reading in theology with a list of titles and authors to consult. Indeed, Broadus would go on to international fame as a theologian, and his books became classic texts relied upon by generations of preachers and laypersons alike. Scott knew his man and his strengths. But his familiarity with Broadus also allowed him to nudge his friend gently toward the pulpit:

> Join to the pursuits to which your aspirations and habits naturally lead you such training as you can get in the neighboring churches and *especially* in the General's Chapel, and you may one of these days, and not long hence, command your position.

General J. H. Cocke, a wealthy planter, operated the school in which Broadus taught, and he offered the young Baptist the opportunity to preach to his slaves in the plantation chapel. Scott urged Broadus to engage in what today would be called applied and experiential learning, to preach to diverse audiences in order to hone his skills.[2]

Broadus did not necessarily heed J. R. Scott's advice. Following his graduation from the University of Virginia, he accepted the position as a tutor at General Cocke's school in Fluvanna County. According to his son-in-law and biographer, A. T. Robertson, Broadus

> resisted the temptation to spoil his University course by too much preaching. . . . He always insisted that it was far better to be thorough in one's educational foundation, so as to have all the more to build on, than to rush headlong through one's school days at breakneck speed.

This reflected Broadus's intellectual inclinations, but he also learned through experience by actually taking up the call to preach and entering the pulpit. Such experience served as the

---

[2] Ibid.; J. R. Scott to John A. Broadus, 23 July 1850, in A. T. Robertson, *Life and Letters of John A. Broadus* (1901; reprint, Harrisonburg, VA: Gano Books, 2003), 76–77; ibid., 75, 78.

perfect complement to his sharp mind. When brought together, Broadus's intellect and experience allowed him to offer profound insights on the ministry.[3]

His unique combination of intellectual erudition and on-the-job training was forged in his early career as he developed under the influence of men like William F. and Andrew Broaddus, Barnett Grimsley, A. M. Poindexter, William H. McGuffey, E. H. Courtenay, and Gessner Harrison. From his conversion at age 16 in 1843 until he became a professor at The Southern Baptist Theological Seminary in 1859, John A. Broadus studied and worked to become a model of the kind of preacher he later instructed others to be during his long career as a theologian and seminary professor.

Family Influences

It was no accident that Broadus became a great preacher. He came from a family with a long tradition of education and ministry. His father, Major Edmund Broadus, a planter in Culpepper County, Virginia, long supported the cause of education, taking particular interest in the University of Virginia. A noted Whig politician and temperance advocate, the major was also a devout Baptist. He suffered financial setbacks in the depression that followed the Panic of 1837, but rather than turning wholly to planting to recover his fortune, he became a steward of the university. The main reason for boarding students in his home was not his own financial situation, however. Instead, the major took the position of steward to give his son the opportunity to go to the university.[4]

His father's example and sacrifices were only part of Broadus's family legacy. His great-uncle, Andrew Broaddus, was widely known as a great preacher and, as a boy, his great-nephew heard him speak on numerous occasions. Remembered by Henry Clay as "the past-master of eloquence," Andrew Broaddus also wrote and published many works for the American

---

[3] Ibid., 76.
[4] Ibid., 12–20.

Baptist Publication Society, including a catechism for children and two hymnals. His rebuttal of Thomas Paine's *Age of Reason* and his published oppositions to Alexander Campbell won him fame as a defender of the faith. He continued his work until his death in 1848 and cast a long intellectual and spiritual shadow that certainly influenced John A. Broadus.[5]

His uncles, William F. Broaddus and Andrew Broaddus, also molded Broadus as a young man. William F. Broaddus labored as a minister in Maryland, Kentucky, and Virginia where he defended Baptist doctrines and missionary efforts against the so-called "Black Rock" or "Hardshell" principles of antimission opponents. His efforts as an itinerant preacher in the mountains earned him a reputation as a successful evangelist, as his "good humor, his keen wit, his facility of speech, his insight into human nature, and his adroit management gave him the advantage in every contest, and constantly strengthened his influence." That influence included an interest in his nephew upon whom William F. Broaddus bestowed the mantle of his ministry. William's younger brother, Andrew, also known as "Kentucky Andrew," did not enjoy the same kind of popular influence and reputation. He entered the ministry much later in life and did not have talents equal to William, although he eventually became more polished and effective in the pulpit.[6]

His own family, then, exerted a powerful influence upon John A. Broadus. He grew up in a Christian family and a long line of preachers. His forebearers also led the Baptists into theological battle, and their legacy was one of education and intellectual activity as well as delivering sermons and ministering to congregations. His father and uncles guided John in his preparation for the ministry and urged him to seek knowledge and education.

---

[5] For the career of Andrew Broaddus and his influence on J. A. Broadus, see: Tom Nettles, *The Baptists: Key People Involved in Forming a Baptist Identity, Volume Two: Beginnings in America* (Fearn, Scotland: Mentor, 2005), 288–89; Robertson, *Life and Letters*, 4–6.

[6] On William F. and Andrew Broaddus, see: Nettles, *The Baptists, Volume Two*, 290–93; Robertson, *Life and Letters*, 7–9.

Early Education and Calling

Broadus's education began at home, where his father encouraged and taught him to read. He later attended schools run by respected teachers, including one operated by his uncle, Albert G. Simms. During his days at Simms' boarding school, Broadus attended a revival meeting at the Mt. Poney Church in May 1843 and converted to Christianity. Baptized by a prominent Virginia preacher named Cumberland George, Broadus joined the New Salem Baptist Church where his family attended. Barnett Grimsley, the pastor of the church, took an interest in mentoring the young convert. A self-educated man with great speaking abilities, Grimsley was considered by many to be one of the best preachers in Virginia. Broadus sat under him in his formative years and later adopted some of his illustrations for use in his own sermons. When Grimsley accepted a new position and moved to Clarke County to preach, he secured a teaching position for Broadus. Still not sure of his course in life, the young man listened to his pastor, finished his studies with Simms, and opened a school of his own.[7]

Things did not go well. For more than three years after his conversion, Broadus struggled with his calling. His bookish inclinations led him to become a schoolmaster but remained unsure of what future God might have in store for him. A young man teaching while seeking his course in life was not unusual, and in hindsight the period was well spent in preparation for Broadus's eventual career not only as a minister but also as an educator. At the time, however, the young man was frustrated and doubted his own abilities. His loneliness added to the difficulty of learning to teach, although his interest in young women earned him a reputation as a "ladies man." [8]

Through it all, his calling lay at the center of his frustration. In April 1845, he wrote to his father expressing his doubts and concerns.

---

[7] Ibid., 33–36.
[8] For this period of frustration and doubt, see ibid., 36–52.

> Sometimes . . . I feel that nature has given me the ability to be something, and I am determined that I will strive to rise. Again I am discouraged by the seemingly insurmountable difficulties that are before me. I have been troubled too, by the fact that I cannot decide what to make of myself.

His father thought he saw things more clearly, but his advice only served to confuse his son, "You advise me to give up other studies for the present and devote myself to my calling. Here I do not understand what you mean, and it is because I wish to explain that I write so soon." After writing about how hard he was working as a teacher and his devotion to his present position, he closed the letter with a plea for more fatherly insight: "Do not understand me now as being unwilling to follow your advice. I only ask you to explain, to tell me what I ought to do, and it shall be done. Please write to me on this subject as soon as you can." [9]

Friends and relatives alike asked him about a possible call to preach. It certainly crossed the mind of a gifted young man from a long line of distinguished divines. In February 1846, Broadus responded to a friend's inquiry about such a possibility. "You inquire if I never think about preaching. I answer, I do; but I always come to the conclusion that preaching is not my office." In part this derived from his confusion about the nature of such a calling, and he said his reluctance was "not because I consider a call to the ministry to consist in some supernatural intimation, for I believe that to be very little more than an earnest and ardent desire for the work, but because I do not think I am qualified for it." Later, having received a divine call to preach, he changed his mind about this and was convinced that the Holy Spirit moved in a supernatural way to bring men to the ministry. But, as a young man struggling with his present situation and possibilities for the future, he tended to rely on his own judgment of his abilities.

---

[9] John A. Broadus to Edmund Broadus, 11 April 1845, in Robertson, *Life and Letters*, 45–46.

I know that my mental capabilities are, in some respects, not inconsiderable, but I was not 'cut out' for a public speaker; I have not that grace of manner and appearance, that pleasant voice, that easy flow of words, which are indispensably necessary in . . . public speaking.

Indeed, his fondness for study and books, his intelligence and insightful mind, had persuaded some of his relatives to urge him to pursue a career in medicine and he spent the winter studying anatomy with a mind toward beginning his education as a doctor.[10]

So Broadus gave up teaching and prepared to enter the University of Virginia to study medicine. It was then he received his calling to the ministry. In August 1846, he attended an association meeting and heard A. M. Poindexter deliver two sermons. Like Broadus himself, Abram Maer Poindexter exemplified the kind of social climbing that Beth Barton Schweiger argued marked the development of evangelical churches in nineteenth-century Virginia. According to Schweiger, early in the century most preachers were self-educated orators who oversaw a rough-hewn revivalism designed to bring about emotional conversion experiences. Over time pastors transformed themselves and their denominations into models of respectability by making education a priority. She argued that the professionalization of the ministry through institutional development, complete with seminaries and large, impressive churches, illustrated the ways in which Baptists moved into the mainstream of society over the course of three generations. They redefined revivalism, polished their presentation, and moved religion into the classroom. In her analysis Poindexter was part of the second generation of that process, and Broadus was a member of the third generation that was the culmination of social progress. Poindexter earned a college degree and published widely on theological matters. Famous for his ability to bring harmony and Christian unity out

---

[10] John A. Broadus to T. W. Lewis, February 26, 1846, in Robertson, *Life and Letters*, 48–49.

of disputes between those who were deeply divided, he served as another important influence for a young man called to the learned ministry.[11]

In his memorial of Poindexter, given nearly 40 years later, Broadus remembered his calling to the ministry in 1846. Referring to himself in the third person, as a "youth," Broadus noted his struggle with his calling, "for three years a professed Christian, he had often thought about the question of becoming a minister, but considered himself to have finally decided that it was not his duty." In the first of his sermons at the association meeting, delivered on Sunday, "Dr. Poindexter preached upon Glorying in the Cross." Broadus admitted that although he "had often heard with enthusiasm and delight such truly eloquent and noble preachers as Barnett Grimsley, Cumberland George, and Henry W. Dodge," on that Sunday he thought "that he had never before imagined what preaching might be, never before conceived the half of the grandeur and glory that gather sublime around the cross of Christ."[12]

The next morning Poindexter preached again, this time "on the Parable of the Talents." Broadus remembered how Poindexter expertly drew his listeners, especially the prosperous planters in the audience, in "by arguing long and earnestly that it is right for the Christian to gather property, and right to provide well for his family. Excellent brethren were charmed." The planters were pleased. "No preacher had ever before so fully justified the toil and sacrifices by which they had been steadily growing rich." But, when he had "gained their full sympathy,"

---

[11] On A. M. Poindexter, see: John A. Broadus, *Sermons and Addresses* (Baltimore: R. H. Woodward and Company, 1886), 373–45; Beth Barton Schweiger, *The Gospel Working Up: Progress and the Pulpit in Nineteenth-Century Virginia* (New York: Oxford University Press, 2000). Many scholars will take issue with various aspects of Schweiger's analysis, particularly when it comes to matters of motivation. While she does not completely ignore other factors, Schweiger insists that economic and political considerations were at the center of institutional growth among evangelicals. In other words, ministers worked to build denominational institutions to make money and gain power. Her conclusion that social improvement by the churches ironically led to less influence also invites further study.

[12] Broadus, *Sermons and Addresses*, 397.

Poindexter turned to the heart of his message, which was Christian benevolence. The "sudden appeal he made to consecrate their wealth to the highest ends of existence, to the good of mankind and the glory of Christ, was a torrent, a tornado, [sic] that swept everything before it."[13]

Then Poindexter "spoke of consecrating one's mental fits and possible attainments to the work of the ministry." Broadus listened intently as the older man "seemed to clear up all difficulties pertaining to the subject." Poindexter "swept away all the disguises of self-delusion, all the excuses of a fancied humility" and "held up the thought that the greatest sacrifices and toils possible to a minister's lifetime would be a hundredfold repaid if he should be the instrument of saving one soul." Broadus was convinced, and he "sought out his pastor, and with a choking voice said, 'Brother Grimsley, the question is decided; I must try to be a preacher.'" At last his calling was clear, and four decades later he was grateful: "For the decision of that hour he is directly indebted, under God, to A. M. Poindexter; and amid a thousand imperfections and short-comings, that work of the ministry has been the joy of his life."[14]

Education at the University of Virginia

A few days after receiving his call to the ministry, Broadus began his college education at the University of Virginia. In his four years there, several professors influenced him tremendously as he earned a degree and was shaped by the influential institution that was so proudly the legacy of Thomas Jefferson. Professors William H. McGuffey, E. H. Courtenay, and Gessner Harrison became trusted mentors as well as teachers and guided the young minister-to-be as he studied in the classical curriculum and prepared for his career.

Broadus soon discovered deficiencies in his preparation for college. Although superior in some subjects, such as Latin, he lacked training in others, including mathematics. He took

---

13 Ibid., 398.
14 Ibid., 399.

advantage of the elective system at Virginia, which allowed him to select courses in a way that fitted his personal needs rather than following a rigid curriculum. He struggled initially but soon blossomed into an outstanding student and was rewarded for his efforts by being selected valedictorian of his class in 1850. While at the university, he joined the Jefferson Society, the largest and most prestigious of the debating societies. This gave him the opportunity to forge lasting friendships and to hone his speaking skills. While no one can judge the influence of a university education with exact certainty, it is clear that the University of Virginia left its imprint on Broadus.[15]

Of course, the impact of an institution derives from the people who labor in its name. While many professors made contributions to his education, McGuffey, Courtenay, and Harrison had the most influence on Broadus. William H. McGuffey, best known for the readers that bore his name, had taken the chair in moral philosophy at the University of Virginia the year before Broadus came to study there. A talented teacher who employed the Socratic Method, McGuffey also appealed to Broadus because he was a devout Christian who often filled the pulpit in nearby Presbyterian churches. In June 1849, having taken sick, he asked Broadus to take his place one Sunday morning and provided the young Baptist the opportunity to give his first sermon. E. H. Courtenay became professor of mathematics at Virginia in 1842 and was considered one of the best math teachers in the country. He worked closely with Broadus to help the student make up for his deficiencies in the subject and set an example for the future seminary professor with his patient repetition and exactitude.[16]

Of all his professors, Gessner Harrison influenced Broadus the most during his days as a university student. Harrison served as professor of ancient languages for 19 years before resigning in 1859 to start a high school. A graduate of the University of Virginia himself, Harrison immediately became a member of

---

[15] Robertson, *Life and Letters*, 55–74.
[16] Ibid., 62–63, 71, 63.

the faculty when recommended for a vacancy by the outgoing professor. Only 21, he developed his own teaching style and took the study of Latin and Greek in new directions in America. His work in etymology and syntax foreshadowed the later German development of "science of language." Using the dead languages "as materials and encouragement for his own laborious studies," Harrison delved deeply not only into the languages but also into history, geography, and literature. He published several important books, but even the admiring Broadus admitted that he might have done more had his "life been less burdened with the overwhelming drudgery of elementary instruction; and had he been more favorably situated for publishing." Teaching, then as now, often got in the way of research.[17]

But as a teacher Harrison won his greatest reputation. Plagued by a number of faults, including not having "a ready command of expression," which meant that "his first statements of an idea were often partial, involved and obscure," he still managed to become an effective lecturer and good teacher. He strove to overcome his inabilities as a speaker by reading the faces of his students, learning to gauge when he had achieved clarity and when he had not. On those occasions when "he saw many clouded faces," he repeated himself, "with all manner of illustrations and iteration, till at last, the greater part of them could see clearly." Broadus remembered Harrison's methods and argued that this "close observation of the class, this sympathy with their efforts to understand, and unwearied pains in helping them through difficulties, is one of the surest marks of the true teacher." The former student fondly recalled that his old professor "made constant use of the blackboard, often drawing quaint diagrams to assist the comprehension of the abstractions of syntax," and also "enlivened attention by frequent and apparently spontaneous gushes of a homely humor, as racy as it was peculiar."[18]

---

[17] For Harrison's life and career, see: Broadus, *Sermons and Addresses*, 303–47; 322; 325.
[18] Ibid., 330.

Beyond his scholarly activity and teaching abilities, Harrison also shaped the university and young Broadus with his efforts as a leader and disciplinarian. He served many terms as the chair of the faculty and worked to improve their lot and the reputation of the university. Jefferson's insistence that liberty required a student honor code meant that discipline was often a problem. Although most students embraced the code, learning to act as a responsible adult was not always easy, especially for young men. Faculty members, including Harrison, were occasionally the victims of violence, and many critics, both inside and outside the university, deplored the students' lack of morality. Harrison worked to improve discipline, largely through his influence as chairman of the faculty. His high moral character gave weight to his efforts, which largely centered on bringing Christianity to campus. A devout Methodist, Harrison worked for the appointment of a chaplain and also cooperated closely with Professor Courtenay to develop discipline policies that were a "combination of liberty and law."[19]

Professor Harrison became a mentor and trusted friend to the young Broadus. He also became his father-in-law in 1850 when Broadus married Maria Charlotte Harrison. In his memorial of Gessner Harrison, Broadus urged that the University of Virginia take the professor's mantle and live by the motto that marked his life: "Sirs, brothers, FEAR GOD AND WORK." Broadus learned much from Harrison, McGuffey, and Courtenay. Their different styles and methods afforded him the opportunity to glean valuable lessons from them that he later employed in his own teaching. Their dedication to learning, to scholarship, and to teaching served as living examples for him to emulate. Their high moral character and piety provided a steady Christian influence on the young convert studying at the state university.[20]

---

[19] Ibid., 334–335.
[20] Robertson, *Life and Letters*, 83; Broadus, *Sermons and Addresses*, 347.

Early Preaching Career

Broadus had started preaching while he was a student but did not immediately enter the pulpit upon his graduation. Instead he accepted the offer to teach at General Cocke's school in Bremo, Fluvanna County, Virginia. The general made the offer on the recommendation of Professor McGuffey, and Broadus spent a year teaching school and reading theology in preparation for the ministry. He considered numerous offers to preach or teach, including a professorship at Georgetown College in Kentucky, but none of them were attractive to the young man and his new bride. Then, in the fall of 1851, he received both a call to the pastorate of the Charlottesville Baptist Church and an offer to teach at the University of Virginia. The two positions could be taken together and offered the opportunity to pursue both his calling to preach and his inclination to teach. He accepted the offers and moved to Charlottesville.[21]

The year Broadus lived in Fluvanna had been spent studying and learning to teach and preach. As his biographer A. T. Robertson pointed out: "As he began, so he went on, so he closed his career—learning, teaching, and preaching." From late 1851 until he became a professor at The Southern Baptist Theological Seminary in 1859, he worked in Charlottesville, laboring at both the church and university. For two years he took a leave of absence from the church to serve as the university chaplain. Throughout this period Broadus lived out J. R. Scott's advice given in the admonition, "The way to learn to preach is to preach." His popularity as a teacher and preacher brought many students to the university and to the church. He learned to preach during this early ministry and his work brought results. His tenure as a pastor was marked by growth and revival, and his influence led to many conversions. Throughout these years he learned to appreciate the labor and methods of the ministry that led to true revival and positive results. One important event that marked his early ministry was a revival in the fall of 1852.[22]

---

[21] Robertson, *Life and Letters*, 75–95.

[22] Ibid., 96.

During his first year as pastor in Charlottesville, Broadus continued his course of study. He taught at the university and preached on Sunday mornings but still found time for a heavy load of reading. His hard work led friends to express concern for his health, and he often suffered from the strain of his new duties. Leading the congregation during the construction of a new church building proved to be a particularly heavy burden. Broadus began the work with enthusiasm and pushed hard to bring it to completion. This set the context for the revival in Charlottesville.[23]

Broadus recorded the revival of 1852 in a journal and reported it publicly to the world in the *Religious Herald*. He marked its beginnings in the spring when "it became a matter of frequent conversation and much regret among the members that we were so cold, and the cause making so little progress." While "some few persons were known to be more or less anxious but most of the unconverted remained careless, though quite attentive, and the professing Christians were all greatly lacking in fervor and zeal." Broadus and some of the church leaders, concerned about the situation, arranged for "a day for humiliation, fasting, and prayer." When held, the "exercises of this day were attended by a goodly number of the members, and a good deal of interest manifested." This began a period of prayer and fasting. "Sunrise prayer meetings were kept up for the next two weeks, and the members, especially the sisters, increased much in fervor of feeling; but most of the male members neglected the meetings, and could not be induced to do otherwise." Like many other ministers in the nineteenth century, Broadus found women more open to spiritual matters than men. Cooperation with women was often the key to revival.[24]

---

[23] Ibid., 96–103.

[24] Broadus, "Some Account of the Revival in the Charlottesville Church in October and November, 1852," John Albert Broadus Papers, James P. Boyce Centennial Library, The Southern Baptist Theological Seminary, Louisville, Kentucky. Broadus's experience with women in the church was similar to that of many other ministers and contradicts the argument of Christine Heyrman, who insists that evangelical clergy relied on the men of the South for access to their families. For Heyrman's view, see: Christine Heyrman, *Southern Cross: The Beginnings of the Bible Belt* (New York: Alfred A. Knopf, 1997), 117–60. For

Hoping to revive his congregation, Broadus tried to bring Barnett Grimsley to town as an evangelist but was unable to secure his help. By the first of June 1852, he and the church leaders decided to wait for revival. Broadus was away much of the summer, attending meetings and trying to recover his health after a period of illness. When he returned to the pulpit in the fall, he found that "the congregations were exceedingly attentive, and even serious, and he hoped." Hope soon turned to excited reality. In October, "he renewed a previously given invitation to Elder Wm. F. Broaddus to come to preach. He promised to do so." Anticipating his uncle's arrival, "with fear and trembling, and yet with some hope and more than ordinary prayerfulness," Broadus "set to work to prepare for a protracted effort."[25]

William F. Broaddus arrived and from Wednesday, October 20, to Sunday, October 24, preached "to large congregations, and with great power and earnestness." Broaddus later recalled the Charlottesville revival as "one of my old-time meetings." Broaddus was a powerful speaker, and his "sermons proved that it was not without reason he had been so long the idol of many hearts in Northeast Virginia." His nephew was among those moved by the evangelist's preaching: "Friday morning, the brethren present were much moved, and the pastor's sorrowing heart greatly encouraged, by a sermon upon 'Be not weary in well-doing; for in due season, etc.'" The effort soon brought results and on "Saturday night an invitation to come forward for prayer was accepted by several, and Sunday afternoon four persons were received as candidates for baptism."[26]

His uncle was "compelled to leave on Monday morning," the 25th of October, but Broadus happily reported that the revival continued until November 5, as "the meetings were kept up every night, with prayer meetings nearly every morning." Others

---

an earlier experience that was similar to that of Broadus, see: A. James Fuller, *Chaplain to the Confederacy: Basil Manly and Baptist Life in the Old South* (Baton Rouge: Louisiana State University Press, 2000), esp. 43–55, 140.

[25] Broadus, "Some Account of the Revival."

[26] Ibid., J. A. Broadus, in *Religious Herald*, 1852, quoted in Robertson, *Life and Letters*, 104.

pitched in to help with the preaching, especially lay preachers and at least one retired minister. They were so eager to help that Broadus only had to deliver one sermon himself. Thus, "The interest increased steadily for a week after Elder Broaddus's departure, and there was still much feeling on the last occasion of extra services." The pastor counted thirty-five conversions by November 5 and noticed that "many of them were cases of exceeding interest." Hopeful that the revival might continue, he tried to enlist the services of another evangelist, including Basil Manly Jr., but none were able to come. The young preacher prayed for the converts, asking that "the Lord grant that each one of them may be truly and faithfully his!"[27]

The Charlottesville revival of 1852 taught Broadus valuable lessons, and he noted them in his journal. His notations included stories of powerful conversions and the humble recognition that his personal role had been limited. The first lesson he learned was, "The power of prayer—the strange fact that God does indeed hear and answer the petitions of his people." To prove this most important point, he related the story of a young woman who "had been more than a week in darkness and grievous anguish, passing through almost all varieties of feeling." Concerned about her spiritual state, Broadus described her condition to his parishioners gathered at one of the early morning prayer meetings and requested the "special prayers of God's people through the day in her behalf." The answer to prayer came quickly as "that night she told him she was converted." Broadus noted her conversion and provided details of how it happened, "She had been reading religious books and tracts during the day and could not tell precisely when any change had come over her, but she was now calmly trusting in Jesus (she was Miss Bettie Purley)." He also remarked on how prayer had lifted his own spirit in the course of the revival. He, "himself, partly doubtless from physical exhaustion, had been feeling on Friday night, October 29, a great lack of fervor and zeal." Broadus "requested special prayer in his behalf and

---

[27] Broadus, "Some Account of the Revival."

he found in himself afterward, a greatly increased interest and efficiency."[28]

In addition to the paramount importance of prayer in bringing about true revival, the events of that autumn also taught Broadus the "fact that good is often done when no one thinks so." He reported that a certain gentleman "was greatly affected by a sermon in the early part of February." The sermon was one that Broadus himself "thought one of his poorest and mourned over it." Another example of good being done when it was not expected came in the story of a lady who "was awakened in the spring by reading *Baxter's Call*, a copy of which the pastor had given her but which he scarcely hoped had produced any effect." Still another example was related in the account of a young woman who "was much moved by a little exhortation made at the prayer meeting, Sunday night, October 17, and went home in an agony of grief. The pastor had hesitated about saying anything and thought afterwards he had spoken to no purpose."[29]

Beyond these two significant lessons, Broadus argued that "protracted effort is most likely to be serviceable where the congregation [had] been inclined before to give attention to religion—the unusual effort serving then to call out what was latent, and bring the halting to decision." Here he carefully delineated between those revivals that were worked up by the use of the so-called "new measures" and those that he considered to be the work of God. Many Baptist leaders worried about the methods used by evangelicals in the Second Great Awakening, fearing that preachers too readily employed the methods of revivalism to create emotional outbursts in order to add to their numbers. Such measures did not mean that true conversion had occurred, and often the so-called converts quickly lapsed back into a life of sin. Protracted meetings were the hallmark of the later periods of the Second Great Awakening, and camp meetings had been the symbol of the early stages of it. Broadus was

---

[28] Ibid.
[29] Ibid.

quick to point out that the Charlottesville revival was not something that had been concocted by the preachers but was built on solid spiritual foundations.[30]

Overjoyed by the revival, Broadus reported that, "upon the whole I have enjoyed during these meetings, a very large measure of happiness. O what joy, in seeing men and women turn to the Lord, over whom my heart had often yearned in anxiety!" He prayed that the "Lord bless all those who have thus lately found Him! O may they be as the apple of Thine eye! May they grow rapidly in grace, may they soon come to shine, and with always increasing brightness, as lights in the world!" Happy for the new converts, he lamented those who had not been saved, "Yet alas! How many there are, who are without hope; who have lived through all this precious season, thus far, and gained no good from it." He prayed, "O that the Divine word may take hold on their hearts! O that the Divine Spirit may pursue them still, and may they have no peace from their consciences, till they find in believing in Jesus, the peace which passeth all understanding."[31]

The young preacher was careful to notice how limited a part he himself had played in the revival. He humbly asked:

> And now, Lord, that thou hast so greatly blessed one, who is indeed "less than the least of all saints," granting him "in due season" to reap, and that so abundantly, help me now to go on my way "rejoicing in hope, patient in tribulation, continuing instant in prayer."

Concerned that success might distract him from his efforts as a minister, he prayed that God would "help me to feel my nothingness before thee, help me to love the souls of my fellow men with an earnest love, and to prefer the prosperity of Zion above my chief joy. And O! deliver me from foolish vanity. Cleanse me of that plague-spot of my soul." Broadus gave the credit for the revival to God: "And help me, in gratitude and adoring love

---

[30] Ibid. For a brief analysis of the Baptist concerns about the new measures in the life of Basil Manly Sr., see: Nettles, *The Baptists, Volume Two*, 278–82.
[31] Broadus, "Some Account of the Revival."

to say, 'Not unto us, O Lord, not unto us, but unto *thy name* give glory, for thy mercy, and for thy truth's sake.'"[32]

In the aftermath of the revival, Broadus set to work to reap fully the spiritual harvest by establishing the new converts in their faith. On November 10, 1852, he baptized 23 people and reported that the "place was quite suitable and convenient, and the morning fine, though at 8 o'clock a.m. it was of course rather cold. The scene was solemn, though I did not feel so deeply as I could have wished." He noticed sinners in the audience and admitted that "I trust that some, who saw their kindred and friends there publicly 'put on Christ,' may be led to think of their own condition, without a Saviour, without God, without hope, and seek the Lord with purpose of heart." He prayed for the newly baptized Christians, "May the guardian care of God be over all those who have thus named the name of Christ, may they be useful, faithful, and thus happy Christians." The preacher hoped "that this may be but the beginning of good things" and prayed "help me to labor, O Lord, to labor earnestly, in faith and hope. O that many more might be converted, and that speedily!"[33]

Such work continued throughout November and included frequent pastoral visits. His calls on parishioners had played a valuable role in the revival, and he would continue the practice throughout his career. They proved especially useful in helping new converts, and after a pastoral visit on November 15, he wrote that, "I do not want to forget Mary Cooke's smiling, joyful countenance, when she sprang to meet me this morning. The Lord bless her in her Christian hope." The young woman's conversion was a special case for Broadus because "I really thought once that she had very little intelligence." Concerned about her, he "sat down one evening, and tried to take nothing for granted, but to explain to her the way of salvation." Apparently, his explanation was effective because "now she tells me that the night after that conversation she was enabled to let go

---

[32] Ibid.
[33] Ibid.

all else, and trust simply in Jesus, and thanks me for 'making it all so plain.'" Broadus happily noted, "I find her now to be quite a sensible girl. What a lesson I might learn from this little incident. Her grandfather was a Baptist preacher, an intimate of Old Andrew and her father was named Andrew Broaddus Cooke."[34]

His reports of baptisms and individual conversions continued for a while. In the summer of 1853, he preached at a protracted meeting himself and reported still more lessons learned. First, he insisted that Christians should not "despise the day of small things. We had very small congregations, and yet good was done." Second, he reported the effectiveness of using personal accounts in his preaching: "It is sometimes useful to mention points as of my *own experiences* (where that is the fact)." He did "not believe in a preacher's 'telling his experience' from beginning to end, which has obvious disadvantages—but only the mention of particular points."[35]

Third, he made note of his attacks on the Campbellites and how it affected his ministry: "I was proud, one day, of having (as a brother thought) demolished the Campbellites, and the next day made another hit at them, in such a spirit as spoiled the earnestness and tenderness of the whole sermon." Alexander Campbell had initially attracted many Baptists when he strongly defended adult baptism, but his insistence on a primitive Christianity soon led to resistance from other churches that questioned his views on doctrinal matters. The continuing power of Campbellism meant that many Baptist preachers frequently confronted the movement. Broadus's final lesson also involved disputes with other Christians as he remarked that,

> in a region where Pedobaptists are frequently attacked,
> one will be apter to convince and win them by preach-
> ing only the great truths in which we all agree. There

---

[34] Broadus kept meticulous records of his pastoral visits. They may be found in several journals in John Albert Broadus Papers, James P. Boyce Centennial Library, The Southern Baptist Theological Seminary, Louisville, Kentucky; Broadus, "Some Account of the Revival."
[35] Ibid.

are cases in which it is doubtless proper to present points of difference, but those cases do seem to me to be very few.

Such a well-armed theologian as Broadus was always ready to do battle over doctrinal differences, especially when it came to such an important matter as baptism. But he advised caution when it came to attacking the beliefs of other churches in the pulpit.[36]

The revival of 1852 coincided with Broadus's efforts to build the new church building in Charlottesville and helped accomplish the task. But the church went into debt to complete the building. Many in the congregation began using the debt as an excuse not to support other work. When a special service for the support of Foreign Missions was planned, church leaders asked Broadus not to have it, arguing that they needed to pay off the debt first. The young minister responded, "Do you think that after being blessed of God in building a house for our comfort and convenience we ought to neglect the lost souls out yonder for whom Christ died?" Worried about the debt, Broadus "went home, fell on his knees, and prayed God for wisdom to lead his people." He prepared and delivered "the best sermon he possibly could on the subject and urged his people to give." At the close of the service, "a glorious collection followed." Impressed by their pastor's leadership, members of the church came to his house the next evening "and paid every dollar of the debt which had been worrying them."[37]

Events like the revival and the repayment of the debt marked the young preacher's tenure in Charlottesville. He developed his own style of preaching, perfecting the ability to convey his message in a way that combined "tremendous moral earnestness with deep pathos and delicate flashes of humor." His power in the pulpit was remarkable, as his "magnetism threw a spell over his audience. People felt that his preaching was one of the events of their lives not to be missed." While many young

---

[36] Ibid.

[37] Robertson, *Life and Letters*, 104–105.

preachers attracted followers and intelligent men won fame, with Broadus it "was more than the glow of youth and genius." Instead, there "was great spiritual power that melted hearts to repentance."[38]

Ever the scholar, Broadus reflected on his own success and shared his insights with others. In 1854 he published an "Essay on the Best Mode of Preparing and Delivering Sermons," in the *Religious Herald*. The piece foreshadowed his later book on the subject and emphasized the importance of study as well as mastering the art of extemporaneous speaking. His own preaching demonstrated his superior abilities and a man who heard him preach at a protracted meeting in Richmond in 1857 later reported that he "threw a matchless spell over the people that carried them away." The observer heard Broadus preach numerous times throughout his career and noted the changes that came with the passing of time, saying that early in his career, "people would worship Broadus, as the most wonderful thing you ever heard. In his later years you went away melted with reverence. There was not more intensity of manner in the early years, but he emitted power more continuously." Broadus "never trifled with his feelings. He preserved his emotions fresh and sweet and there refined piety and the emotion of the Holy Spirit." His profound efforts caused others to imitate him. He was a master preacher, "an artist." In him, "art and nature were married."[39]

Broadus's early career as a preacher came to an end in 1859 when he accepted the call to become a professor in the newly established Southern Baptist Theological Seminary. His years in Charlottesville had brought forth fruit. As he prepared to move into a new phase of his life, he reported on his work since September 1851. In the eight years in Charlottesville, he had preached 761 sermons, 122 of them at the University of Virginia, 421 at the Charlottesville Baptist Church, and 218 elsewhere. Under his ministry 241 people had been baptized. His congregation knew how effective he was and reluctantly let him go. One sad line

---

[38] Ibid., 107.
[39] Ibid., 123–26; 147.

written as he prepared to leave reflected both his legacy and his methods as a preacher, "Leave us not, man of prayer."[40]

The Foundation for Greatness

When John A. Broadus became a seminary professor in 1859, he moved into a larger sphere of usefulness. Not yet the important leader he would later become, he had laid the foundation for future greatness in his early career as a minister. His intellectual bent, his passion for study, his incisive mind, his speaking abilities, his humility, his reliance on prayer, and so much more had been developed on the job in Charlottesville. Shaped by older ministers and university professors as well as members of his own family, Broadus had also made his own way. He struggled with his calling, pursued knowledge at great expense of time and energy, and created his own style of ministry and preaching. In so doing, he emerged as a rising star in the Baptist fold in the years just before the Civil War. The fires of war would further shape him as he served as a chaplain in the Confederate Army and endured the hard times experienced at the seminary during and after the conflict. But he was already prepared for the work that would make him one of the most important Baptists in the world in the late nineteenth century. His education and experience in the antebellum years made him ready to make contributions as a minister, educator, and theologian. Those impressed with his later writings on preaching need only look to his early career to see the roots of his powerful insights. Here was a teacher who had practiced the things he taught. Truly, Broadus had lived out the advice his college friend had given him in 1851. He was an intellectual, a man of great learning and education, much influenced by his reading in the classics and the field of theology. But he was also a man of action. The fruits of his labor in Charlottesville made clear that he had discovered that "the way to learn to preach is to preach."

---

[40] Ibid., 166–67.

Chapter IV

John A. Broadus, Rhetoric, and
A Treatise on the Preparation and Delivery of Sermons

Roger D. Duke

There is much known and written about John A. Broadus the man, the pastor, the New Testament scholar, seminary cofounder and seminary president, denominational statesman, Yale lecturer, and Southern gentleman. But not as much is known about his study of the classics and how they impacted his life. Even less is understood about one specific influence of this classical and personal education, this particular dynamic helped form him into such an outstanding pulpit orator—*classical rhetoric*. This study caused Broadus to "baptize" rhetoric and bring it into Southern Baptist life similarly to what St. Augustine had done.[1] This chapter will seek to demonstrate how this influence affected Broadus as a preacher and as a writer in *A Treatise on the Preparation and Delivery of Sermons.*

---

[1] Reader's Note: For an introductory discussion and analysis of Augustine's *On Christian Doctrine,* please refer to Patricia Bizzell and Bruce Herzberg, eds., *The Rhetorical Tradition: Readings from Classical Times to the Present* (Boston: Bedford Books of St. Marin's Press, 1990), 381–422.

Broadus as Classicist

John Albert Broadus was the fourth and youngest son of Major Edmund Broadus and Nancy Sims Broadus. His older siblings aided in young John's education: "To their instructions was added the teaching of other tutors. From an uncle, Albert G. Sims, he received a careful and accurate grounding in the rudiments of learning."[2] This proved to be a resource upon which he would draw for the rest of his days. "His 'graduation' from his uncle's school was somewhat unusual. He returned home unexpectedly and when Major Broadus inquired the reason the son replied, 'My uncle says he has no further use for me,'"[3] indicating that the young boy had learned all his uncle had to teach. The uncle reassured the father that "he had taught John 'all that he knew.'"[4]

Young Broadus continued his formative education in the mid 1840s. This time of personal study gave him a love for the classics that would change his mode and method of learning. Also during this time he discovered his love for the ancient Greek language. He had considered the ministry and an expertise in the biblical languages would certainly be needed for such a vocation. He had resolved to do what was needed for the task. During this same period he solidified his plans to enter the University of Virginia.[5]

Young John did indeed enter the University of Virginia in the fall of 1846. Since his early education was marred by fits and starts, the next four years were spent in diligent and disciplined study. However, "As a student . . . at the University of Virginia, he was a member of the debating society and enjoyed speaking whenever he had opportunity. During this period his study of Latin and Greek acquainted him with the works of Greek and Roman rhetoricians."[6] He received the master of arts degree in

---

[2] Vernon Latrelle Stanfield, *Favorite Sermons of John A. Broadus* (New York: Harper Bros., 1959), 2.

[3] Ibid., 2–3.

[4] Ibid., 4.

[5] Ibid., 3.

[6] Paul Huber, "A Study of the Rhetorical Theories of John A. Broadus" (Ph. D. diss., University of Michigan, 1956), 3.

1850. Soon he was destined to become one of the best known alumni of his day from this prestigious southern university.[7] His reputation, education, and Christian character illuminated many personal abilities. These brought the young preacher varied vocational opportunities.

When he finished his university course, Broadus rejected various job offers in order to study biblical languages and other theological disciplines. He went to a private school as tutor in Fluvanna County, Virginia. There he preached in small churches as well as studying church history, theology, sermons, and the Bible. Eventually he took a position as tutor of Latin and Greek at the university and became pastor of the Baptist Church at Charlottesville, Virginia. He soon resigned from the University of Virginia in order to pastor the church full time.[8]

During his pastoral tenure Broadus had to face a rather tough personal decision: "In 1858 he was asked to become a [founding] member of the first faculty of the new Southern Baptist Theological Seminary."[9] Initially he turned down the offer to become a professor. This was due to his love of preaching and the pastorate.[10] This invitation pushed Broadus upon the horns of a personal dilemma: "But there [sic] ensued months of struggle with himself over the decision, and he finally agreed to become a member of the first faculty of the Seminary when it opened in Greenville, South Carolina, in 1859."[11]

Broadus was trained both personally and formally as a classicist. He knew and employed the ancient languages, disciplines, and theories and brought them to his students. These were worked out in the classroom before he ever began to write his famous *A Treatise on the Preparation and Delivery of Sermons*.[12] He taught preaching for some 10 years before

---

[7] Stanfield, 4.
[8] Ibid.
[9] Ibid.
[10] Ibid., 4–5.
[11] Ibid.
[12] Reader's note: In the remainder of this chapter, Broadus's *A Treatise on the Preparation and Delivery of Sermons* will be referred to as *Treatise*.

ever compiling and assembling his tome on homiletics.[13] There came a time in the seminary's life when he was no longer able to teach preaching. Broadus's expertise required that he move into administration and other teaching roles. He later reflected on the need to assemble a textbook for his students:

> The desire thus arose to prepare . . . a work which should be [a] full range of topics, and should also attempt to combine the thorough discussion of principles with an abundance of practical rules and suggestions. . . . The author determined, before the subject should fade from his mind, to undertake the work he had contemplated.[14]

Here the *Treatise* had germinated and had begun its incubation.

Broadus began to assemble the *Treatise* and "once carefully rework[ed] . . . his lectures on homiletics for a blind student."[15] As with most professors who must convert classroom notes into a textbook, it was a difficult task of selection. Broadus had preached and taught employing the historic *Canons of Rhetoric*.[16] He employed the classical rhetoricians as his personal mentors. He credited the use of the *Canons*[17] in his *Preface* to his *Treatise*: "The author's chief indebtedness for help has been to Aristotle, Cicero, and Quintilian, and to [contemporaries] Whately and Vinet."[18] The *Canons*, giants of classical rhetoric, and contemporary teachers of oratory all served him well in the classroom as well as the pulpit.

---

[13] John Albert Broadus, *A Treatise on the Preparation and Delivery of Sermons* (1871; reprint, from the Collection of the University of Michigan, Ann Arbor: University Library Scholarly Publishing Office, n.d.), iii.

[14] Broadus, *Treatise*, iii.

[15] Stanfield, 4.

[16] Patricia Bizzell and Bruce Herzberg, eds., *The Rhetorical Tradition: Readings from Classical Times to the Present* (Boston: Bedford Books of St. Marin's Press, 1990), 3–7.

[17] *Canons of Rhetoric* will be referred to as *Canons* throughout the remained of the chapter.

[18] Broadus, *Treatise*, vi.

In addition to the classical rhetoricians, Broadus drew upon another who had adapted rhetoric for preaching. This was none other than St. Augustine. Broadus borrowed heavily from the great theologian and rhetorician. All of the ancient influences shaped Broadus's use of rhetorical theory as well as praxis. He was careful to credit his ancient mentor: "Augustine says, *Veritas pateat, veritas placeat, veritas moveat,* 'Make the truth plain, make it pleasing, make it moving.'"[19] Even a cursory reading of Broadus's *Treatise* demonstrated how these words were his subtext throughout.

Broadus's Use of the Canons of Rhetoric

Aristotle "systematized" the *Canons of Rhetoric* by the end of the fourth century BC. His system would forever serve as rhetorical paradigm. It came to be "fleshed out" later by Cicero and Quintilian.[20] Aristotle's system simply stated what rhetoric should entail:

> The *classical system* of rhetoric [where] there are three principal kinds of public speech: the *legal speech*, which takes place in the courtroom and concerns judgment about a *past action*; the *political speech* in the legislative assembly, concerned with moving people to *future* actions; the *ceremonial speech* in a public forum, intended to strengthen shared beliefs about the *present* state of affairs. In the classical system, these three situations constitute the entire domain of rhetoric (emphasis added).[21]

The seasoned Broadus understood well that rhetoric could be adapted for preaching. This undoubtedly was a focus early in his personal study of Greek and Latin, modern foreign languages, and contemporary sermons. Most contemporary sermons were built upon a learned "eloquence" or rhetoric as it was then known.[22]

---

[19] Broadus, *Treatise*, 20–21.
[20] Bizzell and Herzberg, 3.
[21] Ibid.
[22] See Broadus's pp. 20ff. for a fuller discussion of the "Nature of Eloquence" and the synonymous usage of *eloquence* with *rhetoric.*

Studying the *Canons* was considered essential to become an effective orator in the nineteenth century. Everyone who trained in public address knew "classical rhetoric divides the process of preparing a persuasive speech into five stages:"[23]

> *Invention*, the search for persuasive ways to present the information and formulate arguments
>
> *Arrangement*, the organization of the parts of a speech to ensure that all the means of persuasion are present and properly disposed
>
> *Style*, the use of correct, appropriate, and striking language throughout the speech
>
> *Memory*, the use of mnemonics and practice
>
> *Delivery*, presenting the speech with effective gestures and vocal modulation
>
> This five-part composing process remains a cornerstone of the study of rhetoric (emphasis added).[24]

Without this elementary knowledge one would not be considered as a properly trained orator.

Rhetoric in its classical iterations had a sustained impact on all of Broadus's preaching and teaching praxis. It was because of this influence that he organized his *Treatise* around the *Canons*: "The textbook written by Broadus reflects both his interest in and knowledge of public speaking. . . . Aware that memory is no longer considered in the traditional classical sense, he does not discuss it separately, but only in reference to delivery."[25] For this present discussion then, the *Canons* classically known as *inventio* (invention), *dispositio* (arrangement), *elocutio* (elocution or style), *pronuntiatio* (delivery), and *memoria*[26] will be considered generally and, in turn, from Broadus's *Treatise*.

---

[23] Bizzell and Herzberg, 3.

[24] Ibid., 3–4.

[25] Huber, 3.

[26] Laura Sells, "Greco Roman Rhetoric," [Internet online]; available from <http://www.voxygen.net/rhetciv/GrecoRoman%20Rhetoric.htm> (5 April 2005).

Broadus on Invention

The ancient rhetor selected elements from personal education as well as experience to craft the speech for each occasion. For Aristotle, this was at the heart of persuasion process and event. He observed: "Let rhetoric be [defined as] an ability, in each [particular] case, to see the available means of persuasion."[27] At the center of these observations was the canon of invention. George Kennedy also affirmed Aristotle here: "Invention is commonly defined as the process of determining what to say in a discourse. This process includes both *the choice of a subject* and *the accumulation of materials* which will enable a speaker to transform the subject into a living speech" (emphasis added).[28] This was the essence of Broadus as he prepared any address.

Broadus did not have to "invent" his means of persuasion. He possessed these in abundance: the Scriptures, formal education, wide reading, and life experiences. All of these served as sources of invention for him. He declared: "The chief materials of a sermon are in the great mass of cases not really *invented* at the time of preparation; they are the results of previous acquisition and reflection. . . . The young preacher is not aware that he is drawing upon all that he has thought, felt, and seen, all that he has read and heard, since his childhood."[29] All that a young minister possessed was his intellectual library for preparation in Broadus's schemata.

In the *Treatise* Broadus quoted contemporary pulpit orators to demonstrate that invention must be ongoing for the serious pulpit minister.[30] This was one juncture where his classical training became apparent. He was convinced education helped define, expose, and illumine all of life's experiences. Unmistakably the Bible was his primary source for invention. He argued for this undeniable truth in the *Treatise*:

---

[27] George A. Kennedy, trans., *Aristotle: On Rhetoric; A Theory of Civic Discourse* (New York: Oxford University Press, 1991), 36.

[28] Huber, 10.

[29] Broadus, *Treatise*, 118–19.

[30] See Broadus's *Treatise,* 118ff for a more in-depth discussion.

The *Scriptures* themselves should at every period of his life be a preacher's chief study. When we meet a young brother who has just become convinced that it is his duty to preach, and who is inquiring about preparation for the work, our first word ought to be, the Bible. . . . Young ministers . . . are often sadly deficient as to this general knowledge of the Bible. . . . And every stage of culture and experience, as life goes on, presents fresh occasion and new facilities for studying the Bible.[31]

Broadus recognized the study of Scriptures as paramount to the well-equipped pulpit orator. They were the prism through which all of human existence should be understood and interpreted.

This preacher rhetor had no personal affection or affinity for rules *per se*. However, he did quote Kidder who "'mentions some . . . practical suggestions in reference to *invention* in the form of rules:

Address your mind to the *invention* of thoughts, not words. Words may be employed, but only as auxiliaries. . . .

Pursue *invention* in every variety of circumstance, in the study and out of it. . . .

Make an early selection of subjects in order to secure the advantages of the repeated and incidental action of the *inventive* powers. . . .

Use former studies and preparations as helps to *invention* rather than as substitutes for it'" (emphasis added).[32]

Broadus's use of the Bible as his primary source kept him from having to employ invention in its classical sense. Scrip-

---

[31] Broadus, *Treatise*, 121.
[32] Daniel P. Kidder, *A Treatise on Homiletics* (New York: Phillips & Hunt), 152; quoted in Dargan & Broadus, 119–21.

ture was his ready "textbook for invention." He grieved at the dearth of basic Bible knowledge of those would-be young gospel preachers. He lamented:

> Young ministers . . . are often found sadly deficient as to this general knowledge of the Bible; while the best Sunday Schools, as well as the most admirable family instruction, have usually but laid the foundation for such knowledge as the preacher should make haste to gain.[33]

This "dearth of basic Bible knowledge" seemed to cause him acute personal grief.

Broadus strenuously desired that young men who were "called to preach" should "[Study the Bible i]n the originals, if possible, in the English version at any rate; by the rapid reading of large portions, by the thorough study of a given book, by the minute examination of particular passages . . . [so in] every way, . . . [they would] continually, . . . keep up, freshen, [and] extend . . . [a personal] acquaintance with the precious Word of God."[34]

He drew his invented materials from another source as well. This was the discipline of systematic theology. Here his love and passion were particularly observable:

> *Systematic Theology* is of unspeakable importance to the preacher, indispensable if he would be in the best sense instructive, and exert an abiding influence over his hearers. . . . Exegesis and Systematic Theology properly go hand in hand. Neither is complete, neither is really safe, without the other.[35]

These were symbiotic for the preacher's task in Broadus's idealized construct.

---

[33] John A. Broadus, *A Treatise on the Preparation and Delivery of Sermons*, rev., Edwin Charles Dargan with revised bibliography by C. S. Gardner, vol. 2 in *The Selected Works of John A. Broadus* (New York: Hodder and Stroughton, 1898; reprint, Cape Coral, FL: Founder's Press, 2001), 122. Hereafter referred to as Broadus, *TREATISE*–Dargan rev.

[34] Broadus, *Treatise*—Dargan rev., 123.

[35] Broadus, *Treatise*, 122–23.

All of these sources taken together—a working knowledge of the Scriptures, an education informed by personal experience and wide readings, and a working knowledge of systematic theology—served Broadus as means of invention. He used the Bible for his content and rhetorical invention as his method while both were underwritten by formal education, current events, and life experiences. The integration of exegesis and interpretation of Scripture intersected with rhetorical method of invention. These were the crossroad intersections where Broadus did his best work to prepare a sermon and prepare lectures for the classroom.

Broadus's synthesized methods of invention were plain, straightforward, and quite adaptable for the veteran or neophyte. Everything in life was a tool for use in sermon preparation and delivery. Broadus meticulously captured life experiences in his personal journal. He recorded relevant thoughts, insights, and observations as they came to mind. Well ahead of a particular address Broadus chose the apt materials with care. The biblical text and experiential observations were both adopted with delicate thought. As all sources came together, his applications and adaptations of ancient rhetorical techniques proved quite effective. It enlivened his pulpit manner as well as his classroom teaching of homiletics.

Broadus on Arrangement

The homiletical professor's oratorical acumen proved the necessity and importance of the canon of arrangement. However, he did not treat arrangement as meticulously as other canons such as invention, style, or delivery. He used an eclectic approach as he drew upon the ancient principles for his modern-day iterations needed to teach homiletics.[36] He drew from two classic rhetorical treatises. These were *De Inventione* by Cicero and *Institutio Oratoria* by Qunitilian. However, "he says far less on arrangement than is found in either of these classical works."[37] Here

---

[36] Huber, 45.
[37] Ibid, 45.

Broadus more closely aligned with his contemporaries' use of rhetorical theory. He gleaned what met his needs. Concerning this eclecticism, Huber observed: "The influences he reflects originate from both classical and modern sources, but in giving his [*Treatise*] readers the ideas of others he not only reveals selectivity in his choices, but also offers many conclusions that appear to be based upon his own thinking and experiences."[38] Huber further demonstrated that "almost half of the information given on arrangement . . . concerns organization of various kinds of sermons. In dealing with 'sermon types' and arrangement, he particularly bases his recommendations upon his own experiences as a teacher and preacher."[39]

Broadus employed the metaphor of a general arraying his army for the larger battle rather than the lieutenant deploying individual soldiers in the field. Dargan and Broadus both commented on this stratagem: "The speaker's task may be compared to the organization of an army, and then the concentration of its several divisions upon one objective point."[40]

At this juncture Broadus borrowed from a contemporary orator's understanding of how arrangement should be seen. He knew that any composition should have order. Order holds the discourse together. To vindicate his theory, he cited Vinet's use of Pascal: "'Good thoughts,' says Pascal, 'are abundant. . . . ' I will not go so far as to say that a discourse without order can produce no effect. . . . But we may affirm . . . the power of discourse is proportional to the order in which [arrangement] reigns in it."[41] All of the *Canons* are important, but none was more so to Broadus than that of arrangement.

Although Broadus did not give prevalence to arrangement, nonetheless he gave some extended comments about its appropriation. He demonstrated how "(1) Arrangement is of great importance *to the speaker himself*. . . . (2) Still more important is good arrangement as regards the *effect on the audience*. . . . And

---

[38] Ibid.

[39] Huber, 45.

[40] Broadus, *Treatise*—Dargan rev., 259.

[41] Adolphe Vinet, *Homiletics*, trans. Thomas Skinner (New York: Ivison & Phinney, 1855), 264–65; quoted in Broadus, *Treatise*, 242.

finally, it causes the discourse to be *more easily remembered.*"[42] These three practices governed his sermonic assembly.

Broadus argued passionately that these three arrangement mechanics would serve as a primary rhetorical device. He exhorted the readers of the *Treatise* that order and arrangement made the sermon more persuasive. When "motives and . . . appeals to feeling[s]" are used, "order is of great importance."[43] Always sympathetic to the congregation, he put their needs first. He continued: "The hearers' feelings will be much more powerfully and permanently excited, when appeals are made in some *natural order* (emphasis added)."[44]

As he closed his discussion on arrangement, Broadus summarized by utilizing another contemporary colleague:

> Coquerel says that the lack of [the arrangement] method is the most common fault of preaching, and the most inexcusable, because [it is] usually the result of insufficient labor. "A man cannot give himself all the qualities of the orator; but by taking the necessary pains, he can connect his ideas, and proceed with order in the composition of discourse."[45]

Although arrangement was not as relevant for Broadus, nevertheless, it did serve its purpose in his overall schemata and possessed a high level of credence by him.

Broadus on Style

Broadus took greater pains concerning his discussions about rhetorical style. This was somewhat juxtaposed to his rather short treatment of arrangement. When he began the discussion of style in the *Treatise*, he was greatly concerned with its nature, value, and improvement for the apprentice orator. The three perceived characteristics most important for style were *perspicuity*, *energy*, and *elegance*. Here his *Treatise* demonstrated an

---

[42] Broadus, *Treatise*, 243–47.

[43] Ibid., 246.

[44] Ibid.

[45] Coquerel, *Observ. sur la Pred.*, 163; quoted in Broadus, *Treatise*, 245.

extremely pedagogical nature. It was broken down into minute detail with many examples to serve the reader.[46] Huber picked up Broadus's subdivisions of style here: "He begins his discussion of style by giving what is essentially a conventional definition."[47] Broadus's classical education showed forth here.

Huber captured Broadus's essence with one sharp observation:

> In effect . . . *style* is an orator's characteristic manner of expressing his thoughts whether in writing or speaking. What was emphasized here is the idea that expression or style is invariably the result of the learning, experiences, and interests of a given individual (emphasis added).[48]

There were some reverberations of Broadus's discussions with that of invention. There Broadus demonstrated how the preacher could use the Bible, systematic theology, and a wide variation of personal interest readings to gather sermonic materials. Here he synthesized invention with that of style. This was clearly seen when he declared that "the idea that expression or style is invariably the result of the learning, experiences, and interests of a given individual."[49]

Broadus understood invention and style as symbiotic tools for the young minister. The novice should know both in their classical sense and apply them to contemporary circumstances. Broadus left the young minister the right and privilege to develop his own style through learning, experiences, and personal interests. He understood that "the most important property of style is perspicuity. Style is excellent when, like the atmosphere, it shows the thought, but itself is not seen."[50]

What then was this perspicuity? Broadus again borrowed from a contemporary protégé for insights. Shedd's *Homiletics and Pastoral Theology* shined light on the subject:

---

[46] Huber, 78.
[47] Ibid.
[48] Ibid.
[49] Ibid.
[50] Broadus, *Treatise*, 339.

The thoughts which the religious teacher presents to the common mind should go straight to the understanding. Everything that covers up and envelops the truth should be stripped off from it, so that the bare reality may be seen. . . . When the style is *plain* . . . the hearer experiences the sensation of being touched: and this sensation is always impressive. . . . The preacher should toil after this property of *style*, as he would toil after virtue (emphasis added).[51]

For Broadus, nothing was more important than to bring clarity and plainness to the pulpit. If a congregation could not understand what was declared, what then was the point?

Broadus continued his synthesis of the classical with the contemporary. Quintilian's *The Institutio Oratoria* demonstrated an understanding of perspicuity's character of plainness. He was so impressed that he made it central to his preaching. The address must flood the mind like the sun according to Quintilian. He declared: "We must take care, not that it shall be possible for him [the hearer] to understand, but that it shall be utterly impossible for him not to understand."[52] Broadus drew illumination to lighten the eyes of his young students from Quintilian's classical description.

He spoke at length of his understanding about the rhetorical canon of style. Energy was the essence of style for him. Energy contained three components and among them was "*Animation*, or liveliness, [which] serves to stimulate [the] attention" of the hearers. He used "The term *force* . . . especially with reference to arguments, and the kindred word for power . . . applied both to arguments and to motives." Both must be wedded: "*Passion*—which in its milder and more tender forms we call *ethos*, and in its highest form the sublime." These employed in concert would have their "effect upon the feelings, often by means of

---

[51] William T. G. Shedd, *Homiletics and Pastoral Theology* (New York: Charles Scribner's Sons, 1898), 63–69; quoted in Broadus, *Treatise*, 340.
[52] Quintilian, *The Institutio Oratoria*, Broadus's personal translation from the original language, VIII, 2, 23, 29; quoted in Broadus, *Treatise*, 341.

the imagination: and both force and passion aim at last to influence the will."[53]

Broadus shared a homespun anecdote in the *Treatise* that illustrated well how this energy of style should be delivered. He recounted: "There is a homely story of a preacher who suggested to a sleepy hearer that snuff might keep him awake [during his sermon], and was asked in return, 'Couldn't you put a little snuff into your sermons.'"[54]

These descriptions of style were quite a departure from the sermons of Broadus's day. Dignity was the hallmark of the age. Animation, force, or passion that evoked any sort of emotional feeling was not very well-known among the contemporary pulpit orators. His use of these three ideals of energy was balanced. He argued that "the chief requisite to an energetic style is an energetic nature. There must be vigorous thinking, earnest if not passionate feeling, and the determined purpose to accomplish some object, or the man's style will have no truly exalted energy."[55] This "truly exalted energy" was best understood by Broadus as God's Holy Spirit applying the preacher's message to the hearts of the hearers.

However, Broadus cautioned the extremes of energy if it was left unchecked or an end unto itself. To prove his point he cited contemporary Austin Phelps: "'*Energy* and enthusiasm co-exist in character: they must co-exist in *style* . . . [and] that true *energy* is founded in self-possession.' Extravagance and vehemence by going too far defeat the ends of a true eloquence."[56] So then, an excess of exuberance declared a lack of eloquence or even proper training of the classically trained orator.

Perhaps the most unique element of style was elegance for Broadus. He defined "elegance . . . as 'the product of imagination alone or in combination with passion, and operating under

---

[53] Broadus, *Treatise*, 357.
[54] Ibid.
[55] Broadus, *Treatise*—Dargan rev., 381.
[56] Austin Phelps, *English Style in Public Discourse* (New York: Charles Scribner's Sons, 1883), 208, 217; quoted in Broadus, *Treatise*—Dargan rev., 381.

the control of good taste.'"[57] Broadus contended that elegance
was secondary to perspicuity and energy but was nonetheless
an asset of style that should be used with a bit of discretion and
measure.[58] He noted similarly that "a corresponding evaluation
of elegance [was] formulated by Whately in his popular *Elements of Rhetoric*. He believes that 'when the two excellences
of style are at variance, the general rule to be observed by the
orator is to prefer energetic to the elegant.'"[59] Perspicuity, then,
was the thing for Broadus.

As Broadus concluded his discussions around the issues of
style in general and elegance in particular, he mused: "One must
habitually think his thoughts into clearness, and must acquire
wide and easy command of the best resources of language, if he
would be able to speak simply, and yet really say something."[60]
He understood this to be the chief work of the New Testament
apostles when they preached and taught the gospel. As he was
wont to do throughout the *Treatise*, he called upon a fellow
theologian to mark his point well:

> For the Apostles, poor mortals, were content to take
> lower steps, and to tell the world [the Gospel] in plain
> terms. . . . The Apostles' preaching was therefore
> mighty . . . because [it was] plain, natural and familiar,
> and by no means above the capacity of their hearers:
> nothing being more preposterous, than for those who
> were professedly aiming at men's hearts, to miss the
> mark by shooting over their heads.[61]

The preacher had to think clearly in order to preach clearly. It
was an absolute must for Broadus!

---

[57] John A. Broadus, *A Treatise on the Preparation and Delivery of Sermons*
(1871; reprint, Ann Arbor: University of Michigan University Library, n.d),
403–4, 405 (page references are to the reprint edition); quoted in Huber, 111.
[58] Ibid.
[59] Richard Whately, *Elements of Rhetoric* (New York: Shelton & Co., 1917),
378; quoted in Paul Huber, "A Study of the Rhetorical Theories of John A.
Broadus" (Ph. D. diss., University of Michigan, 1956), 111.
[60] Broadus, *Treatise*, 392.
[61] Henry Rogers, *Reason and Faith and Other Miscellanies* (Boston: Crosby,
Nichols, & Co.), 219; quoted in Broadus, *Treatise*, 393.

Rhetorical style, therefore, consisted at its core foci of perspicuity, energy, and elegance. It was only one of the paramount dynamics that made the pulpit come alive. For Broadus, all of the *Canons of Rhetoric*, *inventio* (invention), *dispositio* (arrangement), *elocutio* (elocution or style), *pronuntiatio* (delivery), and *memoria*,[62] each had its unique place in his "puzzle of rhetoric." None of the canons, however, was more important to Broadus than was the canon of delivery.

Broadus on Delivery

Broadus left his lengthy discussion of delivery until last in the *Treatise*. He presented three chapters explaining factors involved in the delivery of speeches and sermons. This was plain in the layout of his tome: "He wrote his [*Treatise*] text in an era dominated by the influence of elocutionists, he might have devoted greater attention to delivery."[63] Here he jettisoned the Aristotelian tradition. Aristotle had not given much space to this particular canon. Broadus chose, however, to follow neither extreme: "Although he . . . [was] aware of the views of hosts of previous writers, his approach . . . [was] determined by the purpose of his text."[64] For the students and pastors who would read his book, he knew they would face new circumstances or "audience situations"[65] that required them constantly to adapt in their ongoing preparation and delivery.

For Broadus, "everything old was new again." His adaptation of an address or sermon to a particular audience's need was not innovative. This technique had been employed down through the rhetorical tradition. This is also a major focus for communications theorists today. This theory is presently known as *audience analysis*. "Audience analysis *means*" that the speaker discovers all that can possibly be known about the people he is *"talking to or will be talking to so that* [he] *can adapt material*

---

[62] See Kennedy's *Aristotle: On Rhetoric* and Bissell & Herzberg's *The Rhetorical Tradition* for an in-depth discussion of the classical *Canons of Rhetoric*.

[63] Huber, 123.

[64] Ibid.

[65] Ibid.

to their interests, needs, attitudes, fund of knowledge, beliefs, values, and backgrounds."[66] Kenneth Burke, in his *Rhetoric of Moves,* offered another take: "[A speaker] persuade[s] a man only insofar as [he] can talk his language by speech, gesture, tonality, order, image, attitude, idea, identifying ways with his."[67] This was Broadus's method, and he regularly employed it throughout his preaching and teaching career.

Broadus coupled audience analysis with listener's receptivity in his delivery. They were both of utmost concern to him, so crucial to his thinking. He reminded his readers of their collective dual responsibility. He exhorted:

> We are willing to grant . . . that there is not much good preaching; but we beg leave to remark that the proportion of good preachers is quite as great as the proportion of good listeners. . . . One great point of excellence in a preacher, especially to the restless hearers of the present day, will be that he is easy to listen to. . . . Let all preachers strive to be so clear, so sprightly, so earnest and magnetic, that men may hear with ease and pleasure and profit; nay, let them solemnly strive so to speak, in love of their hearers and in the fear of God, that men cannot choose but hear.[68]

There was "anointed" hearing as well as "anointed" preaching in Broadus's understanding.

The *Treatise* discusses the differing views on the major types of delivery. "Reading, reciting, extemporaneous speaking,— which is the best method of preaching."[69] Broadus's response was: "It is a question affecting not only one's manner of delivery, but his whole method of preparation, and in fact all his

---

[66] Larry A. Samovar, *Oral Communication: Speaking Across Cultures,* 11th ed. (Los Angeles: Roxbury Publishing Company, 2000), 67.

[67] Kenneth Burke, *Rhetoric of Motives;* quoted in Samovar, 67.

[68] John A. Broadus, "One Responsibility of Hearers—Good Listening," *Western Recorder* (March 1888); available from <http://www.bereabaptistchurch.org/articles/BroadusJohnA/OneResponsibility.html> (25 May 2005).

[69] Broadus, *Treatise,* 406.

habits of thought and expression."[70] He well understood that the end result would be fashioned by the means to that end for a particular address.

Broadus as Extemporaneous Preacher

Broadus set out in his *Treatise* to show an extemporaneous model for preaching. In the "Author's Preface to the First Edition,"[71] he gave one particular rationale for this chosen style:

> Special pains have been taken, at the proper points of the Treatise, to give practical suggestions for extemporaneous speaking. Most works confine their instruction as regards the preparation of sermons to the case of writing out in full; and many treat of delivery, as if it were in all cases to be reading or recitation. The effort has here been to keep the different methods in view, and to mention, in connection with matters applicable to all alike, such as apply to one or another method in particular.[72]

Throughout his *Treatise* he favored the extemporaneous method above all the others.

Broadus referred to this extemporaneous model of oratory as "Free Speaking."[73] He felt compelled to explain further exactly what he meant by his new idea:

> The technical meaning of this expression requires to be *defined*. Primarily, of course, it denotes speaking without preparation, simply from the promptings of the moment. The colloquial expression for this is "off hand," the image being that of shooting without a rest. . . . This popular phraseology is suggestive. . . . We insist that *free speaking*, after the discourse has been written in full as preparation, but without any effort to

---

[70] Ibid.

[71] Broadus, *Treatise*—Dargan rev., Author's Preface to the First Edition, n.p.

[72] Ibid.

[73] John A. Broadus, *On the Preparation and Delivery of Sermons*, new and rev. ed. (New York: Harper & Brothers, 1944), 325.

repeat the language of the manuscript, shall be called *extemporaneous speaking* (emphasis added).[74]

Throughout his long and distinguished career, he became known for this favored method.

The master orator was quick to offer a strong caveat concerning his preferred extemporaneous delivery before commending its advantages. One of the primary dangers to him was that one might learn to depend on this method without the proper preparation that could be given to memory, recitation, or the reading of an entire manuscript. He also warned, "Really to extemporize [sic] the matter of preaching is as impracticable as it is improper. And it is utterly unfair to represent the advocates of extemporaneous preaching as meaning that men shall preach without preparation."[75] For Broadus there were three primary foci when it came to preaching regardless of the delivery mode. These were preparation, preparation, and preparation.

Broadus advocated this very strongly, "Consider then, the advantages [of extempore]:"[76]

> The extemporary method enabled a person to think more quickly than would be possible if the manuscript was fully written. In a context where time was of the essence, the speaker was able to spend his strength on more difficult parts of the address. This method also had the advantage in that the most-noble thoughts came to the speaker while he was engaged in the task of speaking. New thought might come illuminating the whole of the prepared material in the mind of the speaker as he preached. There might even be a level of inspiration that might come "in the moment" of the spoken word. And in addition to all of this, the preacher could watch for the effect of the message on the face of the audience.[77]

---

[74] Ibid., 326.

[75] Ibid., 326–27.

[76] Broadus, *Treatise*–Dargan rev., 458.

[77] Ibid., 458–62.

Broadus honed his extempore skills throughout his life. During the Civil War he served as a combination missionary and chaplain to General Lee's Armies of Northern Virginia. He recounted that "for three months of that summer [1863] I preached as a missionary in General Lee's army."[78] He reflected that "it was the most interesting and thoroughly delightful preaching I was ever engaged in."[79] During that time there was much confusion because of the war. With all of the goings and comings, he scarcely had time to prepare or study. Broadus remembered that "it is very difficult here to think up an unfamiliar discourse."[80]

During this time he exhibited a certain remiss of preparation time in a letter addressed to his wife on Monday, July 6. It concerned him greatly that he was forced to use old material. His heart was no doubt discouraged due to the great loss just suffered at Gettysburg. He confessed to her that "I haven't got use to the tent, and am constantly making acquaintances. A good many soldiers in attendance both times [I preached] yesterday. . . . You [may] perceive that I am taking my old sermons. . . . The sermons were not particularly good or particularly bad. God grant that they may do some good."[81] He had taken his text from Proverbs 3:17, "Her ways are ways of pleasantness."[82] Dr. J. William Jones later recalled that he employed that particular text on various other occasions.[83]

Broadus also possessed a natural ability to bring to the preaching event the rhetorical mode of *pathos*. He was swept away by personal emotion like unto Jesus Himself when he said, "O, Jerusalem, Jerusalem . . . I would have gathered thy

---

[78] J. W. Jones, "Seminary Magazine," April 1895, quoted in Archibald Thomas Robertson, *The Life and Letters of John A. Broadus* (1901; reprint, Harrisburg, VA: Gano Books Sprinkle Publications, 2003), 198.

[79] Ibid.

[80] Archibald Thomas Robertson, *The Life and Letters of John A. Broadus* (1901; reprint, Harrisburg, VA: Gano Books Sprinkle Publications, 2003), 200.

[81] Ibid.

[82] Ibid.

[83] J. Wm. Jones, [The Southern Baptist Theological] *Seminary Magazine*, April 1895; quoted in Archibald Thomas Robertson, *The Life and Letters of John A. Broadus*, 208–10.

children together" (Matt 23:37 KJV). Pathos may have been Broadus's greatest natural trait. Fant and Pinson observed that:

> The qualities displayed by Broadus will serve any preacher well; *kindness, urbanity, understanding,* and *sympathy* abounded in this Virginia gentleman. He once said. "If I were asked what is the first thing in effective preaching, I should say *sympathy;* and what is the second thing [sic], I should say *sympathy;* and what is the third thing, I should say *sympathy.*" His deep awareness of the needs of people led him to meet the immediate, personal needs of others (emphasis added).[84]

He employed the character of Christ Himself to identify with the people to whom he preached.

Throughout his career this grand pulpit master coupled pathos with his favorite rhetorical method—extempore. The Yale lectures he delivered in 1889 may have been the academic high watermark of this Southern gentleman. The addresses were comparable in notoriety to those of Henry Ward Beecher according to his son-in-law, A. T. Robertson.[85] However, the problem for posterity was this: his use of the extempore style left no complete manuscripts [of the lectures] from which later generations might draw. Fant and Pinson wrote concerning his extempore method: "But as [was his] usual [practice], Broadus had not written them out in full, preferring to speak from notes according to his custom when lecturing. He also expected to incorporate some of them into his *Preparation and Delivery of Sermons.*"[86] But he would be denied his privilege because of his death.[87]

---

[84] Archibald Thomas Robertson, *The Life and Letters of John A. Broadus,* 353–54; quoted in Clyde E. Fant Jr. and William M. Pinson Jr., *20 Centuries of Great Preaching,* vol. 5 of An Encyclopedia of Preaching (Waco, TX: Word, 1971), 51.

[85] Fant and Pinson, *20 Centuries of Great Preaching,* 52.

[86] Ibid. For a more in-depth discussion of the Yale Lectures, see Mark M. Overstreet, "The 1889 Lyman Beecher Lectures and the Recovery of the Late Homiletic of John A. Broadus (1827–1985)," Ph. D. diss., The Southern Baptist Theological Seminary, 2005.

[87] Ibid.

Even before communication theory appeared as an academic discipline, Broadus employed audience analysis to his addresses.[88] He possessed a gift for the extempore and was received well by all who heard him. His freedom from the contemporary use of manuscripts allowed him to look directly at his audience and establish eye contact.[89] Stanfield observed that "he assiduously cultivated this habit and developed the ability to make each person in the audience feel that he was talking directly to him."[90]

In addition to this controversial mode, Broadus developed a conversational manner. His preaching was a "conversation" with the people. He also encouraged his students to "talk like folks talk."[91] He perfected this even to the point where his sermons were referred to as "enlarged conversations."[92] In his quiet delivery he used few hand gestures. His voice was not terribly strong. Broadus could balance between the conversational style on the one hand and being loud enough to be heard on the other. Stanfield further observed: "It [Broadus's voice] was marked by a soft richness, fine flexibility, and often expressed deep *pathos*. He articulated carefully and there was a good distribution of emphasis (emphasis added)."[93]

Broadus's new delivery brought both critics as well as those who would imitate him. Most of his contemporaries "equated 'real preaching' with soaring in the oratorical stratosphere."[94] He was even accused of "ruining the preachers of the South"[95] by this newly minted controversial mode and conversational manner. The students whom he influenced the most recognized his genius and "tried to imitate his tones, his genuine *pathos*,

---

[88] For a fuller discussion of *Audience Analysis,* see Larry A. Samovar, *Oral Communication: Speaking across Cultures*, 11th ed. (Los Angeles: Roxbury Publishing Company, 2000).

[89] Stanfield, 12.

[90] Ibid.

[91] Ibid.

[92] Ibid.

[93] Ibid.

[94] Ibid.

[95] Ibid.

his platform manner, failing to realize that they had only a few of his external characteristics and not the [inner] qualities of his success (emphasis added)."[96]

Perhaps Broadus's method of delivery was most appreciated by the congregations that were blessed to hear him. Audiences have always delighted in preachers who looked at them in the eye and spoke to them directly.[97] This new method was even accepted by the academe of the day. "His Lyman Beecher Lectures on Preaching, which were delivered in this manner, were enthusiastically received by the students and faculty [alike] at Yale University."[98] Since this unique method of preparing and delivering sermons gained wide acceptance from the unlearned soldier to the scholar, "it must be listed as an important element of strength in his preaching."[99]

Many other preachers and orators have been men of renown. But Stanfield declared: "It was, however, the total impact of *man* and *message* that made John A. Broadus such a tremendously popular preacher to his own generation (emphasis added)."[100] Broadus's audience sensed a "reality"[101] that had not been experienced before. Perhaps it is best sensed by "One listener [who] summarized and made articulate what many felt about Broadus's [method of] preaching."[102] He observed: "It was not so much what he said. It did seem that almost anyone might have said what he was saying. But it was the man behind the message. He spoke with the authority of one who tested and knew the truth."[103]

---

[96] Ibid.
[97] Ibid., 13.
[98] Ibid. For a more in-depth discussion of the Lyman Beecher Lectures see: Archibald Thomas Robertson, *The Life and Letters of John A. Broadus*, 375–80; or Overstreet, "The 1889 Lyman Beecher Lectures and the Recovery of the Late Homiletic of John A. Broadus (1827–1985)."
[99] Stanfield, 13.
[100] Ibid.
[101] Ibid.
[102] Ibid.
[103] Claude W. Duke, "Memorial Address of Dr. John A. Broadus," in *Review and Expositor* (April 1927): 172, quoted in Vernon Latrelle Stanfield, *Favorite Sermons of John A. Broadus* (New York: Harper Bros., 1959), 13.

Gleaned Observations of Broadus

In his critique of the electronic media, *Amusing Ourselves to Death*, Neil Postman cited "Marshall McLuhan's [often quoted] aphorism 'the medium is the message.'"[104] Vernon L. Stanfield, longtime professor of preaching at New Orleans Baptist Theological Seminary, once observed: "GRADUALLY, an art or science evolved to assist in the publication of the Christian message. That science came to be called homiletics."[105] Broadus embodied both of these communication truths. To have known Broadus was to experience a genuine preacher: in manner, in mode, in deportment, in character, and in speech. He elevated this science of homiletics to a new height of artistic oratory for his era and following generations.

For the succeeding generations who would not have the blessing of hearing him, Broadus left a rich literary legacy: *A Treatise on the Preparation and Delivery of Sermons* with all of its iterations and succeeding revisions. His *Treatise* was his classical gift to Southern Baptists as well as the church at large. A strong case can be made that the effectiveness of the church rises or falls on the strength of her pulpits. Broadus certainly contributed to the pulpit's lasting efficacy. Stanfield articulated this strongly when he stated:

> Perhaps no book on homiletics has been able to achieve the comprehensiveness, the timelessness, and the simplicity of *On the Preparation and Delivery of Sermons*. Based on solid principles and tested procedures, and drawing upon the very best literature related to the art of sermon preparation . . . [all its revisions and] edition[s] will be indispensable tool[s] for . . . [every] new generation of preachers.

---

[104] Marshall McLuhan, "The Medium is the Message" [Internet online]; available from <http://www.marshallmcluhan.com/main.html> (19 August 2006), quoted in Neil Postman, *Amusing Ourselves to Death* (New York: Viking Penguin, 1985), 8–9.

[105] John A. Broadus, *On the Preparation and Delivery of Sermons*, 4th ed., rev. Vernon L. Stanfield (San Francisco: Harper & Row Publishers, 1979), 9.

Christian history has shown that the strength of the church is directly related to the strength of the pulpit. When the message from the pulpit has been uncertain and faltering, the church was weak; when the pulpit was given a positive, declarative message, the church has been strong. The need for effective preaching has never been greater.[106]

This comment was almost prophetically germane for the twenty-first century. Broadus's life and work has left a powerful legacy for that effective preaching.

Broadus: Ancient Influences, Contemporary Practices, and the Man as Pulpit Orator

Broadus possessed three undeniable as well as admirable traits that will forever live in the memory of any serious student who considers him in even the most general of ways. These are the ancient and classical influences on his life, his contemporary practices of oratory, and his character of life. The Southern Baptist Convention has yet to produce one who embodied all that a Christian scholar, educator, pulpit orator, denominational statesman, and Southern gentleman should be that could equal John A. Broadus—"Preacher Extraordinary."[107]

Early in his youth Broadus found one of his lifelong loves in education. That love and devotion was easily synthesized with his commitment to the ministry. Both simultaneously enhanced his unique and natural endowment for oratory, public address, and preaching. From his earliest learning experiences at his uncle's, Albert G. Sims's "school," he developed a voracious mind of inquiry. This would whet his later appetite with a love for the biblical languages—both Greek and Hebrew—classical Greek, Latin, German, as well as French. Also during his formal education he discovered the ancient texts of classical rhetoric. He especially became familiar with the *Canons of Rhetoric*,[108]

---

[106] Ibid., introductory comments in the front dust cover.
[107] Stanfield, 1.
[108] See notes 16 and 17 above for a fuller discussion of the *Canons of Rhetoric*.

De Inventione by Cicero, *Institutio Oratoria* by Quintilian, as well as Aristotle's definition of rhetoric. There is absolutely no doubt that the influence of Augustine also had a great impact on Broadus as rhetorician. A strong case could be argued that a single quote of the great church father and theologian was the prism through which most of Broadus's public address, preaching, teaching homiletics, and writing of the *Treatise* could be seen: "Augustine says, *Veritas pateat, veritas placeat, veritas moveat,* 'Make the truth plain, make it pleasing, make it moving.'"[109]

This southern gentlemen was not only a renaissance man and classicist; he drew on contemporary scholarship from varied disciplines to incorporate into his writing and teaching. He was well-read in current events and world affairs and would have been considered a "life-long learner" by those today. He synthesized the ancients with the contemporaries for his discipline of homiletics. In the *Treatise* he incorporated upwards of 50 current "Homileticians . . . Rhetoricians and Other Writers"[110] demonstrating well he was not chained to a particular person or school of thought. His use of the extemporary method juxtaposed to that of memory and reading of the written manuscript allowed him an ability "to be in the moment" much more than the other ministers of the day. This was where Broadus was best. He had the uncanny ability to sense the ethos and pathos of those to whom he spoke. These sparked in him and emoted from him those selfsame traits. This natural ability created a spiritual symbiosis that allowed him and the congregation to "feed off" one another and to create a level of immanence in the "preaching event" time and again.

Broadus would craft each sermon and each lecture for its own particular session. His rhetorical skills allowed him to understand another dynamic that would come to be known in Communication Theory as Audience Analysis.[111] He always endeavored

---

[109] Broadus, *Treatise*, 20–21.
[110] Paul Huber, "A Study of the Rhetorical Theories of John A. Broadus" (Ph.D. diss., University of Michigan, 1956), 182–86.
[111] See the prior discussion in Larry A. Samovar, *Oral Communication: Speaking across Cultures,* 11th ed., 67ff.

to spend at least two hours before an address to custom-apply his work to that event even if he had preached it before. He possessed an insatiable desire to be fresh every time he spoke.

This simple preacher was, in his heart of hearts, a man of great moral conviction. As a young man he wrestled within himself whether he would take up the vocation of the gospel ministry. He would also be thrown on the "horns of a dilemma" later in his career. Would he accept the invitation to be one of the founding four professors of the new Southern Baptist Theological Seminary forming in Greenville, South Carolina? He truly loved the work of pastor, so it was indeed an agonizing decision for him. It would, however, be a great opportunity to "enlarge his borders." He had mastered more than one discipline so his expertise was exactly what this new theological venture needed. And once he had committed himself to a task, there was no stopping him or no turning him around regardless of the circumstances or personal costs. This principle was best demonstrated in 1866 after the Civil War when the four founders came back together to carry on the work of the seminary. At the meeting Broadus spoke with conviction: "Suppose we quietly agree that the seminary may die, but we'll die first."[112]

The essence of Broadus's preaching may have been captured best by Vernon Latrelle Stansfield's work, *Favorite Sermons of John A. Broadus*. Broadus was completely devoted to his call to the ministry of proclamation. He never wavered and gave himself body, mind, and spirit to the task all of his days. Even through personal reversals, health issues, and other life circumstances, Broadus was one who could speak to the cultured and refined as well as the plowman or store merchant. He was able to relate to the people of every socioeconomic stratum of society. And this he did well with ethos and pathos. Broadus was not satisfied only to deliver a sermon that was eloquent rhetorically; he had a deep unction to move his hearers to the point of

---

[112] Tom J. Nettles, *The Baptists: Key People Involved in Forming a Baptist Identity*; *Volume Two, Beginnings in America* (Scotland: Christian Focus Publications, Geanies House, 2006), 300.

decision. He preached with the conviction of a lawyer trying
to convince a jury to acquit a man on trial for his life. Lastly,
Broadus gave himself to the study of preachers and preaching.
This he had taken up long before he ever began to teach preaching.[113] He practiced his craft all the days of his life and applied
the ancient art of rhetoric to his artistry early on.

John A. Broadus was one man that could never be replaced.
He was a great orator and pulpit speaker. He may have been
one of the greatest orators of the later half of the nineteenth
century. He was a man who was also "mighty in the Scriptures."
He, like St. Augustine, brought classical rhetoric "right into the
church-house!" He left his fingerprints on The Southern Baptist
Theological Seminary as well as the Southern Baptist Convention. But of all of the accolades that could be piled high, none
was better than: "JOHN ALBERT BROADUS: PREACHER
EXTRAORDINARY!"[114]

---

[113] Stanfield, 5–12.
[114] Ibid., 1.

Chapter V

New Wine in Broadus Wineskins?

Richard Melick

J ohn A. Broadus left a mark on history few have equaled. Furthermore, as a devout Christian man and minister, he had significant impact for the kingdom of God. Generations profited from his insights and valued his scholarship.

Broadus was the forefather of Southern Baptist New Testament scholars. He served as the first New Testament professor for Southern Baptists' first theological seminary. His legacy, however, cannot be measured simply by "the first." As the first New Testament professor, he set the direction for the distinctive contributions of Southern Baptist professors for generations to come. Denominational seminaries share the concern that their resources, and particularly their faculty, contribute to the life of the congregants who comprise their denominations. They expect writings and seminars, as well as classroom lectures, to enrich local congregations. Church-supported theological seminaries should have faculties who exercise their scholarly gifts with a sense of accountability to the churches. They cannot engage in purely abstract scholarship.

John Broadus embodied that as well as any have. He understood his primary calling as a minister of the gospel. In addition to and as an expression of God's call on his life, he became a professor. Yet he never lost his love for preaching and never left the pulpit. Having this understanding of the divine call on his life, he was a scholar who united piety and professionalism, sensitivity and scholarship, and local congregations with seminary classrooms.

Through the years he has received numerous accolades. Many seminaries and colleges have a building or a wing named for him. Virtually every generation of Southern Baptist seminarians know the name Broadus, even those who cannot state who he was or what he did. Few American scholars have been honored more significantly.

Broadus was, first of all, a minister. He was known as one of America's greatest preachers. In 1870 he published his homiletics textbook *A Treatise on the Preparation and Delivery of Sermons,*[1] which he revised in 1890 shortly before his death in 1895. The book may be the most popular homiletics textbook in America since its publication. Like many theological students, this was my college homiletics text. The book has stood through four editions and is still available through most Christian bookstores.[2] Few scholars have written a text that is relevant almost 140 years after its first publication.

Broadus lived in a most interesting era. The 1800s saw previously unparalleled progress in America, with scientific and technological advances, increased immigration, ingenious inventors, and sociological upheaval. Politically and economically, the American Civil War changed life forever, especially in the south where Broadus lived. These various factors, among others, produced a wide gap between life as it was and life as it was becoming.

The Polarization of Society Impacted Religion

The 1800s were a time of great theologians and biblical scholars. In America such a list would have included men like

---

[1] John A. Broadus, *A Treatise on the Preparation and Delivery of Sermons* (Philadelphia: Smith English & Co., 1870).

[2] The later editions update the earlier, particularly in examples given and in more recent bibliographic materials.

A. H. Strong, W. G. T. Shedd, and the authors of one of the earliest large commentary sets in America, *An American Commentary on the New Testament.*[3] European and British scholars influenced significant elements of American religious life. For example, Old Testament scholars Keil and Delitsch, and New Testament scholars Lightfoot, Westcott, and Hort significantly impacted American scholarship.[4]

At the same time, it was an era of great preachers. Perhaps the greatest of Baptists, Charles Spurgeon, was at the height of his popularity. America had its share as well. In addition to the rise of great pulpits with eloquent and relevant preachers, America continued to produce revivalists. The greatest of these evangelists were particularly skilled orators with a variety of personalities and methods in bringing the greatest era of revivals in America. Among them were D. L. Moody and Charles Finney.

The same century witnessed the birth of the Southern Baptist Convention, formed largely over concern to reach the unevangelized areas of the South and Southwest. Like much of America, both the South and the Southwest had their share of great pulpiteers. Perhaps most uniquely, these frontier regions had their own revivalists—frontier preachers with energy, vigor, resilience, and a unique focus on the gospel. Often uneducated, many of these became the preachers whom Broadus would later teach and whose spiritual offspring would seek theological education at The Southern Baptist Theological Seminary.

The ecclesiastical climate of the day brought its own tensions. The church has always struggled with the issues of traditionalism verses modernism, and the 1800s were not immune to this. Among the Baptists, however, there was a consistent theology. The wide gap existed between the formally educated and those

---

[3] An American Commentary on the New Testament, ed. Alvah Hovey (Philadelphia: The American Baptist Publication Society). John Broadus authored the Matthew volume in 1886. It was the first significant American Baptist commentary set on the New Testament.

[4] There were, of course, many other European and British scholars with followings in America. Those mentioned here have enjoyed lasting appreciation for their work and well represent the more conservative perspective.

without. Often pastors and evangelists without formal training and, in some cases, resistant to education's refining and broadening impact, carried the message to the masses. The tensions they produced characterized America from the beginning. From the Pilgrims onward many pastors were expected to utilize the best of scholarship and theological tools in their ministry to the congregations. Indeed, in the early years, often the pastor was the best educated in the community. Yet the gospel mandated an attempt to reach all persons. Men with more zeal and fire than education responded to the challenge of taking the gospel to new areas. Many of these were in the South and West.

Among the mixtures of theological and ecclesiastical varieties in nineteenth-century America, Broadus found wide acceptance. He was eloquent enough for the more refined and passionate enough for the evangelists. He understood academics enough to serve with unique distinction in the classroom, yet he was practical enough to maintain a successful pastorate throughout his life and to serve as a chaplain during the Civil War. He was the ideal scholar-preacher.

This brief sketch of the times of John Broadus sets the stage for his unique ability to succeed in his own times. Other chapters of this volume will consider many of these features. There is no question but that Broadus was a giant of his era. The guiding question of this chapter is: *How would Broadus fare in today's world of biblical scholarship?* Being academically eclectic and pastorally relevant, has he been replaced by the insights of later scholars and the large body of information unavailable to him more than a century ago?

The question must be refined further. Does the current world of New Testament scholarship fit the parameters of his writing? That question gave rise to the chapter title: "New Wine in Broadus Wineskins?" Jesus' answer to His questioners provides the occasion for His famous statement: "Neither do men pour new wine into old wineskins" (Matt 9:17). The old wineskins break. In some senses the metaphor can apply to scholarship as well as to religion. Many scholars have found their conclusions replaced by the work of later scholars. Some are simply irrelevant; others have been shown to be wrong. Each generation of scholars stands on the shoulders of previous generations, but given the significant changes, often advances, in scholarly understanding of the New Testament, the value of previous generations of scholars is often confined to the fact that they served their generation as best they could. Most of us would be happy with that epitaph, for each is called to serve only a generation. A few transcend generations.

The central question reflects a deeper concern. Often past scholars had two limitations compared to today. First, the lack of available information, which enlightens later scholarship, poses an insurmountable barrier. Modern theological students often view past scholars as irrelevant simply because of their lack of information. Second, often past generations of scholars exhibited a lack of interest, or education, in the methods deemed appropriate today. The first limitation cannot be avoided but does not in itself invalidate the work of previous scholars. The second is more critical. Methodological questions often reveal personal commitments. Especially in Broadus's era, new winds of scholarship blew. It was difficult for the practitioner to know, much less implement, ideas and theories born of fresh thinking and research.

These issues strike at the heart of this chapter's inquiry. Obviously, Broadus did not, and could not know, of the many significant changes to be brought by discussions and archaeological findings of the twentieth century. The question here is would he have been open to them, finding them easily fitting into the framework of his teaching. As to the second issue, openness to the new is a philosophical issue. The preacher-scholar who continually preaches the latest theological or biblical fad subjects his constituents to a faith without foundations. Few things are as damaging. Alternatively, refusal to incorporate the genuine insights of scholarship subjects constituents to a parochial understanding promoted by dogmatism.

With this extended introduction we may now turn to the question at hand. Is Broadus irrelevant? Did he anticipate the discussions of today? How would scholarship today fit into the Broadus methodology?

Approaching the subject requires some comments on methodology. First, this chapter is based on information gained from the writings of Broadus himself. Further, they are based on two primary monographs that demonstrate a complementary approach to the value of his scholarship. As mentioned already, the material relies on Broadus's *A Treatise on the Preparation and Delivery of Sermons*. This volume provides a systematic and organized presentation of his methodology. Since the book takes a practical direction, intended for the preacher, the insights found there are cryptic. Yet Broadus knew the foundation for any good sermon was, in part, faithfulness to the biblical text. He therefore included a major section entitled "Materials of Preaching."[5]

In addition to *A Treatise on the Preparation and Delivery of Sermons*, this chapter relies on Broadus's commentary on Matthew in An American Commentary on the New Testament.[6] This major exegetical work should demonstrate the principles with an application to the text. Thus this chapter will compare the two texts representatively in seeking to arrive at an answer to the question of the chapter. There will be many references to these two works, but the references stand as illustrations of Broadus's methodology. They are not intended to be comprehensive.

Second, the methodology of this chapter involves serious choices. Ultimately one cannot say how anyone of history past would relate to the contemporary world. Therefore we acknowledge some guidelines. The first guideline involves placement of almost exact overlap. Strange as it may sound, scholars of today often work with the same issues as those of yesterday. Some of these go back to the apostolic fathers. There

---

[5] "Materials of Preaching" is part I of the book. That, in itself, demonstrates both the importance of the Bible in preaching and the significance Broadus placed on proper exegesis of the text as foundational to all preaching.
[6] See previous bibliographic data.

are many incidences where Broadus spoke to the exact issues of scholarship today. The second guideline is conjecture as to whether Broadus's understanding is likely to have produced a position on the modern issues. There are times when Broadus seems ahead of many of his day in articulating the significance of academic issues.

One final methodological comment is important. Contemporary New Testament scholarship is noted by a proliferation of specialty areas. Probably no one of the nineteenth century could have anticipated the scrutiny with which virtually every area of the New Testament would be subjected. It is further doubtful that anyone could have known that the general advances of society would also impact biblical studies. This has particular reference to the acquiring of knowledge and the current ability to impart knowledge broadly. Any attempt to compare will inevitably fall short of modern expectations. The chapter, therefore, is general in its presentation of the contours of contemporary New Testament scholarship in hopes of developing enough of a profile of Broadus to serve the reader well.

Broadus and New Testament Scholarship

The relationship of Broadus to New Testament scholarship today will involve four areas of investigation. While not being exhaustive of everything that occupies New Testament scholars today, they do represent the large fields of work that must be considered. They are: the biblical text, matters of introduction, exegesis, and hermeneutics.

The Biblical Text

Both in his *Treatise* and *Matthew*, Broadus clearly affirmed his commitment to the text of Scripture as the divinely inspired Word of God. His position was an informed one, not one born only of religious fervor. In multiple places Broadus discussed the importance of the Bible as the foundational text.

The Authority of the Text

Broadus saw the preacher's task as primarily textual, calling people to conform to God's Word. At the beginning of the *Treatise*, he explained, "The primary idea is that the discourse is a development of the text, an explanation, illustration, application of its teachings. Our business is to teach God's word."[7] He stated that there should be a text for every subject, and if not, one should not give the impression that he was speaking from the Bible when the chosen passage did not discuss that subject. He declared: "If there be rare cases in which it is otherwise *[e.g. no text on the subject]*, it will then be better to have no text than one with which the subject has only a fanciful or forced connection."[8]

To make the matter abundantly clear, he provided multiple examples of abuse. In the *Treatise* section on Interpretation, following "Chief Sources of Error in the Interpretation of a Text,"[9] Broadus provided eight pages of "Examples of Texts Often Misapplied."[10] Here he clearly distinguished between preaching without textual base and preaching from a text; offering a reason for abuses, he said:

> It is strange how powerful is the tradition of the pulpit; how often able and thoughtful men will go all their lives taking for granted that an important passage has that meaning which in youth they heard ascribed to it, when the slightest examination would show them that it is far otherwise.[11]

While the specific illustrations included related to the nineteenth century, the force of the argument as well as the kinds of examples given could be easily assumed to be the beginning of the twenty-first century.

For Broadus the preacher had nothing to say if it were not a clear explanation and application of the Bible. He warned

---

[7] *Treatise*, 39.
[8] Ibid., 40. Italics mine.
[9] Ibid., 53ff.
[10] Ibid., 70–78.
[11] Ibid., 70.

the preacher that "he will never say a passage of God's holy and precious Word means so and so, without personal, honest, patient effort to ascertain the fact."[12] While this will be clarified further in pages to come, at the outset it is helpful to understand the platform from which he spoke. The Bible was more than the starting point for an understanding of spiritual realities. It was the locus of God's revelation to us. This was confirmed repeatedly in *Matthew* where Broadus often explained his interpretations in light of the nature of divine inspiration.

The Original Languages

Broadus's confidence in Scripture lay ultimately in the texts of the original languages. While this was and is characteristic of biblical scholars, it often has less value to preachers and other practitioners. Modern practitioners may express surprise at the seriousness with which Broadus took the original languages. Although he did recommend the use of good translations, Broadus offered some careful reflections on them.

Broadus's direct advice to the preacher reflected his concern with the original languages.

He reiterated the point: "If one knows the Hebrew or the Greek, let him never preach upon a text without carefully studying it and its context in the original."[13] Further, *Matthew* consistently demonstrated a reliance on the original languages as well as a desire to explicate their significance in any given passage. The commentary combined the expertise of a good scholar with the heart of a teacher. Passage after passage contained didactic elements intended to inform and instruct in proper methodology.

Yet Broadus knew the limitations of language—any language. He stated plainly: "Language can never do more than approximate to perfect precision of expression, with freedom from the possibility of being misunderstood . . ."[14] The nature

---

[12] Ibid., 78.
[13] Ibid.
[14] Ibid., 53.

of language and differences in the interpreters both call for serious consideration. The options for revelation through language seemed clear, along with their implications. God could either communicate verbally in a familiar style, or He could choose a "uniformly didactic and rigorously scientific style."[15] Thus the Divine Mind chose to communicate with a more normal style. The alternative would be "thoroughly devoid of interest for the ordinary human mind."[16] Thus even the original languages required careful study, a task that the preacher should welcome with joy.

The values of the original languages permeated his writing. People often think that Hebrew and Greek are necessary for the hard passages. Broadus had a more comprehensive view:

> It is often said that one needs a knowledge of the Hebrew and Greek in order that he may understand the difficult passages; it would be more nearly correct, though paradoxical, to say that such knowledge will help him to understand the easy passages, the great mass of Scripture.[17]

First, Hebrew and Greek contain emphases that our language cannot adequately express. There is a "Hebraistic spirit, marked by Oriental modes of conception,"[18] which English people do not understand. Knowing the original languages was analogous to traveling in Palestine. They illuminate emphases and expressions otherwise unknowable.

Second, Broadus saw great value in the power of the words themselves. His classical training brought appreciation for the meaning and function of language. While moderns often speak in different terms, Broadus seemed to understand the values and limitations of the words themselves.

One example of comparative philology occurred in *Matthew*, commenting on the word *preach* found in Matthew 4:17.

---

[15] Ibid.
[16] Ibid., 53–54.
[17] Ibid., 55.
[18] Ibid., 55–56.

He explained the English word *preach* as from Latin through French. It was the equivalent of the Greek *kērussō*. He compared it with *euangelizomai*, partly by providing a survey of synoptic use. His concern was that interpreters not follow the English translations and thus develop a wrong interpretation based on English equivalents.[19] His method was surely correct here.

Yet at other times Broadus was not so clear. He indicated that there are certain significant words that become the key to interpreting the Bible. These are words like "flesh, soul, heart, fear, faith, understanding, foolish, light, darkness, just, righteousness, salvation, grace, good man, wicked."[20] There was confusion since the translators translate only the words—the ideas must be derived from other study of the contexts in which they occur. It may be legitimately asked whether Broadus had properly balanced the impact of the classical meanings with their meanings in given texts. In his exegetical work Broadus seems to have relied more on importing verbal ideas in the form of the words than allowing verbal definition to arise from the contexts. Yet the lack of clarity as to method suggests his own reservation about outside information influencing the interpretation of Scripture.

Third, Broadus understood the necessity of detailed grammatical investigation. He said, in fact, that "this grammatical study of the text can scarcely be made too minute or protracted."[21] The scrutiny included clauses,[22] series of substantives or adjectives being misapplied,[23] as well as to normal grammatical matters. These examples will suffice to reveal Broadus's commitment to the original texts.

Textual Criticism

Broadus showed a remarkably current and open attitude toward the more recent science of textual criticism. This was

---

[19] *Matthew,* 76.
[20] *Treatise,* 56. He is quoting Vinet, *Homiletics,* 111.
[21] Ibid., 79.
[22] Ibid., 58.
[23] Ibid., 59.

obvious in his advice to the preacher regarding spurious passages and his own statements regarding the manuscripts.

Regarding spurious passages, some of his most pointed instruction to the preacher warns about using them. He included now well-known examples: Acts 9:6; Acts 22:10; 1 John 5:7; and Acts 8:37. What was unquestionably spurious "should never be quoted as Scripture."[24] In including this section in the *Treatise*, and in citing these examples, Broadus clearly leaned away from what would now be considered a Byzantine text. Likewise, he freely departed from the Latin Vulgate,[25] the basis of many church decisions as well as popular preaching. His instruction, in effect, encouraged the preacher keeping current with prevailing ideas of scholarship.

The general introduction to *An American Commentary on the New Testament* contained extended information on the current state of extant Greek texts, which were the more important for that commentary series. The introduction, by General Editor Alvah Hovey, showed a preference for the work of Westcott and for the manuscripts that now, at least, would be considered Alexandrian.[26]

Broadus accepted the working methodologies of the editor and the series. When there were uncertainties that affected translation, Broadus "intended to state the preferable reading with a confidence varying according to the evidence; and in all that are of considerable interest the evidence has been more or less fully presented in foot-notes."[27] His method of documentation in footnotes followed the generally accepted procedures for today: internal evidence, transcriptional probabilities, and the

---

[24] Ibid., 48.

[25] The Vulgate and Luther translations are specifically provided in explanation of incorrect inclusions in the text. *Treatise*, 71.

[26] *Matthew*, xlix, n1. "The general contributions to text-criticism made by Westcott and Hort are invaluable, and most of their judgments as to particular passages seem to me correct. But in a number of cases I have felt bound to dissent and to give the reasons as fully and strongly as the character and limits of this work allowed." He continues by expressing reservation about Westcott and Hort's "neutral" text, which he considers to be more Alexandrian. History proved his insights to be correct.

[27] *Matthew*, xlviii–xlix.

evidence from the fathers. In a day when many felt increasingly uneasy about the implications of text-criticism, Broadus spoke with confidence:

> The solicitude, and even alarm, which some persons feel in regard to the encroachments of text-criticism, must be regarded as without cause. Instead of shaking faith in Scripture, these researches will ultimately strengthen faith. When the shock of abandoning a familiar expression has passed, one almost invariably begins to see that the true text is best.[28]

Furthermore, "Neither in text nor in translation do our common Bibles present any such errors or uncertainties as would alter or modify any doctrine of Scripture."[29] He further stated, "The general teachings of the New Testament as to doctrine and duty are now known to be established independently of all passages that contain doubtful readings."[30] Thus Broadus engaged in the science of textual criticism with confidence, while affirming the integrity of the text.

This raises a question related to the nature of biblical Greek. Broadus lived in a time when scholars had no clear definition for the nature of the Greek of the New Testament. Some still believed it was distinctive: a "Holy Spirit Greek." Schooled in the classics, Broadus expressed conviction that the Greek of the New Testament was a more popular Greek than classical. This is a remarkable conclusion, since his writings predate the work of A. T. Robertson, Adolf Deissmann, and James Moulton. After Broadus's death scholars recognized the distinctive nature of *koine* Greek.

Yet when Broadus discussed errors in interpreting the text, he discussed style. The New Testament was "a revelation . . . given in human language, and to be expressed for the most part in that familiar style which would make it 'come home to men's business and bosoms,' would make it a book for men and women,

---

[28] Ibid., xlix.
[29] *Treatise*, 48, footnote.
[30] *Matthew,* xlix.

and boys and girls, for cultivated and uncultivated people."[31] This was accomplished in part by the fact that

> the language of Scripture is, as a general thing, not philosophical but popular, not scientific but poetic, not so much an analytical language, fond of sharp discriminations and exact statements, as a synthetical language, abounding in concrete terms, the representatives not of abstractions, but of facts of actual existence and experience.[32]

Broadus seemed to anticipate the revolutionary discovery of *koine* Greek.

In sum, Broadus understood the authority of Scripture, the primacy of the original languages, and the necessity of textual criticism and these placed him in good company with contemporary scholars. While more archaeological evidence has now accumulated, and more categories of discussion are available, the modern reader is at home with the work of Broadus in the area of the biblical text.

Matters of Introduction

The second major area to consider in this chapter is how Broadus compares with current New Testament scholars in matters of introduction. These will include two basic areas: introduction to the books of the Bible, and questions of harmonization. While harmonization may not be the norm under the category of Introduction, it will be helpful to place it here for this present discussion.

Introduction

Introduction generally includes matters of authorship, date, provenance, integrity, and other pertinent critical issues. On these Broadus gave us little to consider. The primary discus-

---

[31] *Treatise*, 53.
[32] Ibid., 57.

sion was over source criticism: how the synoptics relate to each other.

Initially Broadus handled these issues in a cursory fashion. He stated summarily, "For various reasons, no Introduction to Matthew has been prepared."[33] He did express sympathy with several extant works, giving the impression that repetition would be useless. After the detail given to text-criticism and methodological processes, this is disappointing. The statement did not suggest disinterest, only the economy of time and space. At any rate he did not place a significant value on the typical introductory issues and their influence over the text.

On the other hand, he gave clear affirmation of the importance of knowing these things. In giving examples of disregarding a text's "connection," he spoke of Colossians 2:21, "Touch not, taste not, handle not." He stated "the slightest attention to the connection would show, that in the first place, they are not spoken with any reference to that subject (*e.g., intoxicating drinks)*, and in the second place, that they are given by the apostle as an example of ascetic precepts to which we *ought not to conform.*"[34] While not being definitive as to the specific audience of Colossians, Broadus did indicate the importance of an awareness of the situation. Again, in the Paul versus James debate over faith, Broadus stated: "No trouble need ever have been felt as to the supposed contradiction between Paul and James with regard to justification, if attention had been paid to the theoretical and practical errors at which they are respectively aiming."[35] Obviously knowledge of introductory issues was an important aspect of interpretation.

Broadus did speak to the source criticism issue. This would seem necessary, given the fact that synoptic studies had postulated various theories for almost 200 years. Obviously he knew the issues. He indicated awareness of at least two positions: the priority of Mark and the priority of Matthew. These are the

---

[33] *Matthew*, 1.
[34] *Treatise*, 73.
[35] Ibid., 81.

same two most commonly held views of modern scholarship. Broadus simply stated that those who hold the priority of Mark rely on "examples selected for the purpose." The attempts to try to demonstrate that Matthew built on Mark or that Mark relied on Matthew, "both hypotheses break down." That is in part to the scholars' "unhesitating freedom in manipulating the materials."[36] Therefore in his commentary "no theory has been adopted."[37]

In the actual text of his commentary, however, there are numerous points to relate Matthew to Mark and Luke. Thus while such thinking is unavoidable, Broadus expressed reserve in the conclusions of source critics.

Within the text many issues arise that require critical thinking and have become the subjects of the various textbooks on Introduction subjects. One example was the Sermon on the Mount. Before exegesis Broadus provided an extensive introduction to the sermon. He addressed three issues. First, he considered the unity of the discourse. The basic issue was whether the Sermon on the Mount was to be considered one sermon or a compilation of many. Second, he discussed the relationships between Matthew and Luke. Are they the same sermon or different? Third, he presented the design of the discourse. The basic question was: what is the sermon intended to do; therefore, how is it outlined? After considering these areas, Broadus turned to analysis.[38] Interestingly, the subjects he addressed are the same of many modern introductions and commentaries on Matthew. Many contemporary monographs include more issues, such as the nature of the kingdom of God, but most occupy themselves with the same issues and, strikingly, the same data as did Broadus.

Introductory matters are important to Broadus. Though, again, the data available to him was limited. He knew and addressed the basic issues under discussion today.

---

[36] *Matthew*, xlviii.
[37] Ibid.
[38] Ibid., 83–84.

Harmony

Harmonization was the attempt to make compatible two or more seemingly incompatible texts. In synoptic studies it was the norm for many commentaries. Broadus did make multiple references to the seemingly disparate passages.

Broadus discussed the opening events of Jesus' life, presented differently by the Synoptics and John, and made an extended helpful comment:

> There is no real contradiction between John and the other Evangelists. None of them could record the whole of Jesus' public life, and each must select according to his particular design. Where events are omitted in a brief narrative, we cannot expect to find a wide break as if to invite their insertion from some other source: for this would destroy the continuity of the narrative, and greatly impair its interest and impressiveness. The story must go right on, but must not contain such expressions as would *exclude* the events it omits.[39]

Earlier, in the commentary on Jesus' baptism, Broadus remarked about the synoptic differences:

> As to the authenticity of the narrative, such slight and wholly unimportant variations really confirm it, being precisely such as always occur in the independent testimony of different witnesses. As to the complete inspiration of the Scriptures, we must accept it as one of the facts of the case that the inspired writers not unfrequently report merely the substance of what was said, without aiming to give the exact words.[40]

The statement regarding independent witnesses seemed to counter his stated "nonposition" on the Synoptic Problem, assuming independence. Nevertheless, the realization that the

---

[39] Ibid., 71.
[40] Ibid., 58.

text was reported, rather than quoted, was a significant insight. It will find great acceptance in today's scholarly marketplace.

This brief discussion adequately describes Broadus's methodology and implies two points. First, Broadus did emphasize a correct understanding of Introductory issues as necessary to the proper handling of the text. Second, he had a strong reserve about the issues of source criticism. His commitment to the text, understood in a normal fashion, took priority over theories which he believed to be at times contrived, even by those with the best intentions.

Exegesis

The third major area of comparison is that of exegesis. Here the methodology of the chapter thus far takes a turn. Rather than quote from Broadus himself, the primary discussion will be about his demonstrated methodology primarily in *Matthew.* It should also be noted that so far Broadus had been shown to be adequate in terms of the conclusions of contemporary scholarship. Here questions may be raised.

Exegetical methodology has developed significantly in the last 50 years. Older exegetes normally followed a traditional approach to language and texts. They therefore analyzed grammar, conducted word studies, compared the various texts of Scripture to solve apparent discrepancies, and gave attention to the flow of the sentence. Many placed the primary emphasis on the meaning of words in the text, often following a diachronic approach to lexicography. Others placed emphasis on the sentence, explaining the syntactical relationships between and among the elements of a given sentence. Modern exegetes recognize there are limitations in this approach and have called for a reassessment of its methods. Additionally, texts have been studied from the literary and philosophical disciplines. Today exegesis is a complex matter employing the best of science and art in understanding ancient writings.

At the risk of oversimplification, exegesis may be divided into two major areas. These are structural and literary. *Struc-*

tural refers to the analysis of words, grammar, syntax, and the contribution they make to thought. *Literary* refers to the patterns and conventions employed by the writer to lead the reader to the same conclusion cognitively and emotionally. Literary approaches may, again simplifying, be divided into written devices and rhetorical devices that are reduced to writing in the text. Structural and literary approaches complement each other, though often the proponents of one or another approach believe their method has superiority over others.

Broadus's world was a world of structural exegesis, as I have defined it. Even here, however, there were limitations in both resources and the maturity of the exegetical processes. The literary aspects of exegesis were basically unknown, except by those who understood them by intuition. For example, modern linguistics has given us highly developed systems of discourse analysis, lexical analysis, and functional aspects of language. While some would argue that the origins of the discipline go back into previous centuries in studies of literature, almost no biblical scholars utilized the insights of the discipline until the middle of the twentieth century. It would be highly unlikely, if not impossible, for Broadus to have employed modern linguistic language. The questions therefore are: Did his work anticipate the discussion that would afterward ensue? Do his conclusions suffer from a lack of knowledge of the literary tools employed today?

"Structural" Exegesis

In one sense, *Matthew* was entirely a structural commentary. Its pages are filled with background information,[41] word studies,[42] and structural conclusions.

Yet Broadus displayed little information on issues raised by contemporary philology. His knowledge was drawn almost entirely from classical Greek. He stressed the use of a good

---

[41] For example, see the extended discussions on Galilee (73), Samaritans (218), and Synagogue (80). These represent his intent of supplying information for those without the possession of a Bible dictionary.

[42] For example, p. 76, already discussed in the chapter.

concordance so that each writer could define his own words, but he did little with extrabiblical literature. The fact is, there was little outside of the church fathers available to him at the time. Nevertheless, his desire to employ the Talmud, Josephus, and other Jewish writers suggested a clear understanding of the necessity of contemporary vocabulary use and conceptual similarities.[43]

Similarly, he did little with the structure of macro units so prevalent today. *Matthew* outlined the Gospel of Matthew adequately, but little space was devoted to the structural interests of modern scholars. In this area Broadus is not so much out of date as simply not up-to-date. Yet the commentary provides significant insights even to modern readers. *Matthew* has abiding value because of Broadus's significant exegetical skills.

"Literary" Exegesis

Perhaps the greatest advances in exegesis have been in the literary categories. Here, by modern standards, *Matthew* falls short. Little explains the functional nature of language. Broadus seldom concerned himself with the patterns of the structures and how they were intentionally constructed to make an impact. The tools of modern linguistic theories were, simply, not available to him.

Even so, most of the time Broadus's conclusions of the various sections of *Matthew* are remarkably the same. And ultimately they are in line with those of more recent commentators. There are exceptions where the latest research and the development of methodologies have produced a change in understanding. As will be seen in the next section, on hermeneutics, it would seem that Broadus did avail himself of every acceptable methodology to arrive at a clear understanding of the text. It would be wrong to fault him for living when he did.

Hermeneutics

In the mid-1800s hermeneutics did not occupy the prominent place in biblical interpretation that it does today. Few set forth the "rules" of interpretation, and those who did often presented

---

[43] *Matthew,* xivii.

what would now be considered elementary. Nevertheless, Broadus spent considerable time in these two volumes discussing issues of hermeneutics. All who interpret the Bible should heed his principles.

Broadus's *Treatise* deals with interpretation issues in its opening pages. It was explicit and woven into the fabric of everything Broadus presented. It will be helpful, therefore, to divide the hermeneutics section into the explicit rules and those that are implicit.

Broadus's Stated Rules for Interpretation

The last portion of the chapter in *Treatise,* titled "The Text— Interpretation," contained "the principles upon which one must proceed if he would interpret correctly."[44] Listing them will provide understanding of the core set of principles.

1. Interpret grammatically: "Endeavor to ascertain the precise meaning of the words and phrases used in the text."[45] The available tools for philology, grammar, and comparative study may accomplish this. "Labor at this point saves labor at all after points."[46]

2. Interpret logically: The connections between the text and its surrounding texts usually provided the key to proper understanding.[47]

3. Interpret historically: This called the interpreter to study general historical knowledge such as: the facts of history, geography, culture, and historical sequences in Scripture.

4. Interpret figuratively, where there was sufficient reason. Broadus urged that "in the language of Scripture, as in all other

---

[44] *Treatise,* 78. The following terms of principles for interpretation are taken from Broadus's *Treatise,* 78–85.

[45] Ibid.

[46] Ibid.

[47] Broadus uses two words for seemingly the same idea: *connection* and *context.* The "connection" is the way the text relates to the larger literary units of which it is a part and, it seems, the extrabiblical circumstances to which it relates. Context is the smaller surrounding unit of which the text is a part. There are multiple uses of these two words, but *Treatise,* 79–81, put these two words together in an explanatory way.

language, the presumption is in favor of the literal sense."[48] There were times, however, where common sense required a figurative sense. He gave the example of prophecy, where a literal understanding came only after fulfillment. He was careful to note, however, "that language may be highly figurative without being fictitious."[49]

5. Interpret allegorically, where that is clearly proper. As is true of the last principle, Broadus warned about resorting too quickly to allegory. His basic principle was that the interpreter can only take as allegory what he has a warrant in Scripture to do so. Allegory was not spiritualizing. Rather it was following the guidelines of the New Testament in its interpretation of Old Testament truth.

6. Interpret in accordance with, and not contrary to, the general teachings of Scripture. This prohibited strange or bizarre interpretations. Equally, it provided guidelines for solving interpretive problems where two possibilities exist. The correct one was that which was in accord with Scripture.

These principles are found in almost every textbook on hermeneutics in the twentieth and twenty-first centuries. Broadus did not claim originality for them. He simply urged interpreters to follow them.

Implicit Hermeneutics

Other principles of interpretation must be identified. While they were not in Broadus's stated principles, they were certainly part of his repeated discussions and his methodologies.

1. Meaning was objectively understood. While Broadus did not state his principle in this way, clearly he urged all interpreters to labor to find the meaning intended by the text. While Broadus acknowledged the fact that interpreters had a propensity to make a text mean what they want, he steadfastly rejected that as valid. The words had meaning in themselves, understood as they relate to their "connections" and "contexts."

---

[48] Ibid., 82.
[49] Ibid., 83.

It may be argued that Broadus did not have the advantage of the later philosophers with their subjective understanding of meaning. They had brought various "reader response" hermeneutics to the theory of interpretation. It did seem, however, that Broadus had the advantage of reading extensively in literature (he taught literature on occasion), and the literary critics were already suggesting personalized interpretations. Some of the philosophers and theologians had already ventured in these directions as well. Rather than reply to the academicians, if that were Broadus's intent, he cited numerous examples of common mistakes that were subjective and, therefore, errant.

Broadus did allow for varieties of interpretation based on genre. He warned about taking poetry literally, suggested that law and prophecy demand their own understandings, and urged interpreters to treat parables in a commonsense way. He also warned about excesses in either figurative or literalistic interpretations.

Meaning was always the product of a commonsense approach to the text. But it was always what the text indicated, not what the reader wanted to hear as he read. This approach was the basic thrust of many of the contemporary books on hermeneutics. Broadus anticipated them well. He declared, "We must bring to bear upon men's minds as a part of God's Word, only what the text really means, as best we can ascertain it."[50]

2. The author's intent guided. In the last half of the twentieth century, "author's intent" rang through the interpretive halls loudly and clearly. Broadus proclaimed the same message. This has been implied in previous discussions. A few additional comments may be helpful.

In matters of harmonizing, Broadus respected the plan and organization of the author. Matthew, for example, did not intend a chronological account of events and discourse. Rather his purpose was twofold: (1) to put forth Jesus as Messiah, and (2) to

---

[50] Ibid., 65.

exhibit the true nature of the Messianic reign.[51] These principles must guide both in the arrangement/organization of Matthew and in the specific interpretations.

These major points will illustrate how Broadus approached hermeneutics. Once again, he did not articulate his understanding in contemporary vocabulary. Yet he demonstrated a solid and forward-thinking understanding of biblical interpretation.

Concluding Evaluation

The chapter title, "New Wine in Broadus Wineskins?" may now be addressed more directly. First it was necessary to describe and define the "Broadus Wineskins." Hopefully enough was presented to bring an understanding of: (1) representative statements from Broadus himself, and (2) suggestions as to the approach he would take given today's issues. Second, the chapter suggested some major areas of contemporary thought unaddressed explicitly or implicitly by Broadus. These were often interwoven with the descriptive elements.

Clearly Broadus took an informed and scholarly methodology in his work. His writing demonstrated that he was in the forefront of nineteenth-century scholarship. This is seen in his employment of the original languages, his understanding of lexicography, and his insistence on the proper backgrounds as necessary to proper understanding. He was anxious for his students and preachers alike to follow those methodologies.

Perhaps Broadus's strongest emphasis was on letting the text determine its meaning. Resisting spiritualizing and misrepresentation, he insisted on a sane, commonsense approach to Scripture. This applied to harmonizing seeming discrepancies. For him the text must always be allowed to say what its author wished. Recent books on hermeneutics may differ on the nature and source of meaning, but all have called for a commitment to the meaning of the text. Broadus should be respected for this commitment.

---

[51] *Matthew,* 72. On several other occasions, Broadus stated that Matthew did not intend a chronological account. See for example his discussion of Jesus' miracles, 174.

Broadus demonstrated a proper respect for scholarship and a careful reserve regarding its claims. This may be seen on the one hand in his understanding of the Synoptic Problem, and on the other, his refusal to take a position that to him was based on textual manipulation or selective proof texts. It is also seen in his firm commitment to the results of text-critical investigations. He affirmed the recently found manuscripts and based his work on them. They corrected other manuscripts and early translations. Yet he carefully evaluated texts in light of the church fathers and early translations. He remained open-minded, evidenced, for example, in his appreciation for Westcott's work along with a reservation as to some of his textual conclusions. Confidence and caution characterize good scholarship in every age.

There are, naturally, areas of contemporary scholarly concern unmentioned by Broadus. Most of these reflect the trends of the twentieth century. In evaluating these, it is crucial to see Broadus's attitude toward the scholarship of his day. Many comments contained in *Matthew* reveal an understanding suitable for today's issues, though explained inadequately by today's standards. His studies led him to ask some of the questions which scholars today seek to answer. Beyond the asking of questions, Broadus sought to present a plausible answer reflecting the best of committed biblical scholarship.

John Albert Broadus was an unusual man. He was the preacher-scholar. He was the pastor-educator. He was remarkable in his day with his balanced and sensible approach to his calling. The characteristics he displayed would suit all scholars well—in any era. Furthermore, as scholarly interests have advanced and, in many ways, become more technical, it seems that the issues of today have been well anticipated by Broadus. All who would interpret Scripture today will read Broadus with great profit and, perhaps most significantly, not be led astray by inadequate or ill-informed information. It seems that today's "scholarly wine" would fit into the Broadus wineskins. The wineskins may have to bend, but they would certainly not break.

Chapter VI

Broadus and the Establishment of The Southern Baptist Theological Seminary

Craig C. Christina

A vast difference exists between the dreamer and the builder of dreams. While the dreamer can imagine the truth of the possibilities, the dream builder lays down his life to make the possibilities come true. John Albert Broadus was much more than a dreamer; he was a man who gave his life for the edification of the church, the Southern Baptist denomination, and her founding seminary. Yet it was the establishment and continuance of The Southern Baptist Theological Seminary that became his all-consuming passion later in life, and it is in the building of the Seminary that one finds the heartbeat of this dream builder.

The mid-1800s were a time of much strife and conflict in the nation. Dangerous tensions existed between the northern and southern states that also influenced the life of Baptists. When the Southern Baptist Convention was formed in 1845 at Augusta, Georgia, the fledgling denomination only numbered

300,000 members, 100,000 of which were slaves.[1] The need for Southern Baptist theological education was quickly propelled to the forefront of the denomination's consciousness since institutions like Hamilton Literary and Theological Institute (Colgate University) in New York, Rochester Theological Seminary in New York, and Newton Theological Institution outside of Boston were in the control of the northern Baptists.[2] Thus, several far-sighted Baptist leaders arose who embraced the challenge.

A Seminary in the South

The first man to suggest seriously the idea of forming a seminary in the South was Basil Manly Sr. in 1835.[3] Unfortunately Manly's article met with little response.[4] As W. O. Carver would later describe, several conflicting interests prevented unity on the need for a seminary in the South:

> The State consciousness, pride and jealousy, the provincial claims of the colleges (at least seven) with theological departments, the vested interest and natural feeling of responsibility of the professors of these college departments to state sentiment, all unconsciously exploited the provincialism and unschooled conservatism of the people generally for delaying unity.[5]

Fortunately several men continued to pursue passionately the establishment of a seminary; men like W. B. Johnson, R. B. C. Howell, A. M. Poindexter, James P. Boyce, and Basil Manly Sr. and Jr. urged the formation of such an institution. Howell well

---

[1] W. H. Whitsitt, "Historical Discourse at the 50th Anniversary of the Southern Baptist Convention," *Proceedings of the Southern Baptist Convention*, 1895, 77–90.

[2] In actuality, the need for both missions and theological education controlled by Baptists in the South became two of the driving impulses behind the formation of the Southern Baptist Convention.

[3] Basil Manly Sr., *The Southern Baptist and General Intelligencer* (13 March 1835): 172.

[4] Ibid., 31 July 1835, 72–73.

[5] W. O. Carver, "The Southern Baptist Theological Seminary in the Growing of the Denomination," *Review and Expositor*, XLIII (April 1946): 133.

articulated the basis for formal theological education in an article republished in the "Southern Baptist." As John A. Broadus summarized:

> He [Howell] recognizes that many men have been, and many will be, very useful in the ministry, without formal education at college or seminary. But he argues that the progress of general knowledge, the necessity of encountering trained ministers of other denominations, the demand of many of our churches for better-prepared pastors, all combine to require a larger proportion of thoroughly educated Baptist ministers.[6]

Their combined efforts led to the formation of a study committee in 1847 and an adopted resolution in 1849 at a Southern Baptist Educational Convention meeting in Charleston, South Carolina. Though the issue languished between 1849 and 1853, in part due to J. R. Graves's insistence on a seminary in Nashville, the issue was again discussed at the Baptist Education Society of Virginia meeting in June 1854 and the Southern Baptist Convention held in Montgomery, Alabama, in May 1855.[7] During the Montgomery meeting, a resolution offered by A. M. Poindexter and unanimously passed declared "that in the opinion of this meeting it is demanded by the interests of the cause of truth that the Baptists of the South and Southwest unite in establishing a Theological Institution of high grade," and that a convention be held on the subject in Augusta, Georgia, the next year.[8]

In June 1855, John A. Broadus spoke to the messengers of the Baptist General Convention of Virginia on the need for the theological preparation of Southern Baptist ministers.[9] A year later in April 1856, "the friends of theological education" met

---

[6] John A. Broadus, *Memoir of James P. Boyce* (New York: A. C. Armstrong and Son, 1893), 115.

[7] Cf. William A. Mueller, *A History of Southern Baptist Theological Seminary* (Nashville: Broadman Press, 1959), 11–13.

[8] Broadus, *Memoir*, 118.

[9] James Roland Barron, "The Contributions of John A. Broadus to Southern Baptists" (Th.D. diss., Southern Baptist Theological Seminary, 1972), 45.

in Augusta, and a special committee was appointed to seek the required funding and possible location for a seminary.[10] The committee was to report back to the next Educational Convention to be held in Louisville, Kentucky, in May 1857—two days prior to the SBC meeting there.

On July 31, 1856, upon his induction as professor of theology at Furman University, James P. Boyce delivered an inaugural address that sent shockwaves throughout the denomination among those interested in a seminary. Broadus would later say that this speech "proved to be epoch-making in the history of theological education among Southern Baptists."[11]

In this pivotal oration the twenty-nine-year-old Boyce proposed "Three Changes in Theological Institutions." As Timothy George has well summarized, these changes proposed "openness," "excellence," and "confessional identity" in theological education.[12] Openness meant that anyone called by God, regardless of formal college education, should be afforded the opportunity to pursue theological instruction; for, as John R. Sampey would later point out, "Before 1859 not one of the twelve apostles could have secured admittance as a regular student in any of the standard theological seminaries of our country."[13] Excellence described the content of "special courses" to be offered "so that the ablest and most aspiring students might make extraordinary attainments, preparing them" to teach or write.[14] While making concessions for less educated students, Boyce also desired a seminary comparable to Princeton or Yale that provided the best in academic scholarship. The third change, confessional identity, sought to establish an abstract of principles whereby every professor at the seminary would sign his adherence to

---

[10] Barron, "The Contributions," 45.

[11] Broadus, *Memoir*, 142.

[12] Timothy George, "James Petigru Boyce," in *Baptist Theologians*, ed. Timothy George and David S. Dockery (Nashville: Broadman Press, 1990), 249–66.

[13] John R. Sampey, "The Future of the Seminary in the Light of Its Past," *Review and Expositor*, XXVI (October 1929): 376. Delivered upon the inauguration of Dr. Sampey as the fifth president of The Southern Baptist Theological Seminary in the fall of 1929.

[14] Broadus, *Memoir*, 121.

the doctrines contained therein. Boyce recognized the dangers of "erroneous and injurious instruction in such a seat of sacred learning."[15] Indeed, with the appearance of Unitarianism, Transcendentalism, Landmarkism, Campbellism, and other "blasphemous doctrines," Boyce had the foresight to preserve the theological foundation of the seminary against the disastrous consequences of allowing a single heresy to be advanced upon the minds of her students.[16]

At the time of Boyce's address, Broadus had not been directly involved in the process of founding the seminary. However, after reading Boyce's address on the "Three Changes," he responded publicly through an article entitled "The Theological Seminary," which appeared in the Virginia Baptist paper *The Religious Herald*.[17] In this article Broadus challenged the need for another seminary similar to the other seminaries already in existence.

Many respected Baptists at the time, particularly in Virginia, had great respect for Broadus and his views on religious education. Broadus was called to preach at the age of 19 while on his way to start his freshman year of college at the University of Virginia. He was going to study medicine, but on the way to Charlottesville on August 10, 1846, he attended the preaching services of the Salem Union Association at Upperville, Virginia. A. M. Poindexter, one of the prime movers in establishing the seminary, was preaching when Broadus received the call.[18] Broadus excelled as a student and eventually graduated in June 1850 with the master of arts degree, the highest earned degree offered anywhere in the nation at that time.[19]

Upon graduation, Broadus spent a year teaching school in Fluvanna County, Virginia, while continuing his studies under

---

[15] Ibid.

[16] Quoted by George, "Boyce," 253.

[17] John A. Broadus, "The Theological Seminary," *The Religious Herald*, XXVI (April 9, 1857): 3.

[18] Barron, "The Contributions," 15.

[19] A. T. Robertson, *Life and Letters of John Albert Broadus* (Philadelphia: American Baptist Publication Society, 1901), 61.

the guidance of J. R. Scott, Broadus's chaplain at the university. In September 1851, Broadus embraced a dual opportunity in Charlottesville, to be assistant instructor in ancient languages at the University of Virginia and to be pastor of the Charlottesville Baptist Church. While serving in both positions, Broadus influenced both students and congregants.

Among students, Broadus gained recognition for his scholarship. He eventually served in the prominent position of university chaplain (1855–1857) during which time he led several students to faith in Christ and influenced the spiritual development of others.[20] However, his knowledge of the pedagogical applications of the university's elective system most heavily enabled his later prominence in establishing the seminary's curriculum. As A. T. Robertson observed, "It is impossible to estimate the influence of the University of Virginia over the educational system of the South and of the North as well."[21]

As the pastor of the fourth largest white congregation in Virginia at that time, Broadus gained distinction on several fronts. Obviously, his pastoral ministry impacted numerous lives including individuals like Crawford Howell Toy and Charlotte "Lottie" Moon, both of whom were converted and baptized under his leadership.[22] Yet it was the many other positions Broadus held because he was the pastor of Charlottesville Baptist Church that earned him wider respect.

Though Broadus served as a trustee of Hollins Institute, his greatest educational endeavor as pastor emerged from the establishment of the Albemarle Female Institute—a college level school for women sponsored by the Albemarle Baptist Association. Broadus served as president of the trustees, allowed the school to meet in the basement of the church, and assisted in the development of its curriculum based on the elective system of the University of Virginia. It was also the first school to offer

---

[20] Robertson claims that the enrollment among Baptists at U.Va. increased because of Broadus's presence. For a list of notable Baptists influenced by Broadus's chaplaincy, see Robertson, *Life*, 142–43.

[21] Ibid., 61.

[22] Barron, "The Contributions," 29–30.

English language courses on "parity with the ancient classics and the cultured tongues of modern Europe."[23] Broadus also gained statewide respect through his service on the various boards of the General Association of Baptists in Virginia.[24] Through these varied ministries, Broadus "attracted attention to his ability and earned the position in which he made his contribution to Baptists throughout the South;" namely as professor and eventually president of The Southern Baptist Theological Seminary.[25]

A month after Broadus wrote his article in response to Boyce's inaugural address, the Education Convention was held in Louisville, Kentucky, in May 1857. On May 7 the convention considered a plan proposed by Boyce and South Carolina Baptists to combine Furman University's theology department into a new seminary located in Greenville with the promise of $100,000 in start-up funds provided that another $100,000 could be raised across the South. The plan was adopted, and a Committee on Plan of Organization was formed that included James P. Boyce, Basil Manly Jr., E.T. Winkler, William Williams, and John A. Broadus. Broadus would later say, "In the work of that Committee, began my own connection with the Seminary, though with no dream then that it would ever become an intimate and life-long connection."[26]

In August 1857, the committee met in Richmond, Virginia, to discuss their ideas for organizing the seminary. The three persons able to attend were Boyce, Manly, and Broadus. Boyce offered information on the legalities of beginning the seminary, Manly presented the abstract of principles, and Broadus outlined a plan of instruction. Broadus had suggested in Louisville "that the 'changes' proposed in Boyce's address, especially the

---

[23] H. H. Harris, "John A. Broadus," *The Religious Herald*, LXVIII (March 21, 1895): 2. Broadus later commented that he believed it to be the first college to offer a separate department for English studies; cf. John A. Broadus, "On the Study of English," *The Central Baptist*, XVIII (December 20, 1883): 1.

[24] Barron, "The Contributions," 39; where he suggests that of the six statewide boards of the G.A.B.V. at that time, Broadus eventually contributed to them all.

[25] Ibid., 42.

[26] John A. Broadus, "Editorial Correspondence," *The Religious Herald*, XLVIII (July 15, 1875): 2.

apparently difficult matter of uniting all grades of theological students in the same institution, could be effected through a plan adapted from that of the University of Virginia."[27] The curriculum at the University of Virginia was based on an elective system where, in addition to required classes, students could select other courses of interest to them. Broadus applied this concept to theological education but with a twist. Instead of dictating required courses, Broadus proposed allowing the entire curriculum to be elective. He reasoned, "Men who could attend the Seminary only a single year must be welcomed to such theological studies as would give them the best practical training for their work."[28] If they only have a year to give toward studies, this system would "promote the spirit of freedom" such that "young men can go, with such preparation as they may have, to study what they may prefer, can stay as few or as many sessions as they choose, and can get credit, from time to time, for just so much as they have done."[29]

Broadus arranged the seminary into eight distinct departments or schools. After consulting with Boyce and Manly, the final plan was as follows:

I. Biblical Introduction. In this school would be taught the canon of Scripture and inspiration, with biblical geography and antiquities, etc.

II. Interpretation of the Old Testament. Here there would be two classes—(1) the interpretation of the Old Testament in English; (2) Hebrew and Chaldee, and Hebrew exegesis. It was added that other Oriental languages, such as Arabic, Syriac, etc., might also be taught.

III. Interpretation of the New Testament. (1) Interpretation of the New Testament in English. (2) New Testament Greek, and Greek Exegesis.

---

[27] Broadus, *Boyce*, 150.
[28] Ibid., 155.
[29] John A. Broadus, "The Theological Seminary: Substance of Address by J. A. Broadus, at Hampton," *The Religious Herald*, XXXI (July 29, 1858): 1.

IV. Systematic Theology. (1) A general course, in which the instruction should not presuppose any acquaintance with the learned languages. (2) A special and more erudite course, in which there might be read theological works in the Latin, etc.

V. Polemic Theology and Apologetics.

VI. Homiletics, or Preparation and Delivery of Sermons.

VII. Church History.

VIII. Church Government and Pastoral Duties.[30]

As students completed each school, a separate diploma was granted. In those schools requiring both general and special courses, both courses were required for the diploma. Students able to complete only the general or English course would be granted a Certificate of Proficiency. Those who had already studied theology in college could skip the English courses and go straight to exegetical studies, but no diploma would be earned. Broadus would later observe,

> Not one student in a hundred of those entering the Seminary through its whole history has failed to enter the classes for study of the English Bible; and no one has ever thought of studying the more erudite course in Systematic Theology, without also taking the general or English course.[31]

Academician, theologian, and Baptist university president David S. Dockery has rightly judged, "It was a creative proposal that was fifty years ahead of other advances in theological education in North America . . . [for it offered] something worthwhile for all."[32] Though various emendations were made to the curriculum over time, specialized classes were added, and degrees evolved into the graduate in theology (for English-only

---

[30] Broadus, *Boyce*, 157.

[31] Ibid., 158.

[32] David S. Dockery, "The Broadus-Robertson Tradition," in *Theologians of the Baptist Tradition*, ed. Timothy George and David S. Dockery (Nashville: Broadman and Holman Publishers, 2001), 95.

students), bachelor in theology, master in theology, and doctor in theology—all during Broadus's tenure at the seminary, the basic plan of instruction remained intact.[33]

From this Richmond meeting and the deliberations that ensued, Broadus developed a deep appreciation for Boyce and Manly and they for him.[34] He would need their friendship, for only two months later on October 21, 1857, his wife died after only a week of illness.[35]

By May 1, 1858, the Committee on Plan of Organization reported back to the next Educational Convention meeting in Greenville, South Carolina. It would prove to be the last convention for this purpose. In addition to the other key elements of the plan, Boyce also reported that he had raised almost all of the $100,000 endowment from South Carolinians and had secured the use of the Greenville First Baptist Church's recently vacated facility rent free.[36] Indeed, Boyce boasted that it would be "the great Southern Baptist Theological Seminary."[37] Basil Manly Sr., who presided over the meeting, countered, "Don't say *great* until you succeed in your work of endowment."[38] The delegates accepted the committee's plan and elected four men to serve as the founding faculty: James P. Boyce, John A. Broadus, Basil Manly Jr., and E. T. Winkler. Winkler immediately declined, and Broadus "carried the matter home as a great burden . . . and, after weeks of anxious consideration, felt bound to decline also."[39]

Broadus's resistance to joining the faculty naturally stemmed from his ministry at Charlottesville Baptist Church. On May 8,

---

[33] For an interesting discussion of the changes in Southern's curriculum plan during Broadus's tenure, see Barron, "The Contributions," 49–61.

[34] For Broadus's description of this meeting, see Broadus, *Boyce*, 150–56.

[35] Robertson, *Life*, 146. On February 15, 1858, Manly wrote Broadus to urge him to join him for a week at his home in Richmond to continue their collaborations on the seminary but also, perhaps, to encourage his friend; cf. ibid., 147–48.

[36] Broadus, *Boyce*, 152. The First Baptist Church of Greenville had just moved into "its new and beautiful building."

[37] Ibid., 153.

[38] Ibid.

[39] Ibid., 154.

1858, one friend wrote to him outlining several objections to the offer: (1) If Broadus were truly interested in teaching, he should take an offer from the University of Virginia and, thus, remain in Charlottesville. (2) Other teachers could be found who are adept in their field of study but who cannot preach well, unlike Broadus who is needed in the pulpit. (3) Leaving so many in order to teach 20 to 30 students doesn't make sense. (4) The students won't benefit by seminary education anyway. (5) If Broadus wants to influence young men, why sever his association with the University where he already influences scores of students for Christ. (6) Broadus's ongoing work with the Albermale Female Institute is imminently more important than starting a seminary. (7) No other minister in the denomination can fill the pulpit in Charlottesville as effectively as Broadus.[40] A voluntary committee from the Charlottesville Baptist Church also composed a protest to his departure:

> But take away our pastor. There is left a vacancy which we honestly think no other man in the denomination can at all fill. His relations in past time and now to the University, give him an access to the great mass of mind there, sanctified and unsanctified, which no other man in our denomination can have—which no other pastor in Charlottesville has, or can have, so long as the men remain the same.[41]

In light of such emotive persuasion, one can easily understand why Broadus would wrestle intensely with the decision. He was truly making a difference for Christ in Charlottesville by any standard of measure. Why leave so rich a field of ministry for an endeavor as dubious as the founding of the Greenville seminary?

With only Boyce and Manly willing to accept the faculty positions, it was decided by the delegates in Greenville to postpone the launch of the seminary for a year, to the fall of

[40] Robertson, *Life*, 148–49.
[41] Ibid., 149.

1859, until such time that the two vacancies be filled and additional financial assets from the other states be secured. Though Broadus had declined the professorship, he zealously promoted the plan of organization at every opportunity.

At the Baptist General Association of Virginia meeting in June 1858, he persuasively defended the need for a seminary with an elective curriculum. Perhaps sensing the need to repudiate his former objections to the seminary as published in *The Religious Herald* on April 9, 1857, he admitted that his earlier position was "unfounded, resulting from mere prejudice and lack of information."[42] He reminded the audience of the paucity of pastors with formal theological training due to their unwillingness to spend several years at college studying subjects like mathematics; whereas, in seminary they could invest in a single eight-month session and learn subjects with an immediate application to their preaching.[43] Speaking from personal experience, he told of a young preacher who enjoyed an excellent academic education but lacked a basic knowledge of doctrine. The result was a serious theological blunder on the doctrine of justification by faith. He also defended the need for the abstract of principles on two fronts. First, to the fear that students would be required to sign or adhere to a confession of faith, Broadus defended the necessity for freedom of inquiry to allow the students to formulate their own opinions as to doctrine so that they would never be asked to sign such a confession either upon entrance or departure from the seminary. Second, the professors must sign the Abstract only as a "safeguard against their teaching heresy" and with the understanding that they already ascribe to said doctrines prior to appointment.[44]

Broadus likewise carried his enthusiasm for the seminary back home to his local association. At an Albemarle Baptist Association meeting in September 1858, he presented the annual report

---

[42] Broadus, "Address at Hampton," 1.
[43] Ibid.
[44] Ibid.

of the Committee on Education as strongly supporting the seminary plan and encouraged the audience to do the same.[45]

That same fall, still convinced that his place was in Charlottesville, Broadus was stricken with "a violent and depressing attack of ulcerated sore throat, which threatened to destroy all his hopes and plans for life."[46] He was unable to preach for six weeks. Quite possibly this illness caused him to reevaluate his call to teach at the Seminary. In his tribute to his father-in-law, *Life and Letters of John Albert Broadus*, the renowned Southern Seminary New Testament scholar A. T. Robertson followed the description of the illness with a letter from Andrew Broaddus, John's relative. In this letter Andrew reminded John of the need for humility among preachers; especially in lieu of the inordinate amount of praise received from their congregations:

> Now, lest you should be exalted above measure, be pleased to remember what Brother Jeter said to Brother Farish, and what you were kind enough to apply to me, that 'no matter how mean a preacher a man may be, there are some people who will think him the best preacher in the world.[47]

Could it be that this admonition caused Broadus to ponder the abundant praise of his own congregation; that no matter where he was serving, the congregation's natural inclination is to love their pastor and to praise him above all others?

Robertson followed Andrew Broaddus's letter with another from Manly. In the case of the latter, Manly suggested an outright connection between John's illness and the imposition of God's will for him to teach:

> How is your health now? I heard it was not so good. Perhaps God may be preparing the way to cause you to enter the theological seminary. If that should be his will I should not grieve, for I candidly think that

---

[45] Barron, "The Contributions," 52.

[46] Robertson, *Life*, 154.

[47] Ibid.

the opportunities for permanent and extensive influence there are superior to any other situation in the
South. . . . God bless you, and guide us all according
to his will.[48]

Whether his brief incapacity influenced his reconsideration
of the position is indeterminable. However, for Robertson to
include both Andrew's and Manly's letters, some amount of
influence must be attributable to their input.

In any case, the Lord was already leading Broadus in new
directions. On January 4, 1859, he was married to Miss Charlotte Eleanor Sinclair. By March 29, 1859, Boyce wrote Broadus
to inform him that the provisional committee—to which had
been assigned the responsibility of filling the two vacancies on
faculty—had again nominated Winkler and him to the posts.[49]
In his reply on April 4, 1859, Broadus admitted his reconsideration of the matter.[50] Finally, on April 21, 1859, Broadus wrote
to both Manly and Boyce announcing his decision to accept the
position. Interestingly, he expressed to Boyce that one of the
most influential factors in his deliberations was the prospect of
deepening their fraternal relationship so that "we shall ere long
learn to love each other as brothers."[51] The potential of working
with men like Boyce and Manly in establishing this new work
among Southern Baptists clearly excited Broadus about the
possibilities. After Winkler rejected the offer a second time, the
committee elected William Williams, and the faculty was complete. On May 7, 1859, the board of trustees for The Southern
Baptist Theological Seminary met concurrently with the Southern Baptist Convention meeting in Richmond. They officially
elected John Albert Broadus as professor of New Testament
interpretation and homiletics. That summer, both Richmond
College and the College of William and Mary conferred upon

---

[48] Ibid., 155.
[49] Ibid., 157.
[50] Ibid.
[51] Ibid., 159.

Broadus the honorary title of doctor of divinity (D.D.) "in view of your distinguished attainments as a scholar and divine."[52]

The Early Years of Southern Seminary

The seminary opened its doors in Greenville, South Carolina, on October 1, 1859, with an initial enrollment of 26 students. The largest number of students in each of the first three sessions was from Virginia, in large part because of the efforts and influence of Broadus.[53] Sadly Broadus experienced a prolonged illness of "dyspepsia" that prevented him from teaching his classes for three months during this first session.[54] The other three professors ably covered his classes so that the students could continue their classes without interruption. However, a disruption of another kind waited on the horizon; one which would preclude all studies and threatened the existence of the seminary itself.

With the start of the third session in the fall of 1861, the South was at war with the North. Enrollment declined to 20 students at the start of that session. But as the fall progressed, a new volunteer regiment for the Confederacy was called up from the Greenville area, and Boyce agreed to join the regiment as chaplain. The students, one by one, left the seminary to join their friends in the army. Though young men in the South were often drafted to join the cause as soldiers, ministers were not. However, Broadus felt that ministerial students should not participate in the exemption; otherwise, "[we] would have placed all concerned under a shadow of reproach."[55] With a handful of students left at the end of the session and Boyce already gone, Broadus shared: "We attempted no formal Commencement at the close."[56] The seminary, which had begun so well with a solid class of students and with $200,000 of endowment, closed its doors with no certainty as to a fourth session.

---

[52] As quoted in Robertson, *Life*, 164.
[53] Barron, "The Contributions," 63.
[54] Robertson, *Life*, 171.
[55] Broadus, *Boyce*, 180.
[56] Ibid.

General Stonewall Jackson asked one of Broadus's friends, J. William Jones, to implore Broadus to become a preacher to the Army of Northern Virginia. As Jackson urged, "Beg him to come. Tell him that he never had a better opportunity of preaching the gospel than he would have right now in these camps."[57] Broadus also wrote a tract for the soldiers titled "We Pray for You at Home."[58] Included in the pamphlet was a hymn by Basil Manly Jr. that he called "Prayer for the Loved Ones from Home." Thrilled that Broadus accepted the invitation, General Jackson asked to meet Broadus the moment he arrived. He wanted Broadus to preach from his headquarters because "I wish to help him in his work all I can."[59] Sadly a few days later in the battle of Chancellorsville, Stonewall Jackson "crossed over the river to rest under the shade of the trees," and the two never met.[60]

Broadus eventually became a chaplain in General Lee's army until the end of the Civil War. He also preached in several rural churches and even became their pastor from time to time. The brutality and depravity of the wartime experience burdened Broadus and his family. Survival was challenging. Even at the end of the war, Broadus seemed unaware that it could ever end. On April 11, 1865, he wrote to Manly, "I take it there will now be war in this country fully as long as you or I will live. All thought of doing this or that 'after the war,' must, I fear, be abandoned."[61] Unbeknownst to Broadus, Lee had surrendered to Grant at Appomattox Court House two days earlier.

With the war over, the Seminary's faculty gathered early in the summer of 1865 in Greenville to consider how and when to reopen. With venerable insight, Boyce had originally determined not to encumber the new seminary with thousands of dollars of debt in the construction of a new building. At the Educational

---

[57] Robertson, *Life*, 197.
[58] Ibid., 190.
[59] As quoted by J. William Jones in Robertson, *Life*, 198.
[60] Ibid.
[61] Ibid., 211.

Convention meeting in Greenville in May 1858, a minister by the name of Thomas Curtis had observed the following:

> The requisites for an institution of learning are three *b*'s,—bricks, books, brains. Our brethren usually begin at the wrong end of the three *b*'s; they spend all their money for bricks, have nothing to buy books, and must take such brains as they can pick up. But our brethren ought to begin at the other end of the three *b*'s.[62]

Broadus noted that seven years later, when the question of continuing the seminary was under discussion, "with the endowment lost, and in a land swept as by cyclone," it was gratefully remembered that Boyce's plan was to delay the acquisition of land and buildings; "for even a few thousand dollars of debt would then have sunk the enterprise beyond redemption."[63]

Nevertheless, so many impediments seemed to exist—a lack of funding for the professors' salaries, the question of how to advertise over the summer to enroll enough students for fall classes, etc.—that discouragement fell upon the group. Then, with the greatest determination so characteristic of the spirit in those indomitable Baptists, Broadus declared, "Suppose we quietly agree that the Seminary may die, but we'll die first."[64] Heads were bowed, and the question was settled.

When classes began on November 1, 1865, for the seminary's fourth session, only seven students enrolled. Broadus had only one student in his homiletics class, and he was blind. So Broadus taught him by a series of lectures that were later published in 1870 and titled, at that time, *A Treatise on the Preparation and Delivery of Sermons*. This work not only left an indelible impression upon the young student but also became the standard homiletics textbook in Baptist seminaries for decades to come. As W. O. Carver observed, "No other

---

[62] As quoted in Broadus, *Boyce*, 153.
[63] Ibid.
[64] Ibid., 200. Note that Broadus attributes the quote to "some one," as he was humbly apt to do; but Robertson gives the credit to Broadus in Robertson, *Life*, 214.

work in the field of homiletics has had so wide and extended a use in the history of theological education."[65] In fact, Carver credited Broadus with transforming Southern Baptist preaching from eloquence and oratory to a more conversational, expositional style.[66] In both Baptist and other denominational circles, scholars and ministers alike appreciated Broadus as one of the most gifted preachers of the Word.

During the next five years the enrollment increased from 15 students to 68; however, a lack of adequate finances continued to inhibit the stability of the seminary. Boyce was paying the professors' salaries, but he was privately borrowing the money to do it.[67] Thus, Broadus diligently labored to raise money for the seminary. In 1866 when the Southern Baptist Convention met for the first time after the war, he desperately urged the messengers to sustain the seminary and received $10,000 in pledges. In 1868, his appeal to Maryland Baptists gained another $20,000. When Virginia Baptists met in 1868, Broadus again spoke on the seminary's behalf, and eight men committed to pay a hundred dollars each annually. While Boyce made the greatest advancements in fund-raising, Broadus contributed where he could.[68] By 1869 the seminary's financial situation had improved. Crawford Howell Toy was added to the faculty, and Broadus was allowed a one-year leave of absence to study and improve his health. During 1870, Broadus traveled in Europe with salary and expenses paid.

In the years that followed the war, it became increasingly obvious to Southern's faculty and trustees that the seminary needed to be relocated. As Broadus recognized, the largest contribution of endowment for any academic institution most likely will come from the home state—in this case, South Carolina. For instance, when the seminary was initially founded, half of the $200,000 endowment came from South Carolina Baptists. These funds were mostly given in Confederate money and

---

[65] As quoted in Mueller, *History of Southern*, 67.

[66] Ibid.

[67] Broadus, *Boyce*, 205.

[68] See Barron, "The Contributions," 66; for a concise analysis of Broadus's efforts.

reinvested in Confederate bonds or other Southern businesses prior to the war. After the war the Confederate money, bonds, and other investments were practically worthless. In addition, most of the seminary's benefactors were South Carolinian farmers whose plantations were decimated by the war. With the wealth of South Carolina plundered, the support for the seminary had to come from outside the state. Thus, the momentum for moving Southern Baptists' theological institution was gaining ground year after year.[69]

Boyce scouted multiple options from among the cities with the most alluring appeals and wealthy benefactors. They included Chattanooga, Atlanta, Nashville, Memphis, Murfreesboro, Tennessee, and Russellville, Kentucky. After weighing all the options, Louisville surfaced as the most obvious choice. The city was the most populace of all those considered and the least damaged from the war. It had a large Baptist constituency; but best of all, it had many wealthy families with whom Boyce had already gained favor. In 1872, the trustees voted to relocate Southern Seminary to Louisville, Kentucky, provided that a $500,000 endowment could be raised. Though Boyce did the majority of the fund-raising, Broadus energetically participated where he could. He joined Boyce for the 1874 Southern Baptist Convention meeting in Jefferson, Texas, and raised $18,500 through a three-hour appeal. On May 23, 1874, Broadus preached to the American Baptist Publication Societies' fiftieth anniversary celebration on the subject "The Work of the Baptists for the Next Half-Century."[70] Three days later these Northern Baptists asked him to present the seminary's needs to the American Baptist Home Mission Society. He did, and they gave more than $10,000.[71]

Despite their efforts the goal of $500,000 was not immediately obtained. Nevertheless, The Southern Baptist Theological Seminary moved to downtown Louisville, Kentucky, in 1877.

---

[69] Broadus gives an excellent firsthand account of the situation in *Boyce*, 218ff.

[70] Barron, "The Contributions," 68.

[71] Ibid.

Broadus continued raising money whenever possible for the endowment and for the Student Fund, a fund for needs like books and food.[72] From his popularity in the pulpit, Broadus was invited to preach many times in the northeast. He gained particular influence among Baptists in the northeast. In 1878 Broadus planned a weeklong campaign in Baltimore that netted $12,000 in pledges toward the endowment. During the summer of 1880, while on a trip to New York, Broadus collected more than $40,000 in endowment gifts. By 1882, the endowment reached a place of stability, and the faculty could be relieved that "it was at last certain that the Seminary would live, after twenty-three years of uncertainty."[73]

In 1886, it was decided that a new student dormitory needed to be built. Boyce dispatched Broadus to New York City to raise the needed $60,000. Broadus visited J. A. Bostwick who pledged $15,000. His next visit was to multimillionaire Baptist benefactor John D. Rockefeller who pledged $25,000. In these first two visits, Broadus quickly secured two-thirds of the desired amount. Now the real work began to raise the final $20,000. As the days passed, Boyce sent telegrams to Broadus to encourage him to press on. Broadus recounted: "Hope deferred made the heart sick. But one could almost hear Boyce's ringing voice and merry laugh as he would telegraph, night after night: 'Don't think of coming back without it. Nobody wants to see you here. Stay all winter, if necessary.'"[74] Finally, after three weeks' effort, Broadus prevailed, and the full $60,000 was contributed. Fittingly, at the dedication ceremony for the first building ever constructed on Southern's campus, the dormitory was named New York Hall.[75] It was comprised of lecture halls,

---

[72] Ibid., 71–72, for a discussion of the Student Fund.

[73] Robertson, *Life*, 319.

[74] Broadus, *Boyce*, 282.

[75] Before the construction of New York Hall, the seminary met downtown on the third and fourth floors of The Public Library Hall (later the Polytechnic). Initially, students boarded in homes. After a few years a hotel was rented downtown near the Library Hall more cheaply for the students. These arrangements, as desired by Boyce, allowed the seminary to function without the burden of debt. Once the endowment increased, annual expenses were comfortably met,

professors' offices, a gymnasium, a dining hall, kitchen, and dormitory space for 200 students. If not for the influence of Broadus and the gifts of New York Baptists, the seminary quite possibly would have continued to struggle for years to come.

Yet Broadus's greatest contributions to Southern Seminary were hardly limited to his skills at fund-raising. As the seminary increased in enrollment, so did the size of his classes. Students packed his lecture hall to hear their beloved professor teach them about the mystery of the gospel. An extended quotation from his student, protégé, and son-in-law, A. T. Robertson, exemplifies the depth and range of Broadus's scholarly skills:

> Oh, the rapture of the days when one could hear Broadus lecture in New Testament English or in Homiletics! It was worth a day's journey to any man. He was a consummate scholar, of the widest reading and the most thorough assimilation. He studied the sources of things and worked through everything for himself. To Anglo-Saxon, Latin, Greek, and Hebrew, he had added German, French, Spanish, Italian, Gothic, Coptic, and modern Greek. He had made himself a specialist in homiletics, in the English Bible, in New Testament history, exegesis, in Greek, in textual criticism, in patristic Greek, and hymnology (English and foreign). . . . He was also one of the greatest preachers of his age. It was the rare combination of scholar, teacher, preacher that met you in the classroom. More than all this, there was a witchery or magnetism that entranced you. If the subject was the Greek article, you felt that that was the line of destiny for you. Go and master the article. . . . If it was a scene in the life of Christ, the whole wondrous picture came before you. You found yourself living with the throngs around the

---

and the land purchased on Broadway between 4th and 5th Avenues (as well as additional land across the street fronting 5th), the time was right to erect the first building, which cost about $80,000. Later, in the 1930s the seminary would be moved to its current location among the beech trees; cf. Broadus, *Boyce*, 257, 278–83.

Nazarene. If you exposed your ignorance by a simple, if not presumptuous question, the quick flash of the eye, the kindly smile, the sympathetic voice put you *en rapport*. You were glad to be a fool for such a man.[76]

With amazing candor, Robertson painted a vivid portrait of an academician who was used by God to shape the minds and hearts of future ministers with artistry, oratory, erudition, and love. As another of Broadus's students expressed, "He had marvelous skill in seizing the heart of some great subject on which he had read volume after volume, and giving it to his class in a few pithy sentences of crystalline clearness. . . . It was the most exhilarating experience I ever knew."[77]

With a rare sense of *gravitas*, Broadus captivated the hearts and minds of his impressionable students in order thoroughly to prepare them for service in the kingdom of God. In fact, he was convinced that the fundamental purpose of seminary education was not merely to elevate students to the lofty heights of theological speculation but to equip them to apply the essential truths of the gospel through practical ministry. Even before he taught his first class, Broadus attempted to alleviate the concerns of certain Southern Baptists who feared that formal theological education would produce heavenly scholars who were of no earthly good. So he assured them that:

> Each of the faculty is deeply impressed with the greater importance of the office of the preacher than of the mere scholar; and every effort will be used to make the scholarship acquired of such practical character as to fit the Student the better to proclaim the Gospel of Christ and to build up His people on their "most holy faith."[78]

The focus of theological education, from his perspective, was to empower students to become better servants to Christ

---

[76] Robertson, *Life*, 336–38.
[77] Professor J. H. Farmer, of McMaster University, *The McMaster University Monthly* (May 1895); quoted in Robertson, *Life*, 338–39.
[78] John A. Broadus, "Southern Baptist Theological Seminary," *The Religious Herald*, XXXII (August 18, 1859): 131.

and His church. It was not to produce scholars or professors who had little interaction with the people of God. In Broadus's mind even professors were expected to serve the local church. He set that example by preaching all over the South and North in churches like First Baptist of Chicago, Indianapolis, Richmond, and filling the pulpit as interim pastor of churches like Broadway Baptist (Louisville, Ky.), Emmanuel Baptist (Brooklyn, N.Y.), Calvary Baptist (New York, N.Y.), Immanuel Baptist (Chicago, Ill.), among others. When in Louisville, Broadus faithfully served as a member of the congregation of Walnut Street Baptist Church where he steadfastly supported his pastors like J. W. Warder and T. T. Eaton.

Broadus's influence extended the kingdom beyond his lectures at Southern Seminary or his sermons in various pulpits. He also published numerous books, tracts, and articles. Aside from his most famous work, *A Treatise on the Preparation and Delivery of Sermons*, another celebrated work in the field of homiletics was his *Lectures on the History of Preaching* (1876). He was also well-known and widely respected for his *Commentary on the Gospel of Matthew*. When the 610-page commentary was completed in 1886, J. H. Thayer of Andover Seminary called it "probably the best commentary in English on that Gospel."[79] Alvah Hovey, president of Newton Theological Seminary and the series editor, stated, "No doubt it will prove to be *the Commentary* of the whole series."[80] Though Broadus composed several other books; he also wrote many tracts, Sunday school lessons, and had many of his sermons and addresses published.[81]

In January 1889, Yale University invited Broadus to deliver the highly esteemed Lyman Beecher Lectures on preaching.[82]

---

[79] J. H. Thayer, *Books and Their Uses*, quoted by Robertson, *Life*, 357.

[80] Ibid., 350.

[81] For a collection of his sermons, see John A. Broadus, *Sermons and Addresses* (Baltimore: H. M. Wharton, 1886; reprint, Nashville: Sunday School Board of the Southern Baptist Convention, n.d.).

[82] Editor's Note: For a fuller discussion of the Beecher Lectures see Mark Overstreet's chapter this volume, "Now I Am Found: The Recovery of the 'Lost' Yale Lectures and Broadus's Legacy of Engaging Exposition."

He regularly lectured at Chautauqua in western New York and the Northfield conferences (begun by Dwight L. Moody). In 1890 Broadus delivered the opening lectures on the Eugene Levering Foundation before the YMCA at Johns Hopkins University, which later appeared in book form under the title *Jesus of Nazareth*. Remarkably his influence and appeal extended far beyond the world of Baptists as "Broadus achieved more recognition beyond his own denomination than any of his brethren."[83] With each display of his theological acumen, Broadus gained not only admiration but also respect for the level of scholarship at The Southern Baptist Theological Seminary.

Moreover, Broadus contributed to the Seminary in ways other than academically and financially. He also sought to support the leadership of his colleague and friend, James P. Boyce, who served as faculty chairman from 1859 to 1888. Boyce was given the title of president in 1888 and died that same year. During his tenure an occasional conflict arose that necessitated the advice or appeal of Broadus in order to keep the peace and spare the seminary from external criticism. One such incident involved Broadus's longtime friend and fellow professor Crawford Howell Toy (1836–1919) in what is widely referred to as the Toy Controversy.

The Toy Controversy

As previously noted Broadus led Toy to the Lord, baptized him, and ordained him to the gospel ministry while he was pastor of the Charlottesville Baptist Church. Broadus also guided Toy's theological formation and education in his earlier years as a Christian. From his earliest studies Toy demonstrated exceptional academic abilities. He graduated from Norfolk Military Academy and received the complete works of Shakespeare as "a graduation present for excellence."[84] At the age of 16, Toy enrolled at the University of Virginia where he developed an exceptional giftedness with languages including Latin, Greek,

---

[83] Mueller, *History of Southern*, 63.
[84] Ibid., 136.

Italian, German, and Anglo-Saxon while also pursuing interests in constitutional and international law.

During his days in Charlottesville Toy came under the influence of his pastor and eventual mentor John Albert Broadus.[85] Toy listened intently to the preaching of Broadus at Charlottesville Baptist Church and was led to a saving faith in Christ and baptized by Broadus. Upon graduating from the University of Virginia with the M.A. degree in 1856, Toy took a teaching position at the Albemarle Female Institute where Broadus was chairman of the board of trustees. In 1857, Charlotte "Lottie" Moon entered the institute; and she, too, was baptized by Broadus during a revival in 1859.[86] That same year Toy volunteered as a candidate for foreign missions in Japan and enrolled in the first class at Southern Seminary in Greenville, South Carolina, to prepare for his calling.[87]

At Southern, Toy excelled in his study of biblical languages; especially Hebrew under Basil Manly Jr. His commitment to theological education was so intense that he completed "three-fourths of a three year course of study" in a single year.[88] With war on the horizon, the mission board cancelled new appointments to the field, and Toy's hopes of going to Japan were dashed. After contemplating going to Japan on his own, Toy returned to Virginia to teach Greek at the University of Richmond. He proposed to Lottie Moon, but she declined.[89]

---

[85] Billy G. Hurt, "Crawford Howell Toy: Interpreter of the Old Testament" (Th. D. diss., The Southern Baptist Theological Seminary, 1966), 14–16.

[86] Lottie Moon and C. H. Toy were engaged to be married but eventually parted ways. Lottie became a missionary to China where she gave her life in service to the cause of Christ and on behalf of Southern Baptists. Every year at Christmas, most Southern Baptist churches still collect an offering for international missions entitled the "Lottie Moon Offering."

[87] Although Toy's interest in foreign missions may have been influenced by his relationship with Moon, Toy felt called to go to Japan because he envisioned the Japanese as becoming a major economic world power; Hurt, "Toy," 31.

[88] Ibid., 28.

[89] After establishing himself as a well-respected professor at Southern, Toy again proposed to Moon through correspondence. She accepted, and the two were to be married upon her return home from China in 1879. However, the Toy Controversy caused Moon to have second thoughts, and the engagement was forever severed.

After serving the South in the Civil War as both a private and then chaplain, Toy briefly taught Greek at Richmond College and the University of Virginia. He then traveled to Europe and spent two years (1866–1868) as a student at Berlin University studying theology, Sanskrit, and Semitics. In Berlin Toy was exposed to the views of higher criticism (also known as historical criticism).

In 1869 Toy joined Southern Seminary's faculty as professor of Old Testament. For 10 years Toy taught at Southern and quickly became respected by both faculty and students as "the most learned man on the faculty."[90] However, some of Toy's teachings began to disturb the rest of Southern Seminary's faculty. It became known through Toy's lectures that he had adopted the Darwinian theory of evolution. He had also embraced Abraham Kuenen's and Julius Wellhausen's theory of pentateuchal criticism based on an evolutionist reconstruction of the history of Israel.[91]

As Broadus conceded:

> Dr. Boyce was not only himself opposed, most squarely and strongly, to all such views, but he well knew that nothing of that kind could be taught in the Seminary without doing violence to its aims and objects, and giving the gravest offence to its supporters in general.[92]

Realizing the potential damage to both students and seminary, Boyce shared his concerns with "a colleague who had been [Toy's] intimate friend from his youth;" again, most likely referring to Broadus.[93] Broadus approached his friend and colleague in the hopes of persuading Toy to desist in teaching the adverse "theoretical inquiries" in order to focus on instructing the students "in the Old Testament history as it stands."[94] With grave concern Broadus attempted to convince Toy that the

---

[90] Mueller, *History of Southern*, 137.
[91] Barron, "The Contributions," 74.
[92] Broadus, *Boyce*, 261.
[93] Ibid., 262; a clear reference to Broadus, who most humbly spoke of himself in the third person.
[94] Ibid.

logical conclusion of his theories would inevitably lead within 20 years to his utter repudiation of the supernatural. Toy would not be persuaded.

With the arrival of the next semester, Toy attempted to abide by his colleagues' wishes to refrain from sharing his views. However, word of his unorthodox theories had spread among the student body. Out of inquisitiveness the students questioned their professor about his beliefs; and he, feeling compelled to answer with honest conviction, assuaged their curiosity. Realizing the tension he had created among the faculty, Toy tendered his resignation at the next trustee meeting held in Atlanta in May 1879. Because he did not think his views merited termination, Toy attached an apologetic explaining how higher criticism could benefit the seminarians. Nevertheless, the trustees voted overwhelmingly to accept Toy's resignation.

In spite of his departure from Southern, Broadus and Toy remained good friends. Broadus even recommended Toy to the faculty of Harvard University where he was warmly received because, as Broadus well knew, holding views like those of Kuenen and Wellhausen would have "no objection in Harvard."[95] Indeed, in retrospect, Broadus affirmed that "Dr. Toy had shown himself not only a remarkable scholar, and a most honorable and lovable gentleman, but also a very able and inspiring teacher, and a colleague with whom, as to all personal relations, it was delightful to be associated."[96] Unfortunately his prediction of Toy's inevitable slide into unorthodoxy proved true as Toy eventually abandoned his Baptist identity, denied the supernatural, and became a Unitarian.[97] Broadus, as peacemaker, preserved the unity of Southern's campus and aided his

---

[95] Ibid., 264.

[96] Ibid., 263.

[97] See ibid., 263–64, as Broadus reflects, "He [Toy] was satisfied that his views would promote truth and piety. He thought strange of the prediction made in conversation [probably by Broadus] that within twenty years he would utterly discard all belief in the supernatural as an element of Scripture—a prediction founded upon knowledge of his logical consistency and boldness, and already in a much shorter time fulfilled, to judge from his latest works."

friend. However, his greater achievement was to help preserve the theological integrity of the seminary.[98]

Broadus as President

Over the course of his career at Southern Seminary, John A. Broadus enjoyed numerous prospects for advancement in position, finance, and prestige in both pastoral and educational settings. Speaking of the opportunities Broadus faced during the years of financial struggle after the war, A. T. Robertson observed:

> Brown University, Crozer Seminary, Richmond College, the First [Baptist] Church, Richmond, and Eutaw Place, Baltimore, all clamored for Doctor Broadus's services at a time when there was not enough money to pay the salaries of the professors. But he could not be moved.[99]

In the centennial history of the seminary written in 1959, William Mueller observed that when the seminary was struggling for survival in the 1870s,

> the old University of Chicago sought Broadus as its head. Later, Vassar, Brown University, and Crozer Theological Seminary were eager to call him as president. Newton Theological Seminary wanted Broadus in 1878 as professor of New Testament and homiletics. One influential congregation offered him ten thousand dollars per year as its pastor.[100]

Even his alma mater, the University of Virginia, asked Broadus in 1873 to succeed his admired teacher W. H. McGuffey as professor of moral philosophy. Yet none could persuade him to abdicate his responsibilities to Southern.

---

[98] Ibid, 262 where Broadus says, "It was hard for Dr. Toy to realize that such teaching was quite out of the question in this institution."

[99] Robertson, *Life*, 306.

[100] Mueller, *History of Southern*, 63

Perhaps compounding the temptation to pursue more lucrative offers was the occasional suggestion by laymen that Southern's professors were paid too well. Broadus recalled one instance when he was riding in a buggy with a friend in the Kentucky countryside. When his friend criticized the professors' meager salaries as being too generous, Broadus divulged some recent invitations Boyce had received for advancement:

> Folks in our neighborhood think that your Seminary professors get entirely too big salaries." The other [Broadus], in reply, mentioned the above two offers [$7,000 for Boyce to direct a bank and $12,000 to head a cotton business], and asked what his folks would think of Boyce's having declined such invitations. The old gentleman said, with great naïveté, "Oh, they wouldn't believe a word of it.[101]

Broadus concluded, "A good many well-meaning people think that ministers are always ready to go where they can have a larger salary, and little do they know of the invitations often declined."[102] For Broadus especially, truer words were never spoken. Though the temptations to leave Southern were obvious, Broadus remained steadfast in his commitment and loyalty to Southern Baptist's mother seminary. His fidelity would eventually be rewarded with the highest possible honor, the office of president.

On December 28, 1888, James P. Boyce died at Pau, France, while traveling through Europe. Broadus was particularly devastated at the loss. As his son-in-law, A. T. Robertson, noted, "Doctor Broadus sometimes said that he never felt that he was the same man after Boyce was gone."[103] In May 1889, the trustees unanimously elected John Albert Broadus to become the second president of The Southern Baptist Theological Seminary. They added $500 to his salary for a grand total of $3,000.[104]

---

[101] Broadus, *Boyce*, 283–84.
[102] Ibid.
[103] Robertson, *Life*, 374.
[104] John R. Sampey, *Memoirs of John R. Sampey*, 136.

Ironically, Broadus had disagreed with Boyce over the need to have a president of the faculty. Broadus was content to leave the overall administration of the seminary to the faculty itself under the leadership of a chairman of the faculty as practiced at the University of Virginia (until 1904).[105] As such, Broadus's tenure as president was marked more by a laissez-faire approach rather than autocratic control.

F. H. Kerfoot (1847–1901), who joined Southern's faculty as professor of systematic theology in 1887, explained Broadus's leadership style:

> He was not a projector of plans for administration, nor was he in a strict sense an administrator. He found the work organized, and he trusted his lieutenants implicitly and left them to attend to the departments assigned them, not even inquiring often as to how they were getting along. He was delicately sensitive about seeming to interfere with the work even of a subordinate. . . . In short, it is safe to say that no president ever protruded his presidency less than did Broadus. And yet from the very day of his election Dr. Broadus was *President*.[106]

On the other hand, Kerfoot also noted the imposing presence of Broadus on campus. Of the four founding professors since 1859, William Williams (1859–1877)[107] and James P. Boyce (1859–1888) had gone home to glory, while Basil Manly Jr. had left the seminary to be president of Georgetown College and then returned (1859–1871, 1879–1892). Broadus alone maintained the longest tenure and established himself as the quintessential

---

[105] Barron, "The Contributions," 83; using as his source W. O. Carver, "Recollections and Information from Other Sources Concerning the Southern Baptist Theological Seminary" (unpublished typescript), 15–16. Broadus's reasons stem from the small size of the seminary faculty, little need to discipline faculty, and the abuse of some university presidents to hire and fire faculty. He felt the small faculty could make decisions jointly. See Broadus, *Boyce*, 164–65.

[106] F. H. Kerfoot, "As Seminary President," *The Seminary Magazine*, Broadus Memorial Number (April 1895): 385.

[107] Though Williams remained a professor at Southern until his death, he had been widely criticized and denigrated by Landmark Baptists over his acceptance of "alien immersion."

embodiment of the Seminary's high ideals of scholarship, piety, and service. Indeed, his mere presence cast a spell on students and faculty alike. As Kerfoot further suggested:

> He had a way of binding men to himself personally, and dominating them without seeming to do it. He was also a perfect master of assemblies, and they gladly recognized them by his eloquence, he controlled them by his will, without their seeming to know that he had a will. This power over men showed itself in his presidency. Every member of his faculty was concerned mainly to do what he wanted done.[108]

It is safe to say that Broadus's charisma and influence extended far beyond the classrooms and hallways of Southern Baptists' mother seminary. Perhaps his greatest achievement as president of Southern Seminary was demonstrated in his ability to raise funds to advance the endowment and construct buildings. In 1888, one of his former parishioners at the Charlottesville Baptist Church, Mrs. J. Lawrence Smith, gave $50,000 for a new Memorial Library Building. The gift was in honor of her late husband, a famous Louisville scientist, and the library was opened in May 1891.

At the Southern Baptist Convention of 1890, Broadus spoke for 30 minutes on behalf of the seminary and asked for $10,000; more than $16,000 was given. At the 1891 convention, Kerfoot shared that the seminary was debt free, and Broadus reported a record enrollment of 166 students. The Convention messengers responded by giving $21,000. As the endowment reached $400,000, C. W. Norton and Mrs. W. F. Norton honored a previous commitment to Broadus. The Norton brothers had promised to give $60,000 to construct a new building on the seminary's campus once the endowment reached $400,000. Though W. F. Norton had already passed away, his widow "cheerfully" kept

---

[108] Ibid., 389.

his part of the bargain; and in 1892 Norton Hall was erected containing a chapel, five classrooms, and multiple offices.[109]

In 1893, Mrs. Minnie N. Caldwell gave a piece of property valued at $70,000 in memory of her late husband, William Beverly Caldwell Jr. Later John R. Sampey wrote that the gift was not given in memory of her husband but in honor of Broadus and for the establishment of a Broadus Chair. However, due to Broadus's humility, the gift was entered into the financial records of the seminary as the "William Beverly Caldwell Fund," and no chair for Broadus was established.[110]

During the Broadus presidency, enrollment grew rapidly and new degree programs were established. In 1889, Southern had 187 students. By his last year in 1895, enrollment grew to 312. Sampey later said that the enrollment increased because Broadus personally recruited students while other students were attracted by "the name and fame of John A. Broadus."[111] In 1892, Broadus successfully emended the existing degree programs to offer the titles of graduate in theology, bachelor in theology, and master in theology. The doctor of theology degree was also offered for the first time.

In the spring of 1894, Broadus became weakened from a serious heart ailment. Nevertheless, "he clung to his work from high principle. His colleagues . . . relieved him all that he would allow. But he dearly loved his work and fought the idea of letting go at any point."[112] That winter he spent three weeks in Florida in a failed attempt at recuperation. He resumed his work, but the adverse effects of his sickness had sapped his strength. By March 1895, Broadus lectured in his New Testament English class for the last time. He was speaking on Apollos:

> Young gentlemen, if this were the last time I should ever be permitted to address you, I would feel amply repaid for consuming the whole hour in endeavoring

---

[109] Robertson, *Life*, 398.
[110] Sampey, *Memoirs of John R. Sampey*, 67–68.
[111] Ibid., 64.
[112] Robertson, *Life*, 416.

to impress upon you these two things, *true piety* and, like Apollos, to be men "*Mighty in the Scriptures.*" Then pausing, he stood for a moment with his piercing eye fixed upon us, and repeated over and over again in that slow but wonderfully impressive style peculiar to himself, "*Mighty in the Scriptures,*" "*Mighty in the Scriptures,*" until the whole class seemed to be lifted through him into a sacred nearness to the Master.[113]

On March 16, 1895, John A. Broadus departed this world and was, himself, lifted into the sacred presence of his Master. To continue the legacy of Broadus beyond his death, the trustees authorized the Broadus Memorial Library Endowment so that the interest from the fund could be used to purchase new books for the library in perpetuity. From his proclamation in the local church, his broad study of varied topics, his authorship of numerous works, his oratory skill in the classroom, his unwavering support of the administration, and his public promotion of the seminary's best interests, John Albert Broadus exemplified the highest ideal of the Christian academician; and the Lord has used him well.

Conclusion

At the Southern Baptist Educational Convention meeting in Greenville in May 1858, Thomas Curtis had observed: "The requisites for an institution of learning are three *b*'s,—bricks, books, brains." If this be true, then the Lord worked through Broadus in an amazing way. During his 36 years of service to Southern Seminary, Broadus raised much of the necessary funds for the founding of the seminary, its relocation from Greenville to Louisville, and the construction of its first three buildings—New York Hall, Memorial Library, and Norton Hall—with plans to add a gymnasium. He continually sought to raise money for additional library books, so much so, that a library endowment fund was begun at his death to ensure the continued

[113] C. L. Corbitt, "Seminary Magazine," April 1895; quoted by Robertson, *Life*, 430.

availability of new books. Finally, Broadus, who more than any of the great founding faculty members of the seminary exemplified the "brains," the Christian mind, was used by the Lord to increase student enrollment, not merely to achieve record numbers but to shape the minds of future ministers of the gospel so that the man of God might be "thoroughly furnished unto all good works" (2 Tim 3:17). In the end this pastor, professor, and dream builder gave his love, his life, his all; and The Southern Baptist Theological Seminary shines brightly to this day.

Chapter VII

Now I Am Found:
The Recovery of the "Lost" Yale
Lectures and Broadus's Legacy of
Engaging Exposition

Mark M. Overstreet

T he contributions of John A. Broadus to the arena of homiletics and the enduring influence of his ministry among Southern Baptists bear witness to a life invested as a preacher, teacher, and scholar. His influence from the pulpit and the classroom transformed homiletics within the Southern Baptist Convention and beyond. A. T. Robertson, Broadus's colleague and son-in-law, wrote, "No man ever stirred my nature as . . . [he] did in the classroom and the pulpit."[1] His works as professor and preacher yielded the production of the most widely used book on homiletics in the nineteenth century.[2]

---

[1] A. T. Robertson, "Broadus the Preacher," *Methodist Quarterly Review* 69 (1920): 244. Robertson continues, "It has been my fortune to hear Beecher and Phillips Brooks, Maclaren, Joseph Parker and Spurgeon, John Hall and Moody, W. J. Bryan and David Lloyd George. At his best and in a congenial atmosphere Broadus was the equal of any man that I ever heard," 244–45. See also A. T. Robertson, "Broadus as Scholar and Preacher," in *Minister and His Greek New Testament*, A. T. Robertson Library III (reprint, Grand Rapids: Baker, 1977), 118, cited in David Alan Smith, "Introductory Preaching Courses in Selected Southern Baptist Seminaries in the Light of John A. Broadus's Homiletical Theory" (Ph.D. diss., Southwestern Baptist Theological Seminary, 1995), 1.
[2] See A. T. Robertson, "Broadus the Preacher," 247.

Flowing from his influence in the pulpit and classroom, Broadus began early in ministry producing volumes for use at seminary and beyond. He published his magnum opus in 1870, and *A Treatise on the Preparation and Delivery of Sermons* (*PDS*) served as the most influential text on preaching through the first half of the twentieth century.[3] Ironically Broadus had to subsidize the first printing himself. The work went through more than 50 printings before Broadus's colleague and successor in the chair of homiletics, E. C. Dargan, revised the volume. More than a century later and through three major editions, the text remains among the most popular and significant volumes on the traditional methodology of preaching.[4]

Broadus established his homiletic by tracing the history, function, and propositional nature of biblical preaching. He ordered his book with divisions representing the canons of classical rhetoric, and Broadus cited more than 100 authors of oratory, including Aristotle, Cicero, and Quintilian. He identified numerous eighteenth- and nineteenth-century orators, displaying a remarkable familiarity with the sources and progress of public speaking and preaching. Indeed, those nearest Broadus understood his desire to teach and preach with clarion precision and perspicuity.[5] With his indefatigable preaching schedule and scholastic ability, Broadus enjoyed a position among the most prominent preachers in the American pulpit.[6]

---

[3] Robertson notes that his text, in its first half century, was used more than all other textbooks on the subject combined. Ibid.

[4] For example, the new homileticians consider Broadus's work the most influential of the traditional methodology. See Lucy Atkinson Rose, *Sharing the Word: Preaching in the Roundtable Church* (Louisville: Westminster John Knox Press, 1997), 8. A close examination of the third and fourth editions reveals significant changes in the direction of the text. Many contemporary scholars, though dismayed about the changes made through the third and fourth editions, still hold the volume in high regard. See R. Albert Mohler Jr., "Classic Texts Deserve Valued Spot on the Preacher's Bookshelf," *Preaching* (March–April 1989): 34.

[5] Harold K. Graves, "Broadus, Robertson, and Davis—Southern Seminary's Contribution to New Testament Scholarship [1958]," TMs (photocopy). Special Collections, Boyce Centennial Library, The Southern Baptist Theological Seminary, Louisville, 5.

[6] Robertson, "Broadus the Preacher," 247.

In January 1889, this rank earned Broadus an invitation to deliver the influential Lyman Beecher Lectures on Preaching at Yale Divinity School.[7] The Beecher lectures began in 1871 through a grant from Henry W. Sage of Brooklyn, New York. Henry Ward Beecher, who named the lectures in his father's honor, served as Sage's pastor and delivered the inaugural lecture series. Since their inception the Yale Corporation has appointed the speaker for the annual lectureship, seeking "a minister of the Gospel of any evangelical denomination who has been markedly successful in the special work of the Christian ministry."

The instruction of the corporation changed through the years, but the prominence of the lectures only grew, becoming the most renowned lectureship of its kind in the world. Phillips Brooks, P. T. Forsyth, J. H. Jowett number among the historic names added to the distinguished list of lecturers.

From the beginning the eminent preachers who have been invited to lecture have created from their lectures the content of their homiletic text.[8] Because of the eminence of the preachers who have delivered these lectures, the Yale lectures have achieved unequalled distinction among the various lecture-

---

[7] Also known as the "The Lyman Beecher Lectureship on Preaching." For a brief summary, see Batsell Barrett Baxter, *The Heart of the Yale Lecture* (New York: Macmillan, 1947). Also, see Edgar Dewitt Jones, *The Royalty of the Pulpit* (New York: Harper & Brothers, 1951).

[8] For example, see John Hall, *God's Word through Preaching* (New York: Dodd and Meade, 1875); Phillips Brooks, *Lectures on Preaching* (New York: Dutton, 1877); Howard Crosby, *The Christian Preacher* (New York: Nelson and Phillips, 1880); P. T. Forsyth, *Positive Preaching and the Modern Mind* (New York: Hodder & Stoughton, 1907); J. H. Jowett, *The Preacher: His Life and Work* (New York: Doran, 1912); George Buttrick, *Jesus Came Preaching* (New York: Scribner, 1931); Francis John McConnell, *The Prophetic Ministry* (New York: Abingdon, 1930); Halford E. Luccock, *Communicating the Gospel* (New York: Harper, 1954); Henry Mitchell, *The Recovery of Preaching* (New York: Harper, 1977); Gardner Taylor, *How Shall They Preach?* (Elgin, IL: Progressive Baptist Publishing House, 1977); C. F. Buechner, *Telling the Truth: The Gospel as Tragedy, Comedy, and Fairy Tale* (San Francisco: Harper, 1977); Fred Craddock, *Overhearing the Gospel* (Nashville: Abingdon, 1978); John Claypool, *The Preaching Event* (Waco: Word, 1980); and Walter Breuggemann, *Finally Comes the Poet: Daring Speech for Proclamation* (Minneapolis: Fortress, 1989).

ships in the field of homiletics. Among the influential lectures within the field of homiletics, whether Hester, Payton, Mullins, Sprunt, or Warrack, none can claim the influence of the Yale lectureship.[9]

Since Beecher's first address, Broadus displayed an interest in the Yale lectures. As soon as the lectures appeared in print, Broadus added the text to his homiletics syllabus.[10] His delivery of the lectures marked the crest of more than 40 years experience as a preacher and 30 years as a professor of homiletics.

At the time of the lectures, almost 20 years had elapsed since the first printing of his *PDS*. The structure and function of his lectures revealed a seasoned understanding of the minister, and the content and purpose of his addresses delivered to the university in 1889 differed in style from the first edition of his homiletics manual. His lectures at Yale filled the aisles of the Marquand Chapel with chairs and left many standing in the corners and peering in from outside.[11] Broadus contributed to the "highest enthusiasm" the lectures had experienced since Henry Ward Beecher's first delivery nearly two decades earlier.

Members of the Yale faculty expressed their "high appreciation of the suggestive and stimulating series of lectures." Furthermore, they expressed hope that the lectures would soon be

---

[9] Warren Wiersbe, *Walking with the Giants* (Grand Rapids: Baker, 1976), 203, cited in Steve Reagles, "One Century after the 1889 Yale Lectures: A Reflection on Broadus's Homiletical Thought," *Preaching* 5 (1989): 32.

[10] Miscellaneous syllabi from 1872 through 1891 contain instructions for the students to acquire either Beecher's lectures or "some volume of the Yale lectures." See Broadus papers, including notes on the Yale Lectures. Special Collections, Boyce Centennial Library, The Southern Baptist Theological Seminary, Louisville.

[11] One listener remarked of the deep impact he had on the campus, even outside the divinity school: "The audience might have been doubled or quadrupled if there had been room for those who would have gladly come. . . . Many students expressed in private the warmest appreciation of the work Doctor Broadus had done for them this year, and declared that this is the universal feeling among the young men. . . . Doctor Broadus approaches so closely one's ideal of a lecturer to students that one hardly sees how the ideal could be more nearly satisfied." H. C. Vedder, "The Examiner," Feb. 7, 1889, cited in A. T. Robertson, *Life and Letters of John Albert Broadus* (Philadelphia: American Baptist Publication Society, 1901), 376–77.

published.[12] The pinnacle of Broadus's homiletic thought late in life was condensed in his lectures delivered at Yale. Tragically, unlike all previous lectures in this historic series, his eight lectures were never published in their entirety. Broadus had not written his lectures out in full but spoke from notes, as was his custom in formal lectures. Reporters summarized his material; but, religious periodicals notwithstanding, no other contemporary material has been available to evaluate these acclaimed lectures. Thus, the lectures have been called the "The Lost Yale Lectures on Preaching."[13]

Background

These unpublished lectures reveal a void in the intellectual contribution of Broadus. The press reported Broadus's delivery was marked by a conversational delivery that condensed his mature thought and practical advice for the young preachers in the audience. Furthermore, instead of receiving the content of a formal treatise on homiletics, the audience received a personal, intimate, and detailed accounting of the preacher's ability and desire to prepare and deliver sermons appropriately, as the beginning of another century approached.[14] Indeed, the absence of any primary source material from these lectures presents a problem in the comprehension of his homiletic as Broadus neared the end of his life. The void created by the absence of these lectures for years pressed many to speculate whether the

---

[12] Robertson, *Life and Letters,* 376–77.

[13] Ibid.

[14] In the late twentieth century, mainstream homiletics called for the discharge of Broadus's theory, accusing the traditional school of a distanced rigidity that no longer related to the audience. The new methodology argues for a "new homiletic," represented by a preaching style rooted in relational preaching. While Broadus's style called for persuasion of the audience toward some propositional truth claim, this new homiletic rejects universal truth, exchanging truth propositions for a "proposal offered to the community of faith for their additions, corrections, or counterproposals." See Rose, *Sharing the Word,* 5. Also, cp. Fred B. Craddock, *As One without Authority* (Nashville: Abingdon Press, 1971). In his work Craddock blames the death of traditional theory on the "sag in the pulpit," which results from "the loss of certainty and the increase of tentativeness on the part of the preacher" (11).

substance of the lectures appeared in any of Broadus's later writings. Some have presumed—without due merit—the lectures' full presence in his posthumous second edition.[15]

My discovery of Broadus's Yale lecture notes sheds fresh light on the substance of Broadus's homiletic at the end of his life. The recovery of these manuscripts enables another generation of expositors to survey the work of Broadus with added precision and personal depth.

The content of Broadus's 1889 Yale lectures reveals Broadus's homiletic near the end of his life. This chapter will summarize Broadus's Yale lecture material and demonstrate their content as a late endorsement of his homiletic. In the lectures Broadus reinforced and expanded his homiletic corpus, offering no substantial change in his philosophy of preaching. The lectures complemented and reaffirmed the earlier writings of Broadus, providing a clearer and more comprehensive understanding of his homiletic.

Broadus's Yale lectures displayed the preacher's keen awareness of both the history of rhetoric as well as contemporary communication theory. Furthermore, he displayed an intimate familiarity of the demands the modern audience had placed upon the communicator.

Broadus remained committed to the classroom throughout his ministry. Broadus prepared students for ministry, desiring to impact the next generation by remaining a preacher to preachers.[16] After delivering the Lyman Beecher Lectures on Preaching at Yale University, Broadus planned to compile his notes to write a second edition of his magnum opus. His death on March 16, 1895, prevented the update of his seminal work for preachers.

---

[15] Cf. Baxter, *The Heart of the Yale Lectures*. Also see Jones, *The Royalty of the Pulpit*.

[16] For the most recent reflection on Broadus's impact on students, see David M. Ramsay, "Boyce and Broadus, Founders of The Southern Baptist Theological Seminary: Founder's Day Address [1941]." TMs (photocopy). Special Collections, Boyce Centennial Library, The Southern Baptist Theological Seminary, Louisville. Ramsay, a student of the founders, delivered this address in Broadus Chapel, at 85 years old. For more on Broadus's commitment to teaching, see A. T. Robertson, "Broadus in the Class Room," *The Review and Expositor* 30 (1933): 157–69.

The Lectures

The recovery of the information in the Yale manuscripts requires some explanation. During my early studies as a doctor of philosophy student, many hours were spent perusing early Baptist periodicals and documents in The Southern Baptist Theological Seminary's archives. During a search for materials related to Broadus and his early preaching ministry, this writer discovered seven notebooks scattered through boxes of manuscripts and documents among the Broadus material. After reading the titles of several of these notebooks, I recognized the notebooks contained the materials of Broadus's lost lectures at Yale. The lecture manuscripts were handwritten in pencil and pen on the medium of a bound folio notebook. A total of 193 pages of Broadus's notes comprised the manuscripts. Only the manuscript of the lecture, "The Minister's Private Life," was absent.

The content of the Yale lecture material will be reviewed within the context of Broadus's homiletic as outlined in both editions of *PDS*. Each source will be examined and evaluated for emerging trends of homiletic development. Finally, these will be compiled and appraised as Broadus's late homiletic contribution that provides the context to consider Broadus's homiletic legacy for a new century of homiletics, whether in the classroom or the pulpit.

Canon One: "Materials of Preaching" in Broadus's Homiletic

Within the first canon of Broadus's homiletic, his lectures material included "On Freshness in Preaching" and "On Sensation Preaching."[17] The material included in these lecture manuscripts provides new detail and practical materials that offer perspective on Broadus's late homiletic. He addressed the "helps" and "cautions" associated with the inventiveness of freshness and the creativity of sensational preaching.

---

[17] The lecture notes surveyed in this chapter include 29 pages and 24 pages, respectively, of handwritten text.

Freshness in preaching, Broadus contended, ensured boldness of thought and relevance for the audience. As a discipline, the notion of freshness brought to the contemporary audience the historic message of the gospel together with the demands of human nature, life, culture, and society. The preacher had to be involved in the creative act of constructing a message that included both the old doctrines in truth with new perspective.

Building upon the example of Scripture, Broadus argued the preacher should describe similar events to different audiences in varied ways. For Broadus, the herald must first arrest the attention of the listener, interest the audience in his monologue, convince each of his message's importance, and impress him toward a decisive change of will.

Although the young minister may intrigue his audience through his youthful novelty, Broadus reminded the preacher that freshness must be established as a regular exercise early in ministry. This practice would prove helpful as the minister ages and loses his youthful vigor and novelty in the pulpit, Broadus argued. Lack of freshness, Broadus asserted, yielded an uninterested and disconnected audience. Thus, the investment of freshness in preparation must be maintained in order to progress upward and onward in the ministry of proclamation. The minister should maintain freshness through the study of Scripture, systematic theology, and other formal academic endeavors combined with an increase in the preacher's ability to address difficult subjects in common terms from the pulpit.

Additionally, the minister should study through observing the "occasions of life." Preachers should observe the currents of their congregations in order to deliver the message rightly for maximum impact. Sermons should be updated, changed, modified, and tailored each time for its new setting. Whether studying individuals, culture, the church, or self, strength, and freshness in preaching would come through the labors of study.

Through continued study and maturation, the Yale lectures served as the pinnacle and fulfillment of his instruction to students. Broadus urged upon the preacher the duty to bring fresh and engaging dialogue to the pulpit year after year. The herald must process and analyze both the text and the context within which the sermon was preached. Beyond analysis, the preacher should study associations in order to create a sense of perspicuity in freshness. Preaching should instruct by communicating the principles of the text into the lives of the audience through analogical or inferential references. This complex process must be repeated in order to increase effectiveness in proclamation. Finally, freshness should be stimulated through vigorous mental activity or other physical stimuli. Whether from engaging conversation or through intensive reading of great books, Broadus argued the best sources of invention came through freeing the mind to clear and creative thought. Through reading and taking time to consider these studies, the preacher should compile and analyze his thoughts in a notebook for reference.

The distinction between freshness in preaching and sensationalism remained difficult to distinguish concretely. Partly on the times, partly on the character of the preacher and the audience, the minister should exercise caution in the employment of creativity in exposition.

In the end the preacher had to avoid the objectionable and guard against frivolity, but the herald must remain fresh and creative. While provocative rhetoric and striking language must be used, the preacher was to build his ministry on a sense of aim and purpose for the sacred and spiritual. With spiritual aim at the fore, the preacher must seize the attention of the listener.

Broadus cautioned against advertising sermons by naming specific sins, the horrific, art and literature, or other subjects because the genre created a downward spiral as the audience demanded more sensation and edge. On the other hand, preaching within the arena of politics should be pursued, so long as the aim remained spiritual. Likewise, humor may be carefully employed, while applause should be avoided. In the end preaching should be focused on the Christian principle of proclamation together with the creative to cultivate reverence and an appetite for the spiritual.

While Broadus carefully warned the student of homiletics of the dangers of sensational preaching, his argument for the preacher to maintain freshness and disciplined invention provided convincing appeal for the power and usefulness of the prepared preacher.

Canon Two: "Arrangement of a Sermon" in Broadus's Homiletic

The second canon of Broadus's structure was "Arrangement of a Sermon." Since none of Broadus's Yale lectures dealt explicitly with the formal elements of sermon construction and preparation, the materials included in *PDS* and *PDS2* should be considered. Broadus included within this canon the vital elements of his homiletic, including an essay on the importance of arrangement, as well as the formal construction and elements that comprise a sermon, including introductions, discussion, and conclusion. Also, various forms and "species" of sermons were discussed and evaluated.

An examination of the *PDS* and his Yale lectures revealed similarities throughout his discussion on the formal and functional elements of sermon construction. Broadus built his homiletic legacy by arguing that the sermon derives its power first from the Bible and its authority. Indeed, he contended expository preaching best corresponded with the idea and design of preaching.

Broadus articulated a persuasive argument for the proper arrangement of a sermon. For every preacher each sermon should display the necessary materials and arrangement in order to arrive at the desired end. Though Broadus refused to take notes into the pulpit, the sermons that remain clearly indicate that the preacher who wrote the world's most popular homiletics text had applied his theories to his ministry of proclamation. For Broadus clear divisions and proper arrangement served to strengthen the substance of the sermon. Broadus argued that each sermon should be ordered with respect to the importance of structure and necessity of purpose in every subject. Broadus reflected this conviction consistently throughout his lectures at Yale.

In both the *PDS* and his lectures, Broadus contended that order assisted the audience in their receipt of the message. While Broadus spurned show and arrogance in the pulpit, he praised the genuineness of extemporaneous proclamation. The combination of proper arrangement wed with extemporaneous delivery conveyed the most powerful form of speech, Broadus argued.

Indeed, Broadus's discussion on the formal elements of sermon construction provided a constructive argument for expository method in contemporary homiletics. Broadus established the importance of the introduction and conclusion as well as the structured division of the text into an orderly arrangement. The structure of the sermon served the audience and enabled the listener to receive the message more effectively.

Throughout his Yale lectures, Broadus affirmed the significance of the functional elements of the sermon. The Yale lectures served as a late affirmation of Broadus's conviction that engaging explanation, argument, illustration, and application were tools for proper preaching. Renowned for his explanation, Broadus argued for the importance of perspicuity in the pulpit. Careful and plain explanation served as the preacher's gift to the listener in the audience. Also, argument and illustration should be joined together in order to convince the audience toward some desired Christian end. For Broadus, application served as the means to elucidate the truth of the Bible for the context of the Christian life.

Finally, both *PDS* and his lectures reflected the strength of Broadus's commitment and dependence on the authority of Scripture and its sufficiency for preaching. While the expository sermon included the arguments and applications of the preacher, the message must derive its substance and power from the Scriptures. For Broadus, expository preaching endured as the form of proclamation that best strengthened the pastor and his preaching ministry. Thus, through both *PDS* and the

Yale lectures, one can see Broadus's unchanging instruction to preach sermons grounded in the exposition of Scripture.

Canon Three: "Style" in Broadus's Homiletic

The third canon in Broadus's text discussed "Style" in sermon delivery. Broadus discussed the importance of style and the necessary work of improving as an orator. His work detailed Broadus's continuous labor to drive the event of proclamation with relevant and perspicuous discussion. Energy, imagination, and elegance were considered. Yale lecture material considered in this section will be "The Minister's General Reading" and "The Minister and His Hymn Book."

As a pastor, linguist, Bible scholar, and homiletician, Broadus displayed a broad knowledge of both historic and contemporary literature. In this division of lectures, Broadus argued that the discipline of reading and study are vital to the minister and his preparation for preaching. Furthermore, Broadus's lecture on hymnology argued for the importance of a working knowledge of the hymns and the songs of Christian faith.

At the beginning of the third major division of *PDS,* Broadus stated that the preacher's style remains a characteristic original to himself. Whether in writing or in speech, the minister should develop a characteristic style that continued to improve through "discipline and indefinite improvement."[18] Broadus consistently affirmed this concept in his lectures, expanding his content for his Yale audience.

The content of these Yale lectures offered detailed insight into Broadus's homiletic. For Broadus, the development of pulpit excellence, while rare, remained attainable and should be pursued. Through constructive imagination and perspiration, he concluded, any man who will try can learn to "say what he means." The foremost means of improving style, Broadus argued, was the study of the language and the study of literature. Beyond the acquisition of mere language through reading,

---

[18] Broadus, *PDS,* 320.

the preacher who reads both supplements his vocabulary and enhances his ability of expression.

Broadus argued reading develops in the preacher a healthy appetite for principles of proper style and good taste. Reading should be pursued as the first form of intellectual recreation for the minister, he said. While reading does provide general knowledge for the preacher, it also provided requisite mental stimulation necessary for the work of preparation in preaching. Furthermore, in addition to cultivating literary taste, reading provided the elementary substance that contributed toward the development of the herald's sense of style in preaching.

Spanning the spectrum from ancient to modern, Broadus directed the preacher to read voluminously. From short works to tomes, the preacher must work to develop his preaching through reading, Broadus argued. Beyond literature, hymnology must also find its way to the minister's study, Broadus said. As a form of poetic expression, the study of the "poetry of the church" must be pursued by the preacher. From the early hymns of Scripture to the songs of the contemporary church, Broadus contended for the study of songs through the major developments in hymnody. In *PDS*, Broadus argued that the preacher must know hymns to serve the church more effectively. Reflecting this consistency, "The Minister and His Hymn Book" commended the minister to study and benefit from an expansive knowledge of hymns, their substance, and their relation to public and private worship.

Beyond the knowledge of hymns, Broadus asserted singing improves the voice for preaching. Also, it provided an emotional connection with the audience, he concluded, especially the choir. Furthermore, singing prepared the mind and body for the physical requirements of preaching.

Like hymns, reading in general provided a necessary element in the development of the preacher. His argument for the acquisition of style, energy, imagination, and elegance in the pulpit was driven by his instruction to read and study language, literature, and hymnology. In these lectures Broadus provided a thorough and compelling argument for the importance of literature and hymnology in the development of style in the preacher.

Canon Four: "Delivery of Sermons" in Broadus's Homiletic

In the fourth canon of *PDS,* Broadus described the subject of oratory with respect to the pulpit. Broadus argued that far too many preachers ignored the means through which the message of God was preached. He reviewed a brief history of the three major methods utilized in homiletics and argued for "free delivery." The Yale lecture "On Freedom in Preaching" commended freedom to the preacher who aspires to greatness in the pulpit.

In "On Freedom in Preaching" Broadus proposed a model of extemporaneous preaching that was comprehensively informed, summarily prepared, and passionately encompassed by the subject. Freedom was controlled by the responsibility of mastering the subject to be addressed, Broadus argued. This comprehensive preparation was to be arranged in an orderly structure. With this knowledge and structure, Broadus contended the audience should be considered with respect to their ability to comprehend the contents of the message. The preacher must keep the understanding of the audience at the fore of his preparation. Broadus also contended for a free model of speaking from the pulpit that was logically arranged, perspicuous, properly articulated, and free from the fear that liberty may lead to failure.

Broadus drove the preacher to embrace extemporaneous preaching. They must learn to trust themselves, he argued. The preacher must trust his preparation and entrust himself to God by preparing a sketch of the sermon, leaving it at home, and preaching with freedom, Broadus said. Broadus provided ample historical evidence to suggest that the most gifted of preachers engaged themselves, if not at first, in the practice of free delivery.

The herald had to build confidence in this freedom through certain disciplines. Habitual correctness of speech in conversation will likely procure the same in the pulpit. In addition to correctness of speech, the herald should also strive toward excellence in delivery. Broadus hailed the important concept of being liberated from hindrances or shackles to freedom of delivery. Areas of concern that ought to be discarded include fear of forgetting, repeating, failure, or preaching too long. Fears should not rule the minister but freedom.

The freedom of extemporaneous speech combined with proper preparation and the creation of a sketched outline enabled the preacher to respond to the stimulus of the audience and react appropriately in order to deliver the most effective message. Looking through annals of history, Broadus contended this methodology to be the most effective.

Broadus concluded his argument for his method of extemporaneous preaching by describing methods of public address outside the church. From the floor of Congress to the stump of a political campaign, Broadus contended that the most persuasive elements of speech are possessed by those who wed education with pleasure, combining aesthetics with instruction.

In "On Freedom in Preaching," Broadus combined his vast knowledge of rhetoric and oratory with his conviction for expository preaching resulting in a proposal for impassioned and informative proclamation. He built a strong case for the young minister to strive toward freedom in exposition in order to persuade the audience to a decision of direction. For the preacher, Broadus argued, his fulfillment as prophet was found in the lives of his audience and the change effected as a result of his bold proclamation. In his lecture Broadus provided a fresh, detailed, and powerful argument for freedom under control in the delivery of sermons.

Canon Five: "The Conduct of Public Worship"
in Broadus's Homiletic

In the concluding canon of material for ministry, Broadus's final lectures addressed myriad issues in the minister's public and private life. Broadus discussed many practical issues ranging from Scripture reading in worship to service length and pulpit decorum. Likewise, he addressed a wide range of subjects in the lectures "The Young Preacher's Outfit" and "The Minister and His Bible."

Broadus addressed in these lectures the disciplines of the young man in ministry. Leadership in the church required humility and the realization that preaching and ministry must be a call, not a profession. Broadus elucidated the call that required the indwelling of the Holy Spirit and significant religious experiences.

Moreover, the ministry demanded good health, strong mental facility, and disciplined study of the Bible and beyond. The preacher ought to work on the improvement of his ability to articulate clearly and powerfully. Beyond clarity of statement, the preacher should seek to improve his command of argument in the arrangement of a sermon. With these, the preacher must remember the audience and employ the powers of creative imagination. Combined with proper preparation, the herald must deliver the message through appropriating passion, sympathy, and a strong will. Each of these themes was present in Broadus's homiletic text.

Beyond the requisite internal strengths of the minister, the preacher must acquire the skills of his office. The herald must develop and maintain the lasting habit of study. Preparation through study laid the foundation of every message. Beyond the foundation the herald was to maintain the discipline of observation as well as the practice of reflecting upon those observations.

Among the strengths Broadus described as necessary to the ministry, perhaps no discipline was more important than personal holiness. Broadus consistently emphasized the importance of piety in the life of the preacher. Whether he was in public conversation or private meetings, the preacher should practice habitual grace and temperance of language and actions. Also, the man in ministry should maintain proper posture and gesture as well as habitual good manners. Finally, the minister who worked to maintain these habits and build a ministry should aspire to greatness for the Lord. Ambition to achieve, if properly motivated, should mark the life of the minister, Broadus asserted. The young minister should attempt to achieve great things for God through hard work, discipline, and ministry.

Additionally, Broadus developed the habit of Bible study into an entire lecture on the important concept of the voluminous study of Scripture. Broadus articulated a defense of reading the Bible for devotional and spiritual benefit. Moreover, the minister should read to gain materials for preaching and pastoral ministry. Also, the preacher should read for both a general knowledge of Scripture and memorization. This knowledge would aid in the public reading of Scripture in worship and meetings. Furthermore, regular reading of Scripture will improve expository preaching in general.

Broadus provided a schedule for regular reading of the Bible that included many challenges. The preacher should begin with a thorough reading and study of a small portion of Scripture. Broadus suggests 45 minutes of study. Then the minister would read the Bible in the original languages. After 30 minutes of reading in Hebrew and Greek texts, the herald would spend another half hour in the rapid reading of the English Bible.

While many read through whole books or chronologically, Broadus encouraged reading through prominent lives and regions of Scripture. Also, some theme or questions could be explored through rapid reading. Broadus additionally suggested reading rapidly in some foreign language. This could help clarify and illuminate the English reading. Finally, the minister should spend 15 minutes reading a brief passage devotionally. The importance of reading and growing in the knowledge of the Scripture should remain at the forefront of the minister's pursuits.

These lectures served as a late endorsement of Broadus's great homiletic work, providing a clearer understanding of his contribution to Christian pulpit ministry. As a result, Broadus's mature thought on the demands of ministry deserves renewed observation today and for future generations of those called by God to preach His gospel.

Conclusion

Broadus's invitation to the sacred desk of Marquand chapel at Yale Divinity School produced in a single locus the corpus of his late homiletic. The recovery of these unpublished lectures reveals the consistent contribution Broadus made to preaching and the Christian pulpit.

Broadus's 1889 lectures unleashed a personal, intimate, and detailed instruction for success in the preparation and delivery of sermons. As the end of another century approached, Broadus bestowed on the audience the culmination of his teaching ministry—a late affirmation of the homiletic he had expressed many years earlier in his first edition of *PDS*.

Beyond anecdote and hagiography, Broadus's Yale lecture materials revealed his acute awareness of both the history of rhetoric as well as contemporary communication theory. Indeed, the materials evaluated above display a distinct familiarity with the demands of the modern audience. As a result, Broadus's content reveals a fresh and informed perspective on the craft of preaching at the end of the nineteenth century. The Yale lectures reinforced and affirmed Broadus's early philosophy of preaching. These addresses served as the pinnacle of his homiletic corpus, and the recovery of these manuscripts allows Broadus's homiletic to be examined and displayed for another generation of expositors.

Broadus's Yale lecture material deserves further study in our seminaries for the sake of the pulpit and engaging exposition. Throughout his lectures at Yale, Broadus sought to describe a model of biblical preaching with an applicational style that drove each listener to a powerful impulse of the will.

Broadus's lectures displayed superior knowledge and informed theory on the nature and character of preaching. His contribution to homiletics was unparalleled among Baptists, and the Yale lecture content broadens his relevance for renewed study today.

Baptist preaching will remain indebted to the passions and discipline that reigned in the works of the Southern Baptists' first professor of homiletics. Throughout his ministry Broadus displayed an unwavering commitment to the authority of Scripture, and he provided the functional and formal elements necessary for the proper delivery of a sermon.

While traditional homiletic theory loses its influence over the Protestant pulpit, Broadus's lectures provide a new reason to rediscover his vast contributions to homiletics. This study unearths the latest addition to Broadus's homiletic corpus. The Yale lectures reveal creative new materials Broadus believed critical for the preacher, young and old alike.

The presence of this lecture material provides a new perspective on Broadus and his style in the pulpit. Indeed, these Yale lectures display Broadus's vivid and engaging homiletic, reaffirming his earlier convictions, and thus refreshing it for another generation of expositors.

At Broadus's death Dr. William Rainey Harper, president of the University of Chicago, declared:

> No man ever heard him preach but understood every sentence; no one heard him preach who did not feel the truth of God sink deep into his heart. As a teacher of the New Testament as well as of homiletics, it is perhaps not too much to say that he had no superior in this country.[19]

Affirming the late contributions of his colleague, E. C. Dargan said:

> As a preacher, John A. Broadus was one of the greatest of his age and country. The circumstances of his career . . . hindered the full measure of recognition to which his extraordinary merits as a preacher surely entitle him. Had he kept himself to a pastorate in some conspicuous place like those to which he was often invited, and had he written and published more sermons, there is no doubt that his enduring fame would

---

[19] Cited in Bernard R. DeRemer, "The Life of John Albert Broadus," *Christianity Today* 6 (1962): 22.

have been at least more nearly commensurate with his actual rank among the great preachers of the world.[20]

From his first edition of *PDS* in 1870 to the lost lectures of 1889, Broadus remained clear in his commitment to conversational preaching that embodied the art and discipline of proper biblical preaching. The principles he established in his 50 years as preacher-teacher are timeless. As he approached the end of his productive ministry, the Yale lectures marked the pinnacle and culmination of his lifelong promotion of powerful, practical, and engaging proclamation. Evangelical preaching remains indebted to the passions and discipline that reined in the life of Southern Baptists' first—and most prominent—professor of homiletics.

---

[20] Edwin Charles Dargan, "John Albert Broadus–Scholar and Preacher," *Crozer Quarterly* 2 (1925): 171.

Chapter VIII

The Enduring Impact and Relevance of
A Treatise on the Preparation and Delivery of Sermons

Thomas J. Nettles

Topknot come down!" On this text John A. Broadus supposedly announced at several churches around Louisville that he would preach on the biblical view of women's hairstyles. His text—Mark 13:15: "Let him that is on the house top not come down." Thus wrote homiletician John Killinger. He then drew, with a markedly demonstrated sense of superiority, the application: "This was thought to be very clever, but it is the kind of carnival pitch that teaches people to be distrustful of ministers."[1]

For an instructor in the art and sober call of preaching to ignore John A. Broadus more than a century and a third after the publication of his "watershed" text is understandable. But to represent him with such an absurd and demonstrably false anecdote borders on sinfulness. Any reading of Broadus's *A Treatise on the Preparation and Delivery of Sermons* would demonstrate *a priori* that such a tale could not be true. It would violate every nerve of Broadus's highly sensitized commitment to honesty, integrity, doctrinal soundness, exegetical clarity, the majesty of Scrip-

---

[1] John Killinger, *Fundamentals of Preaching* (Philadelphia: Fortress Press, 1985), 178.

176

ture, the need for careful selection of texts, and the necessity of avoiding sensationalism. Pity that Killinger gives no evidence of consulting Broadus—the unsavory anecdote constitutes the only entry he has of Broadus in his text, *Fundamentals of Preaching,* even omitting him from the bibliography—for it would have been much more useful to the church of the Lord Jesus Christ had he looked more honestly to Broadus. Thankfully Killinger's cavalier dismissal of Broadus has not been universal.

The Ironies of Its Inception

Under the most inauspicious circumstances, John A. Broadus began the work on his classic textbook on preaching, *A Treatise on the Preparation and Delivery of Sermons.*[2] The foundational lectures that formed the basic substance of Broadus's approach came in the first session after the Civil War. As A. T. Robertson recalled the incident:

> Everything was paralyzed by the effect of the war. When the Seminary did reopen on Nov. 1st, it was with only seven students. In homiletics Doctor Broadus had only one student, and he was blind. But it was like Doctor Broadus to give this one blind student the best he had. The careful preparation of full lectures for the blind brother led to the writing of *Preparation and Delivery of Sermons.*[3]

Initially two students enrolled in the class; but one, Mr. Getsinger, had to leave, with the blind Mr. Lunn alone remaining. Broadus proceeded—he considered Mr. Lunn a good listener—but had his struggles with the apparent futility of such arduous efforts with such little promise. He wrote Charlotte, his wife,[4]

---

[2] John A. Broadus, *A Treatise on the Preparation and Delivery of Sermons* (Philadelphia: Smith, English & Co., 1870).

[3] A. T. Robertson, *Life and Letters of John Albert Broadus* (Philadelphia: American Baptist Publication Society, 1902), 214.

[4] Ibid., 442–43. Broadus had married Maria Harrison, November 13, 1850. She died October 21, 1857, before her twenty-sixth birthday, leaving three girls. Broadus remarried January 4, 1859, to Charlotte Eleanor Sinclair and spent the rest of his days in her splendid company, though she was infirm much of the time. Dr. W. S. Ryland wrote her the day after Broadus's death, "How much of his power and usefulness, even of his life, was thus due to your loving, thought-

on February 1, 1866, "Really it is right dull to deliver my most elaborate lectures in homiletics to one man, and that a blind man. Of course, I whittle it all down to a simple talk."[5] Later Broadus wrote, in light of the course under such circumstances promising so little,

> We were determined to keep up the instruction in every department; and as the student could not read text-books, the professor tried to lay out a somewhat complete course, and give it to him in lectures, to which the brother listened with unfailing manifestation of kindly interest.[6]

Broadus went on to comment on how such an unpromising course of action accrued an immense future interest on the investment of energy. He stated:

> A work which appeared five years later, entitled "Preparation and Delivery of Sermons," and which a good many persons have found useful, quite possibly owed its origin to that year's lessons with the blind student. We often find that by "doing the thing that is next" to us, even though it is be "the day of small things," we find the way opening for undertakings which otherwise might never have been planned.[7]

A second irony concerning the composition of the *Treatise* was that Basil Manly was to be the chief beneficiary of its completion. Originally the writing of the book came so that Broadus could relinquish teaching homiletics and turn it over to Manly. Robertson recorded that by May 1869, Broadus struggled with greatly impaired health. The trustees, however, had added a new professor, Dr. C. H. Toy, to teach Old Testament so that Manly

ful care, the world can never know. God only knows and can reward it. May he greatly comfort you in your bereavement, in the thought that you have helped, as a true yokefellow, a great man to extend and diffuse himself, widely and strongly; and to multiply his labors through others."

[5] Ibid., 216.
[6] John A Broadus, *Memoir of James Petigru Boyce* (New York: A. C. Armstrong and Son, 1893), 201.
[7] Ibid.

could assume the course in homiletics.[8] Broadus, in fact, mentioned in the preface to the first edition that since "it was necessary to relinquish Homiletics" he wanted to undertake the work "before the subject should fade from his mind."[9] In fact, adding to the irony of these events, the transfer of homiletics to Manly played a role in his resignation from the seminary in 1871 to accept the presidency of Georgetown College in Kentucky. "Somewhat to the surprise of his colleagues, he took no fancy in teaching Homiletics."[10] Faculty peers as well as Broadus saw Manly as "eminently adapted to the interesting and helpful correction of written sermons," but Manly saw it as drudgery and his dislike of it only increased through the year.[11]

In the throes of writing, Broadus responded to a suggestion in a letter from J. L. M. Curry in January 1870, that he "should work towards the task of preparing a life of Christ." Broadus valued this as "the goal of my literary aspirations." He also felt pleased that one of his "wisest and most cherished friends should have suggested the same thing." The arduous task, however, of careful composition, Broadus found to be "wearing." Moreover, he had begun the past summer a treatise on the "Preparation and Delivery of Sermons." This was to provide "a text-book for Manly, and at the same time meet the wants of young ministers who have no course of instruction in homiletics, and give some useful hints to older ministers." These hopes for its acceptability tottered on several disadvantages: "Such books do not get a wide sale, and no publisher is willing to take one from an unknown Southern author." Though his summer's work fell short of completion, he hoped to finish it before the school session ended. "I

---

[8] Robertson, 232. See also Broadus, *Memoir*, 211–12.

[9] John A. Broadus, *A Treatise on the Preparation and Delivery of Sermons,* New (37th) edition, ed. Edwin Charles Dargan (New York: George H. Doran Company, 1898), ix. Dargan adds this note to Broadus's statement in the original preface. "This relinquishment was only temporary, being required by the author's state of health, though he at the time supposed it would be permanent. After one year [a year of travel in England and Europe] he resumed Homiletics, and taught it with enthusiasm and success to the end of his life."

[10] Broadus, *Memoir*, 214.

[11] Ibid., 214.

don't want my intention to issue the book publicly known till I am prepared to announce it," he told Curry.[12]

A third irony was that he had to finance the publication at his own expense (since he was "an unknown Southern author") and the first edition appeared when he was out of the country for a year. In May 1870, with the homiletics text still incomplete, Broadus arranged to supply the pulpit in Orange, New Jersey, for the month of June. His physician advised him to rest some weeks before writing. For two weeks he would follow the doctor's orders then go to Virginia for 10 days. There he would begin writing a few hours a day and on his return bring his books in an effort to finish by the end of June. "I mean to slight the latter part as far as will be endurable" he confided to Boyce.[13]

Within a week, however, a new situation had arisen. The trustees had strongly suggested that Broadus take a 12-month trip to England and Europe. Feeling he could not be spared at the seminary and believing his wife could ill afford to have him go, he refused. Boyce, however, who had contemplated leaving the seminary to go into business in order to manage its financial support himself, decided to stay and argued that the time for Broadus's trip was as propitious as it ever would be. His wife also insisted that he go for the sake of his health; so he wrote Boyce, "If therefore it is not now too late, I can undertake to go in July."[14] He now felt renewed urgency to complete the *Treatise*.

Broadus began to plan his writing schedule carefully since "pecuniary and other considerations require that I shall not go away without finishing it." He believed he could do this while keeping his commitment to preach the first, third, and fourth Sundays of June in Orange.[15] Working with steady diligence through June, he wrote Basil Manly on June 27 to say:

[12] Robertson, 233–34.

[13] Broadus to Boyce, 23 May 1870, in *"Our Life Work": The Correspondence of James P. Boyce and John A. Broadus, Founders of the Southern Baptist Theological Seminary, 1857–1888,* ed. Sean Michael Lucas and Jason Christopher Fowler (privately bound collection in the James P. Boyce Centennial Library, Southern Baptist Theological Seminary, Louisville, 2004), 83. Further quotations from this volume will be noted as Lucas and Fowler.

[14] Ibid., 85.

[15] Ibid.

I have sent to Fagan all of the book except Delivery as respects Voice and Action (two chapters) and Public Worship (one chapter). These I can finish this and the next week, if nothing happens. I have been taking it very easy. The hot weather last week prostrated me considerably. Today, I feel much better.[16]

As Manly read Broadus's manuscript, he sent suggestions to him. After all, it appeared that he would be teaching the text instead of Broadus. Broadus incorporated pertinent suggestions and on July 9 wrote Manly: "Nearly done on Action. Profiting by your notes."[17] By July 25, 1870, Broadus wrote to Boyce:

My book is done, and all stenotyped, except the last chapter. Rev. J. C. Long is preparing the index, and will correct the last proofs. It ought to be out by 15 August. I did all the managing I could at the North towards making it go. . . . I have explained to Manly all about the financial arrangements for my book, and asked Smith, English, and Co. to report to him. I could not trouble you with it, knowing how much you have to do.[18]

Broadus had arranged to publish at his own expense through Smith & English in Philadelphia. This plan had good prospect of succeeding because he had received incognito from Richmond, transferred through Wm. B. Isaacs & Co., a healthy gift of financial aid in completing his project. With promises from Boyce and Manly to do all they could to promote it, Broadus left for his trip. He was eager to know how it would be received. From Harrogate in Yorkshire he wrote Boyce on August 30, (after a long letter about travels over and in England, and some sickness), "I should be glad if anybody would cut out and send me notices of my book—or just send a newspaper, postage 2 cents."[19]

---

[16] Robertson, 236.
[17] Ibid., 237.
[18] Lucas and Fowler, 88.
[19] Ibid., 91.

The Enthusiasm of Its Reception

Broadus's desires to see reviews soon began to be fulfilled. On September 24, 1870, in the middle of a long letter full of news and friendly banter, Boyce inserted bits of news that he knew would interest his friend. A most worthy review had appeared in the *Religious Herald* of September 8, 1870. Boyce also had managed to get substantial notices in three papers, one in the *Charleston Courier*, one in the *Columbia Phoenix*, and another in *The World*, published in New York. In addition, he enclosed a personal letter from Dr. N. M. Crawford from Georgetown College.[20]

Later that month Broadus received a copy of the *Religious Herald*, read the review, and wrote:

> This morning I received the 'Herald' of the eighth, with Bro. Long's review of my book, the first information I have had of its appearance. I am exceedingly indebted to Bro. Long for a notice so very carefully prepared, so very kind, and calculated materially to promote the acceptance of the book. I mean to write to him.[21]

J. C. Long, who succeeded Broadus as pastor of First Baptist Church, Charlottesville, had produced the index to the *Treatise* and had corrected for the press the last proofs. He knew the book well and felt qualified to make the most positive evaluation. His introductory paragraph set a tone that would be duplicated not only throughout his review but in many that would follow. "A book on preaching, by a master of the art," Long began, "may very well excite high expectations; and in this case the expectations will not be disappointed."[22]

Long's mention of "expectation" made its way into several reviews. The words reflected a perception of Broadus's greatness as a preacher that had been developing for two decades. An 11-year-old girl who heard his very first sermon on June 4,

---

[20] Ibid., 95.

[21] Robertson, 244.

[22] [J. C. Long], "Literary Notices," a review of *The Preparation and Delivery of Sermons* in the *Religious Herald* (September 8, 1870): 2. All quotes from this review appear on the same page of the *Religious Herald*.

1849, remembered in adulthood that he "spoke as I never heard man speak before of our gracious Saviour."[23] By 1851, he had such a reputation that people crowded to hear him preach, to catch a "glimpse of the young preacher," when they heard he was to be present at a meeting. On one such occasion, when the intensity and high expectation made the situation ripe for failure, an eyewitness recorded, "And fail he did not; he fully sustained his early fame" preaching a sermon "equal to the demands of the great and trying occasion." It contained "no gush, no attempt at mannerism or display of learning; it was the pure gospel in simple, earnest, well-chosen diction, and impressively delivered."[24]

In 1854, Broadus was selected to speak before a group of ministers in Virginia on the subject "The Best Mode of Preparing and Delivering Sermons." At the urging of those that heard his oral presentation, he published an essay in December 1854 in the *Religious Herald* by that title.[25] In 1867, J. William Jones, an early graduate of the seminary wrote to James P. Boyce:

> Bro. Broadus's sermon produced a profound impression here. All (of every name) agree in pronouncing it the finest sermon ever preached in the community. Prof Harris says he is the best preacher on the continent while Gen'l Lee, Dr. White, Dr. Kirkpatrick, Gen'l Smith, Ex Gov. Letcher &c are scarcely less enthusiastic.[26]

In January 1869, Broadus published "Suggestions for Expository Preaching" in *The Baptist Quarterly*.[27] In January 1870, in the same publication, Broadus published "The Three Methods of Preaching."[28] Both of these articles appeared as chapters in the *Treatise*.

---

[23] Robertson, 71.

[24] Ibid., 92.

[25] Ibid., 123–25.

[26] J. William Jones to James P. Boyce, Boyce Collection in the archives of the Boyce Memorial Library at The Southern Baptist Theological Seminary. Located in box 1/7. Letter of August 12, 1867.

[27] John A. Broadus, "Suggestions for Expository Preaching," *The Baptist Quarterly* (January 1869): 69–84.

[28] John A. Broadus, "The Three Methods of Preaching," *The Baptist Quarterly* (January 1870): 91–116.

Having exaggerated none at all, therefore, in the mention of such high expectations of a book on preaching by John A. Broadus, Long went on to entice the reader:

> Dr. Broadus has written from a deep conviction that he had something to write which was worthy to be written. Everywhere in his book there is that intensity of earnestness which is at once the charm and characteristic of his preaching. From the first sentence of his introduction to the close of his last chapter, he makes you feel that he is dealing with things of the utmost importance. Twenty years' experience as a preacher, ten years' experience as a teacher of homiletics, profound and varied scholarship, a calm and critical judgment, extraordinary powers of observation, an intense love of his calling, and the one purpose to excel in it—these are his qualifications for the task he undertook. It is nothing more than the simplest justice to say that he has produced a volume worthy of himself and of his subject.[29]

Long provided a full summary of each part of the book. He included fitting, and sometimes lengthy, quotations and pointed out the appropriateness and pertinence of several poignant ideas and stylistic devices developed by Broadus. "More than any other man we have ever known," Long testified, "Dr. Broadus excels in making brief, pointed remarks." Sometimes these make one smile, sometimes pause and think, and sometimes "he lifts you to a solemn and earnest tension of soul." In the end the book was effective "upon the ministry of our State, in which its author is so highly esteemed, must be in the highest degree beneficial," Long observed.[30] Many laymen also will discover "quickening of their Christian energies, and learn from it a more intelligent sympathy with the minister of Christ."[31]

The notices sent by Boyce, though not nearly so elaborate, expressed just as much confidence in the superior quality and

---

[29] Long, 2.
[30] Ibid.
[31] Ibid.

usefulness of the book. To the New York readers of *The World*, Boyce intended to gain a hearing both for Broadus and the seminary. He informed them that though the author was from the "far South," he was active among the scholarly circles of the North and indeed the world. The American Baptist Publication Society at Philadelphia engaged him to prepare a commentary on Matthew. Also he is connected with the "translation and editing of the famous commentary of Dr. Lange, now publishing under the supervision of Dr. Schaff." His preaching in Orange, New Jersey, his address at the Baptist Education Convention at Brooklyn, and his speech at the Baptist Home Mission Society in New York had significant impressions on the Baptist clergy of the North. These opportunities "secured for him here the reputation he had long possessed at the South of one of the first preachers of the day."

As one would expect of such a scholar, the book is "full of the evidences of thorough scholarship applied with conscientious care to the development of the subject." His massive bibliographical knowledge allows him to gather "from the Greek and Roman classics, from the fathers and writers of later ages, and from the best writers of modern days in Germany, France, England, and America." The whole field of homiletics "has been carefully surveyed," the materials "thoroughly digested" and subjected to "the patient thinking of an independent and vigorous mind, guided by an unusually suggestive experience."[32] Among its most potent contributions, Broadus's *Preparation* teaches how one may speak extemporaneously "with all the power of unfettered and living oratory." Broadus's own success in this mode combined

> his wide-spread opportunities of analyzing the powers of others, and especially his ten years' experience in teaching large classes in the largest Baptist theological seminary of America, make his suggestion worthy of the most careful examination.

---

[32] Long, 2.

To assure its widespread advantages to many classes of people, the volume "is exceedingly readable, and charmingly written."[33]

Boyce reminded the readers of the Charleston *Courier* that Broadus, "one of the best scholars of the age," had fully sustained his reputation in this book. One peculiarity that "render[ed] it eminently suitable to this section of the country" was its concentration "on the art of speaking more than on that of writing." He readily understood and communicated "those points of difference between the orator and the author, which give the speech of the former an efficiency beyond the printed page of the latter." This made it valuable not only for the preacher but also for the lawyer and others that must make an impression and bring conviction to minds by the medium of the spoken word.[34] The same material appeared in the *Phoenix* at Columbia, South Carolina, artfully rearranged.

W. D. Thomas, who as a student at the University of Virginia in 1850 heard a young Broadus preach, himself became a minister of the gospel, remained a loyal friend through the years, and presented a beautiful eulogy at Broadus's funeral, wrote to Broadus in November 1870 from Greenville. The news had wild variety:

> Dr. Boyce is working like a hero and the Seminary is going well, though you are sorely missed. . . . You have heard before this of the death of General Lee. . . . Your book is going like hotcakes. . . . I hope you are taking notes for a book of travels.[35]

---

[33] [J. P. Boyce], "Book Notice," *The World* (November 5, 1870). Unless otherwise noted all of these reviews are collected in the Archives of the Boyce Memorial Library at The Southern Baptist Theological Seminary, The Broadus Collection, Box 22, folders 7, 8, 9. Some of them have some bibliographical information, others have none, but it is almost always incomplete. Virtually without exception they are headed with the bibliographical information of the first edition of the work. Very soon, however, other publishers printed versions. Each of these was called an "edition" though not differing at all in content or pagination.

[34] [J. P. Boyce], *Courier* (Charleston, 1870).

[35] Robertson, 249.

It was all true. Boyce was working hard, the much lamented friend of Broadus, Robert E. Lee, was dead, and Broadus's book was selling like hotcakes, rapidly and in abundance. J. M. Pendleton bought 37 copies to give to every student in the recently established Crozer Theological Seminary in Upland, Pennsylvania.[36] J. L. M. Curry wrote in December from Richmond: "Your book has received more favorable commendations from the religious journals than any book of the kind ever did in America. I have seen notices in Methodist, Presbyterian, and Congregational journals."[37]

It seemed that the number of reviews in such a wide variety of publications and across denominational lines had seldom been duplicated by any single book, particularly on its first printing under such apparent disadvantages. The *American Literary Gazette* wrote, "It is easy to see that the volume is the result of much reflection; it abounds in suggestions which may be turned to profitable account, not only by preachers, but by lawyers. . . . Some of the sentences are quite pointed and pithy." An Episcopal journal drew a conclusion that Broadus would not have anticipated or approved, "With this book at hand we see no need of a person going to a Seminary to learn the art and mystery of sermonizing."[38]

The Standard of Chicago, on September 22, wrote, "Dr. Broadus writes with an earnestness which is conclusive as to the fact that he is thoroughly alive to the magnitude of his theme." The writer particularly appreciated Broadus's emphasis on

> piety as first in order and importance in the requisites for the preparation of a sermon. This proposition will receive ready assent everywhere, for without a knowledge by faith and love of Jesus, how can

---

[36] This very brief bit of information appeared on a small bit of newspaper in the files with no evidence front or back as to where or when it appeared.

[37] Robertson, 249.

[38] John A. Broadus Papers, Archives and Special Collections, James P. Boyce Centennial Library, The Southern Baptist Theological Seminary, Louisville, Kentucky. Also, see note 33 above for all such subsequent review citations.

a preacher comprehend and exhibit spiritual truth to others?[39]

From Boston, *The Christian Era* remarked,

> No pastor could attentively read the book without profit, and preachers who have not enjoyed the privileges of a course of study, either in college or in a theological seminary, will find in it instruction which cannot fail to augment their power in the pulpit.

A summary of contents concluded that the book was "a complete work on this subject, and one which commends itself by its intrinsic merit to the favorable consideration of the religious public." These compliments bracketed a series of mild and minor criticisms. One concerned the intended breadth of Broadus's purpose. "No man can accomplish such a task with entire success," the reviewer noted. "The nearer a treatise approaches the standard of a first-class text-book, the more is it shorn of those attractions of style" in a book simply to be read. "The nearer the style of a book approaches the popularity and elaborateness necessary for attractive reading, the more is it rendered unfit for a text-book" he went on to say. Broadus had done well in the attempt, but the disparate goals were too wide apart for the possibility of satisfying success.[40]

In another criticism the review contended that Broadus communicated "too much of the assimilated material of other authors." While making good selections, "he would have added to both the strength and attractiveness of his book" had he first "fused this material in his own brains and then given us the result permeated with his spirit and bearing his stamp." This observation seems debatable, for several other reviews note a characteristic described in the *Christian Index*. "Numerous productions of Rhetoric and Homiletics have been boiled down in the alembic of an active brain," the reviewer observed, "and are here distilled, in pure healthful consistency for our benefit."

---

[39] Ibid.
[40] Ibid.

From South Carolina, after acknowledging that "we have read the book with absorbing interest, and have been impressed at almost every page with its many excellencies," the *Associate Reformed Presbyterian* noted, "It is not a compilation from other authors, nor a stale repetition of common places, but is a valuable and original work, enstamped with that strong common sense which is a marked peculiarity of the author." In addition, "rich, deep thoughts and eminently practical suggestions abound through these pages, and are clothed in a style that is transparently simple."[41]

From Philadelphia, the *Methodist Home Journal* recommended this "judicious and exhaustive treatise on the general subject of preaching." They believed that it would "occupy a very prominent—if not the highest place among books on Homiletics." The *Watchman & Reflector* agreed saying, "As a text book for theological schools, and as a book for private study it has no superior." A periodical of the Cumberland Presbyterian Church, *The Medium,* judged that "among the many treatises which have been published on this important subject, we know of none superior to this as a text-book for Theological Seminaries." The *Presbyterian Banner* in Pittsburgh came close to such an estimation in calling it "one of the very best works of the kind which has come to our table for some time" and "a work of unusual merit . . . not superficial, but thorough."[42]

A Methodist newspaper from Richmond in March 1871 agreed by saying: "We unhesitatingly recommend this book to *Methodist* preachers, especially to young preachers, and beginners, as the very best book, everything considered that we have seen on the subject of the preparation and delivery of sermons." Looking at every aspect and perspective, "it is a first rate book, as unexceptionable as we shall ever see, and as such is heartily commended to Methodist preachers." Beyond that they saw other stellar qualities in Broadus's approach. Though a Baptist, Broadus "is so large and liberal in his views as to place him

---

[41] Ibid.
[42] Ibid.

beyond the contracted and petty sphere in which bigots and sectaries move and revolve." Nothing in the book "can be offensive or objectionable to any man of like Christian liberality with the author. It is as clear and perspicuous in its style, as it is elevated in its tone, and Christianly in its temper." In addition, Broadus advocated a preaching style for which the reviewer manifested great interest and zeal.[43]

> It contains views on *extemporaneous* preaching which should be carefully studied by our young preachers, at a time like this, especially, when there is such a tendency, (a tendency so much to be deplored) in our pulpit, to reading sermons from manuscript. Would to God that something could bring us back [as a people] to the custom and habits of our best preachers, in the earlier days of Methodism, of thorough study and careful preparation of the *matter* of our sermons, and to the free extemporaneous delivery of them in the pulpit. This new book will help in that direction.[44]

Another Methodist paper, *The Christian Advocate* of Nashville, called it "a capital work," pronounced it "excellent," and confided to its readers that if called on to write such a book and able "we should do it generally just as this author has done it." This reviewer also approved Broadus's tone even though he detected "a grain or two of Calvinism with a slight admixture of anti-pedobaptism." These appeared, however, only as a "homeopathic dose" and produced "little effect." He should drop illustrations from Spurgeon "as his works abound in twaddle" and should not be "cited as models, in any sense." He then suggested seriously that some "large-hearted Baptist brother" send a free copy "to all the ministers and candidates for the ministry in the Southern Baptist Connection." Moreover, "some of the wealthy and zealous sisters—the Hannahs, and Huldahs, and Priscillas—who adorn the Baptist communion" should provide

---

[43] Ibid.
[44] Ibid.

every Baptist Sunday school library in the South with a copy. Likewise for the Methodists, he continued "for we need such works as much as the Baptists." Methodist preaching includes an "immense amount of bungling" and "it is high time that vigorous measures were adopted to bring about a reform."[45]

When compared with the recently published *Office and Work of the Christian Ministry* by James M. Hoppin,[46] reviewers preferred Broadus. The *Christian Advocate* said:

> Our bishops have done well in putting Hoppin's *Office and Work of the Christian Ministry* in the Course of Study for candidates for the sacred office in our Connection. We are not sure that they would not have given this book [Broadus's *Treatise*] the preference, had it been issued before, as it is the work of a South Carolina Virginian.

---

[45] Ibid.

[46] James M. Hoppin (professor of homiletics and pastoral theology in Yale College), *Office and Work of the Christian Ministry* (New York: Sheldon & Co., 1869). Hoppin stated in the preface: "This volume is chiefly designed as a textbook in Homiletics and Pastoral Theology, for those who are in a regular course of training for the ministry of the Gospel. While I hope that pastors may find in it something of value to themselves, it is mainly intended to be used by theological students in the class-room, for the purpose of recitation; and this will account for the broken-up and analytical style of the book, that being necessitated by the treatment in condensed, rather than expanded, forms of discussion of so many and varied themes." In a review that appeared in *The New Englander and Yale Review*, vol 28, issue 108 (July 1869), the reviewer summarized Hoppin's view of the ideal sermon. "We might conceive the ideal of a Christian sermon, not yet attained, or not attained by all, but which is adapted to the needs of our highest modern civilization, while it does not lose the earnestness and practical aim of the Gospel. It is unpretentious, devotional, springing from the meditation of a holy soul upon the Scriptures, with Christ as the central burning theme; tender and full of love, but strong in apostolic faith, like the preaching of masculine Paul and Luther; courageously hopeful for man, and filled with the true enthusiasm of humanity; thoughtful and substantial in reasoning, but not intellectual so truly as spiritual; not confined in any set forms, but free with that liberty wherewith Christ makes free; with an internal rather than external method of thought; of the highest literary style, because fresh and simple, almost plain and homely, so that the ignorant man and the child may understand what feeds the most highly educated hearer; as well fitted for backwoodsmen as for philosophers, because it is deep and penetrating, is drawn from the common wells of truth and salvation, appeals to the common wants and desires of the heart, and is fitted to convert men from sin, and to lead them to the life of God."

A bit more opinionated and forcefully stated, the *Christian Era* observed: "It is vastly superior to the work of Professor Hoppin, issued about a year since. The press generally praised that, but without reason, for it is brim-full of the most ludicrous mistakes." But with Broadus, "It is a pleasure to greet a book generally so correct."[47]

Several reviews remark at the coincidence of Dabney's *Sacred Rhetoric,*[48] that had appeared early in 1870, and Broadus's *Treatise.* The *Southern Presbyterian* of Columbia, South Carolina, remarked:

> It is striking, and to us a pleasing fact, that the present year should have produced, in the Southern country, two able works on the same subject. Dr. Dabney of Union Theological Seminary in Virginia, and Dr. Broadus of the Baptist Theological Seminary at Greenville, S. C., have both laid the religious public under lasting obligations for their masterly productions on the same general theme.[49]

The *Biblical Repertory and Princeton Review* in January 1871 published a review of the two volumes together. As to style they opined that "the treatise of Dr. Broadus is in some respects the opposite of Dr. Dabney's." They viewed it as "more complete as a compilation, probably the most complete, for a text-book, that has yet appeared in Homiletics." It fell short of Dabney in "force and freshness" and therefore was "less entertaining to the reader." Broadus tended to be redundant, less scientific in analy-

---

[47] John A. Broadus Papers.

[48] Robert L. Dabney, *Sacred Rhetoric or A Course of Lectures on Preaching* (originally published 1870; Edinburgh: Banner of Truth Trust, 1979). In his preface Dabney writes, "If this work has any peculiarities to which value may be attached, they are these: that the necessity of eminent Christian character is urged throughout as the foundation of the sacred orator's power, and that a theory of preaching is asserted, with all the force which I could command, that honours God's inspired word and limits the preacher most strictly to its exclusive use as the sword of the Spirit. If my readers rise from the perusal with these two convictions enhanced in their souls—that it is grace which makes the preacher, and that nothing is preaching which is not expository of the Scriptures—my work is not in vain" (7).

[49] John A. Broadus Papers.

sis, and "loose and confused" on a minor aspect of his distribution of sermon-types. Broadus, despite some minor flaws, "has made a good book full of instruction, rich, varied, and exhaustive." Broadus investigated several methods of preparation and pulpit delivery with "great candor and wisdom," but the most strategic contribution to pulpit eloquence of both Dabney and Broadus concerned extemporaneous delivery. Both had done a great service in their "masterly demonstration" that "preaching the gospel can regain its power and success only when the eye in delivery is emancipated alike from the manuscript and the recitation of words committed to memory."[50]

Many of the reviewers transferred their deep respect and affection for Broadus as a person to their evaluation of the merit of his book. Two examples show the tone of these observations. G. W. Samson, writing for the *Watchman and Reflector* noted:

> In the first place, Dr. Broadus is admired from New York to South Carolina as a successful preacher; his sincere piety, deep experience, comprehensive knowledge, earnest spirit and attractive manner winning every class of hearers wherever he is called to speak or preach.[51]

A reviewer for the *Christian Index* of Georgia shared this high estimation:

> If we may judge from the extent of the practice, talking behind one's back must possess a strong fascination for human nature; and we are glad of the opportunity to indulge it, just this one time. Dr. Broadus is parted from us, at present, by the width of the ocean; and we can tell our readers to the full what we think of him, with no risk that our words will ever reach his ears in Europe. . . . "Take him all in all," he is the Prince of Preachers, within our sphere of (adequate) personal knowledge; and we have sometimes thought that if

---

50 Ibid.
51 Ibid.

we were condemned to hear but a single voice from the pulpit for the residue of this mortal pilgrimage, and were allowed liberty of choice in the premises, it should be the voice of Dr. Broadus. No pen could more appropriately undertake a work like the one before us than his—and this is worthy even of that.[52]

Although accolades piled up in review after review, a writer for the *Lutheran Observer* said he was "unable to discover from the book before us any special aptitude of the Professor for the work he has undertaken." What would southern evangelicals think of such ecclesiastical innocence! "He may be scholarly, and at home in dogmatic theology," the review continued, "but his style is heavy and clumsy, and wanting the grace and elegance of diction peculiar to the rhetorician." One wonders; was he speaking of John A. Broadus? In addition, while homiletical books multiply, "the most conspicuous and impressive pulpit orators have paid little attention to them." Does he omit Broadus himself from the category of "impressive pulpit orators?" Besides all this, the *Treatise*, though "sound in its instruction upon the structure, materials, discussion, and delivery of sermons" had "nothing new; no new line of thought; no suggestion; no method—nothing that I have not found in every work on homiletics, from Scholt down to Ripley." At the end of the day, one must ask, "What is the use of another such book after Theremin, Tholuck, Harms, Pulmer, and the scholarly and exhaustive work of Dr. Shedd?" And so, while "there is no need of such a work," because the writer was a Baptist from the South, "his chapter on the management of the voice in preaching is specially commended to his brethren in the South" he continued. Many of them are "addicted to a *sing-song* or 'holy whine' so offensive to refined taste and delicate nerves."[53]

As a startling anomaly a Lutheran review presented a context of evaluation to which other views may be compared. From Aberdeen, Scotland, David Brown wrote Broadus in England. Having

---

[52] Ibid.
[53] Ibid.

received a copy and intending to read only the preface and contents, he finished all before he set it down. "You have collected a large amount of the best matter from the best writers on homiletics and writers on kindred topics," Brown acknowledged, so far in agreement with the less enthusiastic observation above, but added, "And besides this have contributed much that is weighty and well worth attending to of your own." In fact, the volume seems "everything that one requires as a manual" on preaching.[54]

The *Christian Intelligencer* of New York must not have read the same book reviewed by the *Lutheran Observer*, for its observations were virtual contradictions. The *Intelligencer* expected "to find it a mere compilation of the thoughts of previous writers" but discovered instead that it was "fresh, original, and of solid, practical value." Far from a mere redundancy, "it is the most complete and comprehensive work of the kind that has yet been published in this country." Not just the holy whiners of the South may benefit, but "it is also so suggestive and scholarly, and pervaded by so excellent a spirit, that all preachers, whatever their experience, may find in it much that they can turn to practical account."[55]

A Virginia paper, the *Enquirer*, said that before Broadus appeared, it despaired of finding a truly helpful book on preaching. The reviewer observed, "We have read the various well-known treatises on homiletics, but have always felt unsatisfied upon laying them down. They were not practical enough. They lacked the very details a young clergyman should know, and yet cannot unless 'some man tell him.'" They lacked fullness and were ill-arranged and "on no point less instructive than with reference to the composition and delivery of extempore sermons." But Dr. Broadus himself must have sensed those same defects and "deeply to have sympathized with the yearnings of theological students for simple, practical directions" and written his book specifically to address "this interest and sympathy." Far from clumsy, the book is "earnest, well written, and lays stress

---

[54] Robertson, 248.
[55] John A. Broadus Papers.

on many points hitherto neglected." Even with many other texts on preaching, Broadus is essential for "it combines the excellencies of Russell, Shedd, and Alexander, while urging attention to many important matters that to some may appear very trivial, which they have failed to notice."[56]

The Abiding Impact of Its Conception

Broadus, having received copies of the book from the publisher, gave a copy to C. H. Spurgeon. An American newspaper editor reported: "We have received a private letter from Rev. C. H. Spurgeon, of London, from which the following is taken: 'I was delighted to see Dr. J. A. Broadus. His book is invaluable.'" By October 1870, Broadus's *Treatise* had made its way to England via another route. He recorded a visit on October 11 to Regent's Park College where Dr. Davies introduced him to Dr. Angus, the college president. Dr. Angus had received a gift copy of the book when in America and read it on the way across the Atlantic. Broadus noted, "He proposes to use it as textbook in the college, which will probably help me." Eventually Nisbet & Co. of London issued a reprint of "Preparation and Delivery of Sermons," with introduction by Dr. Angus.[57]

Twenty-eight years later, Edwin C. Dargan (1852–1930) could write, "The book was a great success." He claimed that "it became the most popular and widely-read text-book on Homiletics in this country." As evidence of the claim, he could point to 22 editions, that was, separate printings, and its having been "adopted in many theological seminaries of different denominations as the text-book, and in many where no text-book is used it is highly commended for study and reference." Besides its use as a text, it obviously had wide circulation. Two separate editions had been published in England, it was used in mission schools in Japan and China, and a Portuguese translation was under way.[58]

---

[56] Ibid.
[57] Ibid.
[58] John A. Broadus, *A Treatise on the Preparation and Delivery of Sermons,* ed. Edwin Charles Dargan (New York: George H. Doran Company, 1898), v–vi.

When Jesse Burton Weatherspoon (1886–1964) wrote a preface in 1943 to his edition of Broadus, he testified, "That the book has been in constant and increasing use since its first appearance and after three quarters of a century remains the outstanding text-book of Homiletics is full justification for its continuance."[59] Instead of writing his own text, he chose a revision "in the belief that a revised Broadus will have greater worth for the next generation of preachers than a new book."[60] He believed that "few if any books" had achieved the "comprehensiveness, the timelessness, and, withal, the simplicity of Broadus." Broadus's focus on "principles and tested procedures" as well as the "classical works of the centuries," meant that the book "still lives" and needed revision "only in secondary matters."[61]

Vernon Stanfield (1920–1991), beginning in 1942, studied Dargan's revision taught by Weatherspoon. In 1946, he began teaching Weatherspoon's revision at The Southern Baptist Theological Seminary.[62] In 1979, he wrote:

> For thirty-two years I have used *On the Preparation and Delivery of Sermons* as a text. I have not done this out of loyalty to the Broadus tradition or to my former professor Dr. Weatherspoon. I have done so because it remains the most complete text for the study of homiletics.

Though he had used many other supplemental texts, Stanfield still believed "no other text has matched Broadus for complete basic material."[63]

A text written in 1963, *Steps to the Sermon*, condensed the methods of three professors of preaching on the task of sermon

---

[59] John A. Broadus, *On the Preparation and Delivery of Sermons,* new and revised edition by Jesse Burton Weatherspoon (San Francisco: Harper & Row, 1944), v.

[60] Ibid.

[61] Ibid.

[62] Stanfield taught for three years contractually and was elected to the faculty in 1949. He taught until 1959 and then went to teach at New Orleans Baptist Theological Seminary.

[63] John A. Broadus, *On the Preparation and Delivery of Sermons,* fourth edition revised by Vernon L. Stanfield (San Francisco: Harper & Row, Publishers, 1979), xi.

preparation.[64] In their introduction they expressed indebtedness to the texts of John A. Broadus and Edwin C. Dargan and acknowledged the powerful influence of their classroom teachers Jesse B. Weatherspoon and Vernon Stanfield. These will be recognized immediately, of course, as the author and the subsequent revisers of *A Treatise on the Preparation and Delivery of Sermons.* When they quoted this volume, they used the Weatherspoon edition, which at that time was the most recent. On one occasion they used illustrations that clearly are not the product of Broadus.[65] Otherwise, they cited him legitimately on a number of occasions as an authority. They quoted Broadus on the function of a text, the necessity of developing a proper interpretation of the text, on sources of illustration, on imagination, on developing force and energy in one's style, on the use of quotation in extemporaneous preaching, and on the distinction between preaching and reading.[66] Though developing their text on a much narrower, more condensed scale than Broadus's, the authors cited him when his ideas fit the discussion.

David Alan Smith sought to determine the level at which Broadus's use of classical rhetoric as a foundation for sermonic construction still operated in Southern Baptist ministerial education as of 1995. Broadus openly acknowledged his indebtedness to Aristotle, Cicero, Quintilian, and Christian approaches to preaching that built on those orators and rhetoricians. In light of this, Smith traced the influence of classical rhetoric on Broadus's understanding of the purpose of oratory, his gathering of material compared with the rhetoricians' "canon of invention" and his theory of arrangement and style compared with the same ideas in classical rhetoric.[67]

---

[64] H. C. Brown Jr., H. Gordon Clinard, and Jesse J. Northcutt, *Steps to the Sermon* (Nashville: Broadman Press, 1963).

[65] Ibid., 43. The quote cites a sermon thesis from Harry Emerson Fosdick and another from James Reid.

[66] Ibid., 34, 47, 48, 72, 77, 155–56, 187, 190.

[67] Editor's note: For a fuller discussion of Broadus's use of classical rhetoric, see this volume's chapter "John A. Broadus, Rhetoric, and *A Treatise on the Preparation and Delivery of Sermons.*"

Using a questionnaire, examining class syllabi, and examining written materials of the professors of three seminaries, Smith drew his conclusions. He found that many elements of Broadus's theory still are diffused through the preaching instruction of today. "Much of Broadus's theory is still being taught to Southern Baptist preachers today" [1995], he summarized but continued, "Yet for the most part the preaching departments sought to maintain a balance between traditional and innovative forms."[68] Though persuasion still is a goal of the sermon, they showed less commitment than Broadus to deduction and rational discourse as means of accomplishing it. Several defensible reasons led to the gradual use of innovative forms. Revolutionary changes in communication, the breakdown of a pervasively held worldview in society, and rapidly shifting views of how people process information for the purpose of life change has made the task of teaching homiletics polyformed and open-ended.

In 2006[69] this author constructed a simple and modest survey of Southern Baptist seminary homileticians and their use of Broadus. Nine respondents answered three questions:

1. Do you include Broadus's work on preaching as a suggested (not required) reading in your preaching classes?

2. Do you personally derive any of your homiletical theory taught to your classes from your acquaintance with Broadus's "Preaching and Delivery of Sermons"? Any section more than others?

3. Do you have any assignments from Broadus included in any of your courses? If so, what?

The results showed a consistency with Smith's conclusions but with some increase in the intensity of appreciation for Broadus.

---

[68] David Alan Smith, *Introductory Preaching Courses in Selected Southern Baptist Seminaries in the Light of John A. Broadus's Homiletical Theory* (Ann Arbor: UMI, 1995), 172. This is a dissertation written for the Ph.D. at Southwestern Baptist Theological Seminary.

[69] Tom J. Nettles, Personal Homiletical Survey.

Question 1 had seven "yeses" and two "noes." Question 2 had seven "yeses" and two "noes." (These were not the same two persons, however, that answered "no" to question 1). Question 3 had five "yeses" and four "noes." None of the assignments for Broadus were in the basic course on preaching but were in elective M.Div. and D.Min. and Ph.D. courses.[70]

On question 2, one respondent wrote that he believed "Broadus has published the finest work to date in the field of preaching in his book." Though this respondent possesses every revised edition, he still preferred Broadus's original and states specific areas in which he was greatly influenced. "Part I, Chapter V—Explanation; Part I, Chapter VI—Argument; Part I, Chapter VII—Illustration; Part I, Chapter VII—Application; Part II, Chapter I—Importance of Arrangement; and Part II, Chapter II—The Several Parts of the Sermon."[71]

Another professor remarked on the overall impact of Broadus on his homiletical theory:

> Broadus's work was the first I read on the subject of preaching, and I am certain that it has been more influential in my thinking and teaching than I am aware. I cite him frequently in my lectures, not so much for a comprehensive theory, but rather for particular insights that he expressed. For example, I cite his definition of expository preaching; I advocate his approach of extemporaneous delivery. I refer to his materials on argument to some extent—in fact, I wrote an M.A. thesis that looks at this theory of argument, including, but not limited to, his treatment of presumption and burden of proof. These are only a few examples of the sorts of things that I draw from Broadus's text.[72]

Still another respondent commented on his convictions concerning the present usefulness of Broadus's *Treatise* and the historic impact of the work:

---

[70] Ibid.

[71] Ibid.

[72] Ibid.

In my judgment Broadus will continue to be considered a great book by true expositors. It was the classic text for a hundred years in Evangelical Seminaries. My homiletics' professor at Duke, Dr. James Clelland [sic: Cleland], a conservative Scotchman said that Broadus was an outstanding treatment on homiletics and had been so regarded in all Evangelical Seminaries from the time of its publication. We are living in a day of serious aberrations in homological [homiletical?] methodology, and I am confident that Broadus's viewpoint would be considered passé by many so called Evangelicals. But in my mind it is very insightful and valuable to the true expositor of the infallible Word of God.[73]

A remarkable element of many of the recent evangelical books on preaching was the revitalization of appreciation for Broadus and even immediate dependence on his ideas. In a 1992 book written by the faculty at Master's Seminary, the importance of Broadus came into prominence at several points.[74] John MacArthur cited Broadus's *On the Preparation and Delivery of Sermons* as the first important influence on his concepts as an expositor of the Bible.[75] James F. Stitzinger's chapter, "The History of Expository Preaching," gave a brief space to Broadus as one of "several important biblical expositors" of the later nineteenth century. Broadus has been termed "the Prince of Expositors."[76] According to Stitzinger, subsequent editions of the 1870 *Treatise on the Preparation and Delivery of Sermons* "have reduced its original thrust and value."

Irvin A. Busenitz, dealing with the subject of "Thematic, Theological, Historical, and Biographical Messages," cited Broadus in areas of general concern on these issues as well as each specific type of sermon. He pointed out that "Broadus

---

[73] Ibid.

[74] John MacArthur and the Faculty at Master's Seminary, *Rediscovering Expository Preaching* (Dallas: Word, 1992).

[75] Ibid., 347.

[76] Ibid., 60. Stitzinger quoted Nolan Howington, "Expository Preaching," *Review and Expositor* 56 (1959).

cautions against a restricted focus on one's immediate concerns" if devoted too much to subject-type messages. One must not be tempted to "think more of his ideas and his sermons than of 'rightly dividing the word of truth' and leading men into the Kingdom of God."[77]

Busenitz quoted Broadus as an authority on "Thematic preaching" who issued all the proper caveats on the subject.[78] He continued his reference to Broadus on "Theological Preaching" utilizing his entire section on that subject. He noted this suggestion in particular: "Doctrine, i.e., teaching is the preacher's chief business." Some fear such matter on the grounds of possible "dryness" or stirring unnecessary controversy, but Broadus suggested:

> It would seem to be a just principle that a preacher should never go out of his way to find a controversial matter or go out of his way to avoid it. He who continually shrinks from conflict should stir himself up to faithfulness; he who is by nature belligerent should cultivate forbearance and courtesy. . . . Let us avoid needlessly wounding the cause of our common Christianity.[79]

On the subject of "Historical Preaching," Busenitz showed the doctrinal and biblical relevance of Broadus's ideas, relying heavily on Broadus's treatment of "Historical Subjects." "In the Bible the designs of Providence are not left to be judged of by our sagacity," Broadus wrote, "but are often clearly revealed, so as to show us the meaning of things obscure, and the real co-working of things apparently antagonistic." Busenitz continued the quote: "Thus the Bible histories act like the problems worked out in a treatise of Algebra, teaching us how to approach the other problems presented by the general history of the world. The oft-quoted saying of an ancient writer that 'history is philosophy teaching by example,' applies nowhere so

---

[77] Ibid., 258. Busenitz cited the 1944 edition of *Treatise*.
[78] Ibid., 265.
[79] Ibid., 267; Broadus, 76 in 1898 version.

truly as to the inspired records, which are God himself teaching by example."[80]

MacArthur's article, "Delivering the Exposition" referenced Broadus's discussion of the methods of delivery and cited at least one pertinent Broadus quote:

> Delivery should be the spontaneous product of the speaker's peculiar personality, as acted on by the subject which now fills his mind and heart. . . . Delivery does not consist merely, or even chiefly, in vocalization and gesticulation, but it implies that one is possessed with the subject, that he is completely in sympathy with it and fully alive to its importance, that he is not repeating remembered words but setting free the thoughts shut up in his mind.[81]

John Carrick, in *The Imperative of Preaching*, discussed four modes of speech to be used in preaching, gave a biblical defense of the use of each mode, biblical examples of their use, and preaching examples. He quoted Broadus in a positive, and somewhat prescriptive, way on three of the modes of rhetorical address. Carrick made the point that "the indicative mood is, then, in its very nature, ideally suited to that element in preaching described by the Reformed tradition as *"explicatio verbi Dei,"* the explanation of the Word of God. He sealed his proposition by quoting Broadus: "There is in preaching very frequent need of Explanation," and again, "To explain the Scriptures would seem to be among the primary functions of the preacher."[82] In speaking of the use of the exclamation having quoted Dabney, Carrick observed: "It is, however, very important to sound a *caveat* here, precisely because the exclamative presents certain

---

[80] Ibid., 268–69. Broadus (1944), 71; Broadus (1898), 93.

[81] Ibid., 328, 330. He quotes the revised edition, a Harper & Row reprint of 1979. In the 1898 Dargan edition the quote, for the most part, is found on pages 477–78.

[82] John Carrick, *The Imperative of Preaching* (Edinburgh: The Banner of Truth Trust, 2005), 14. He quoted Broadus in the 1898 edition, 153, 155.

potential dangers to the preacher. John A. Broadus recognizes well both its dangers and its usefulness for the preacher."[83]

> Impassioned preachers are somewhat apt to use it too freely. Some say *Oh! Ah!* Or *Alas!* So often that it loses all power. Others indulge too much in such exclamations as *How Grand! Momentous Issue! Fearful thought!* And the like. On the other hand, we must not be over fastidious in avoiding exclamation, where it is naturally prompted by actual feeling.[84]

Later in his discussion of the same mode, Carrick affirmed, "Broadus and Alexander are absolutely right. Exclamation belongs to what is sometimes termed *the language of passion* and as such it is essential that it be characterized by genuineness and reality." When he explained the interrogative style, Carrick noted:

> John A. Broadus observes that "interrogation is with all orators a frequent means of giving animation to discourse. Not only may an antagonist, real or imaginary, be questioned, in such a manner as to awaken lively interest on the part of the hearts, but questions are constantly addressed to the hearers themselves. Their minds are thus aroused as if called on actually to answer."[85]

In his widely used book, *Christ-Centered Preaching*, Bryan Chapell referred to Broadus for confirmation, definition, or illustration throughout. Chapell used many other works, mostly recognized twentieth-century evangelicals, but he respectfully acknowledged Broadus as a formative authority on expository preaching.[86] Broadus's influence came at a crucial time for evangelicals. "During the past 150 years, expository preach-

---

[83] Ibid.

[84] Ibid., 53 quoting Broadus, 401.

[85] Ibid., 68. Broadus, 401.

[86] Bryan Chapell, *Christ-Centered Preaching* (Grand Rapids: Baker Book House, 1994). Chapell used Weatherspoon's edition of 1944. References to Chapell and *Treatise* will be bracketed in the text, the first number being the page of Chapell's discussion and the second being the location in Broadus to which he draws attention.

ing has gained prominence in conservative Western churches for at least two reasons," Chapell contended. "The evangelical search for a means to stem the erosion of commitment to biblical authority; and the nearly universal access to biblical material." He then pointed to Broadus in a footnote:

> Although Broadus argues for the antiquity of the expository method, his book, *On the Preparation and Delivery of Sermons,* first published in 1870, is the seminal volume for the codification and popularization of the expository method as we now know it. The erosion of scriptural commitments that would soon sweep this culture after the initial publication of Broadus's work indicates how critical was the timing of his methodology and why it was so widely adopted by evangelicals.

He followed the quote by noting several evangelical works that give evidence of Broadus's impact on their homiletics [129].

Chapell discussed the Reformed emphasis on *sola scriptura* and compared *lectio continua,* that is, consecutive preaching through a book, as preferable to *lectio selecta.* On this point he footnoted Broadus: "John A. Broadus refers to this as 'continuous exposition' in *On the Preparation and Delivery of Sermons*" [57, 146–47]. As he illustrated by a graphic his preference for sermon form, he acknowledged:

> Figure 4.2 is more in keeping with the understanding of John A. Broadus, the father of modern expository preaching. In his classic, *On the Preparation and Delivery of Sermons*, this master teacher and preacher concludes that in an expository sermon, "the application of the sermon is not merely an appendage to the discussion or a subordinate part of it, but is the main thing to be done." Broadus's conclusion has ample biblical precedent [79; 210].

Chapell referred approvingly to Broadus on each component of an expository sermon. He observed that homileticians "once divided sermons into three basic components: exposition (the explanation and arguments for what the text says); illustration (the demonstration of what the text says); and application (the behavioral or attitudinal implications of what the text means)." His footnote led the reader to Broadus "who divides exposition into the categories of explanation and argument separate from illustration and application" [83; 144,155]. In explaining how each of these components relates to the others and to the sermon as a whole, Chapell wrote, "Each component has a vital role in establishing listeners' full understanding of a text," with a reference to Broadus; and again, "As your expertise grows, the components of exposition will blend and bond to drive the truths of God's Word deep into the hearts of his people" with another reference to Broadus. Again, "In a traditional expository message each component of exposition occurs in every main point of the sermon because it makes no sense to explain something that can be neither demonstrated nor applied" with Broadus cited again for support [84; 155, 211].

When discussing the process of explanation in relation to the clarity of Scripture, Chapell footnoted Broadus after asserting, "There are no dark passageways through twisted mazes of logic to biblical truth that require the expertise of the spiritually elite" [99; 157]. Chapell deferred to Broadus rather than give space to a discussion of types of formal argument. His footnote informed, "For some traditional distinctions among the types of formal argumentation see Broadus, *On the Preparation and Delivery of Sermons,* 167–95" [122; 167–95].

Should a preacher make his outline obvious in his preaching? After mentioning several ways to answer this question, he referred to Broadus [132; 11–13: 257; 118]. Chapell taught that "Sermons are built on propositions. Classic homiletics describes a proposition as 'a statement of the subject as the preacher proposes to develop it,' " he gave the footnote to Broadus [139; 54]. He taught that application justifies the exposition and gave a strong defense of application. Following Broadus he concluded "application is the main thing to be done" [201; 210]. Broadus again carried freight for Chapell in his discussion of the introduction ["Ill begun is apt to be wholly ruined:" 229; 103; "Listeners do not want a porch on a porch:" 242; 105; "The best introductions start with specifics" 243; 106–7]. Further material concerning the importance of the introduction for the tone and eventual success of the message included the Broadus warning: "Introduce the message without spoken or implied apologies even if you feel unprepared. The outset is not time to prejudice a congregation against you, your message, or the potential of the Holy Spirit to work beyond human weakness" [244; 104].

Chapell continued with the importance of the conclusion and drew from the wisdom of Broadus: "The message that starts with a gripping introduction should end with an even more powerful conclusion" [244; 123]. For the importance of exhortation as an element of conclusion, he also drew energy from Broadus on more than one occasion. "In the conclusion the preacher exhorts people to act on what the sermon has already made clear" [246; 125], and again, "Sage preachers once taught, 'If there is no summons, there is no sermon'" [246; 210]. On the subjects of avoiding anticlimax, drawing focused and poignant conclusions, making skilled transitions, Chapell referred to Broadus [250; 127, 128: 252; 120].

David Larsen demonstrated the same deep appreciation for Broadus and the abiding relevance of his homiletical method. "Truly one of the Olympians in the history of preaching," Larsen acknowledged, "John A. Broadus (1827–1895) is called by some the father of American expository preaching."[87] Though Larsen pointed out that Broadus's "minimal interaction with narrative in homiletical theory" betrayed a serious underestimation of "the importance of biographical narrative in Scripture,"[88] he still touted Broadus as "a gifted homiletical theoretician" and "an immensely popular and able preacher" who in 1870 "spoke more about narrative than did Haddon Robinson in 1980."[89]

Even under the pressure of some modern homileticians to pass beyond Broadus's preponderating emphasis on discourse

[87] David Larsen, *In The Company of the Preachers* (Grand Rapids: Kregel, 1998), 551.

[88] David Larsen, *Telling the Old, Old Story* (Wheaton: Crossway Books, 1995), 196.

[89] Larsen, *Company*, 552.

and argument, Larsen found Broadus still intriguing and instructive. On an issue as modern as the use of imagination in preaching, he went to "John Broadus, no less," to identify the "factors in cultivating the imagination." He listed five suggestions thus derived: (1) Study art and nature. (2) Read imaginative literature and drama. (3) Be a people watcher and a people lover. (4) Find within your prayer and devotion to the great Creator a source of creativity. (5) Do not lament a lack of imagination but cultivate it by saying, "Let us suppose, or imagine that, or, Can you conceive?"[90] This issue of imagination deserved notice in one of the earliest reviews of the book. A reviewer for *The Baptist Quarterly* drew special and commendatory attention to "the chapter on imagination in its relation to eloquence, in which a much higher and wider sphere is assigned to imagination than is customary among writers on rhetoric."[91]

Another contemporary homiletician that has demonstrated a recent and earnest zeal for Broadus is Joseph Webb, professor of global media and communications at Palm Beach Atlantic College. Webb gathered an extensive and impressive professional and teaching resume in journalism and communications before obtaining his theological education at Candler School of Theology and Claremont School of Theology. Among his seven books on communication, journalism, and preaching is *Preaching without Notes.*[92] He believed that Broadus had given the best defense of the practice available in homiletical literature. By way of general commendation, Webb also began a Web page article: "Few books, if any, have had more 'staying power' in preaching over the past century and a half than John Broadus's 550-page volume called *A Treatise on the Preparation and Delivery of Sermons.*"[93] He reminded the reader that "Between 1870 and 1899, it went through 37 printings; and it was in print, under various editors, throughout the Twentieth Century. It still

---

[90] Larsen, *Old, Old Story*, 250–51.
[91] *The Baptist Quarterly* (October 1870): 504.
[92] Joseph Webb, *Preaching without Notes* (Nashville: Abingdon Press, 2001).
[93] Joseph Webb, "Broadus on Sermon Delivery," accessed at http://contemporary_preaching.typepad.com/all_about_sermons/.

is." In mainline seminaries only rarely will a student have heard of John A. Broadus, though he is alive and well in evangelical seminaries where "changes in the nature of sermon preparation have been downplayed." But "Broadus knew his stuff" and "one can say unequivocally that there is still—to this day—NO BET-TER GUIDE to sermon delivery than the 100 plus pages on sermon delivery in John Broadus's book."

Webb summarized Broadus's discussion of the three methods of sermon delivery—the fully written-out sermon, the memorized sermon, and the extemporaneous sermon—with the advantages and disadvantages of each. This complete presentation Webb called "good inductive scholarship." He highlighted the salient features of "extemporaneous preaching" and considered Broadus's defense of its advantages and his suggestions as to how to overcome its disadvantages a *tour de force.*

> As to delivery itself, it is only in extemporaneous speaking, of one variety or another, that [the sermon] can ever be perfectly natural and achieve the highest effect. The ideal of speaking, it has been justly said, cannot be reached in any other way. Only thus will the voice, the action, the eye, be just what nature dictates, and attain their full power. And while painstaking culture vainly strives to read or recite precisely like speaking, the extemporaneous speaker may, with comparative ease, rise to the best delivery of which he [or she] [[Webb's brackets]] is capable.[94]

Webb closed the article with a helpful exhortation: "Should you happen to find a good second-hand copy of Broadus's book someplace, buy it. Read it. Few books on preaching today are as comprehensive, or even as insightful about so many things related to preaching, as this great classic." And not to leave out the advantage that Broadus might bring even to him he suggested, "And to learn HOW to do what Broadus proposes about sermon delivery, order a copy of my book, *Preaching without Notes.*"[95]

---

[94] Ibid.
[95] Ibid.

Conclusion

Many texts on preaching of the last 40 years do not state any reliance on John A. Broadus in their theory of preaching. This is quite understandable given the changes and challenges in theories of communication, Bible interpretation, worship styles, the importance of preaching, the possibility of grasping truth through declamation, or the possibility of grasping truth at all. Scores of texts on preaching endured for a short time within a restricted circle and perished with their initial devotees. That so many texts and teachers of preaching still do, however, find Broadus fresh, stimulating, and helpful gives quite remarkable testimony to the unrestricted usefulness of Broadus's discussions of all the issues concerning the birth and delivery of the sermon event. Virtually every section of Broadus's resilient *A Treatise on the Preparation and Delivery of Sermons* finds expression in the developing corpus of evangelical works on homiletics. From the initial defense of the importance of preaching to his concluding remarks on pulpit decorum, contemporary writers have found much to imitate and recommend.

We opened this essay with a characterization of Broadus by one who apparently knew virtually nothing about him but characterized him by a silly and insulting fable. It seems that with Broadus, those who knew him most intimately had the highest regard for him and employed the most unbounded words of adulation for his character and his accomplishments. It is not inappropriate to allow one who, in his own right, was no mean scholar and an astute judge of scholarship to weigh the quality of Broadus's work. From his perspective on Broadus in 1882, A. T. Robertson composed the following evaluation and included the judgment of a respected contemporary on *A Treatise on the Preparation and Delivery of Sermons*:

> Soon Doctor Broadus found himself confronting large classes that at last gave full scope for his magnificent powers as teacher. But he had nevertheless given his best to the small classes through all the years at

Greenville. If he could only have had large classes all his previous life! But, though [he was only] fifty-five years old, he was in his prime and glory now. Oh, the rapture of the days when one could hear Broadus lecture in New Testament English or in Homiletics! It was worth a day's journey to any man. He was a consummate scholar, of the widest reading and the most thorough assimilation. He studied the sources of things and worked through everything for himself. To Anglo-Saxon, Latin, Greek, and Hebrew, he added German, French, Spanish, Italian Gothic, Coptic, and modern Greek. He had made himself a specialist in homiletics, in the English Bible, in New Testament history, exegesis, in Greek, in textual criticism, in patristic Greek, and hymnology (English and foreign). His "Preparation and Delivery of Sermons" had become the standard and most popular work on the subject. Prof. W. C. Wilkinson, of the University of Chicago, speaks of it as "on the whole, the best single treatise existing on its subject. This judgment is one neither hastily formed nor extravagantly expressed. It is a conviction arrived at after long and careful comparative consideration of the principal works in any language that could be regarded as rival claimant for the praise bestowed."[96]

One may apply Broadus's own closing words of his textbook to this attempt to evaluate his enduring contribution to the purity of biblical preaching:

Nor must we ever forget the power of character and life to reinforce speech. What a preacher *is*, goes far to determine the effect of what he *says*. There is a saying of Augustine, *Cujus vita fulgor, ejus verba tonitrua,*— if a man's life be lightning, his words are thunders.[97]

---

[96] Robertson, *Life and Letters,* 336. His citation of William C. Wilkinson, "John Albert Broadus: The Scholar, the Preacher, the Teacher, the Man of Affairs, the Man, the Christian," in *The Biblical World* (May 1895): 327–35.

[97] Broadus, *Treatise* (1898), 541.

Chapter IX

How to Preach Marketable Messages without Selling Out the Savior: Broadus on the Role of Sensationalism in Preaching

Beecher L. Johnson

What can a homiletician from the nineteenth century possibly add to the twenty-first century "conversation" on preaching? After all, when John A. Broadus was alive, PowerPoint and video clips had not been invented, the contemporary concept of a "seeker" was unknown, clerically casual fashion was not in vogue, and the "pulpit" was still decades from being commonly referred to as a "stage." The answer is actually quite a lot! Broadus could not have been familiar with the modern terms and methodologies that surround and inform current discussions on preaching. He did, however, hold an exceptionally firm grasp on the irreducible and timeless principles associated with the communication of God's Word. One such axiom of effective communication was that a speaker must attract and hold the attention of the listener in order to inform and persuade. The question was not the necessity of this but the means by which it would to be rightly accomplished in the context of Christian preaching.

Some veins of the contemporary church are using increasingly diverse and even questionable tactics in order to attract the masses. Steven Lawson has noted:

> Pressure to produce bottom-line results has led many ministries to sacrifice the centrality of biblical preaching on the altar of man-centered pragmatism. A new way of "doing" church is emerging. In this radical paradigmatic shift, exposition is being replaced with entertainment, preaching with performances, doctrine with drama, and theology with theatrics.[1]

At the dawn of this twenty-first century, many prominent churches promote sermons and sermon series designed to entice attendees by toning down formality and tuning up a so-called relevancy that accentuates the temporal and offers practical advice for Monday-morning living.[2] Even a cursory look at the modern church landscape reveals that the use of this approach has been extravagantly successful at attracting crowds.[3] Is that the ultimate goal? If so, where does the preacher draw the line in reference to the means used to reach that end? Certainly the aim of the church and the preacher is to bring glory to God by proclaiming the gospel biblically and compellingly to as many people as possible. Is that objective best fulfilled by simply

---

[1] Steven J. Lawson, *Famine in the Land: A Passionate Call for Expository Preaching* (Chicago: Moody, 2003), 25.

[2] The reader is referred to recent sermon series delivered in influential evangelical churches around the United States such as the "Sexual Revolution," offered with the admonition that "it's time to put the bed back in church and church back in the bed" and adorned with sermon titles such as "Stripped" and "Do Your Thing." Other examples include messages and series such as "Two Myths about Sex" and "How to Have an Affair," http://isite78285.intellisite.com/225499.ihtml?id=225499; "How to Deal with How You Feel," "Managing Stress," and "Figuring out Your Finances," http://www.pastors.com/en-US/Sermons/DownloadableSermons/default.htm. The author wishes to be clear that it is not the evangelistic motives but the methodological choices made in regard to sermon content, themes, and/or titles of the above that are in question.

[3] For example, according to the Hartford Institute of Religion Research, the churches referenced in the footnote above in 2005 listed 19,500, 3,400, and 22,000 members respectively. http://hirr.hartsem.edu/cgi-bin/mega/db.pl?db=default&uid=default&view_records=1&ID=*&sb=1.

filling the church pews by any means? Does the pretense under which they are attracted matter? R. Albert Mohler, president of The Southern Baptist Theological Seminary, has an interesting insight:

> One of the fundamental issues of misunderstanding that leads to corrupt churchmanship in our genera-tion is the failure to distinguish between a crowd and a church. The failure to distinguish between a crowd and a church is . . . to misunderstand everything about preaching, everything about ministry, everything about our task. If we think our business is to build a crowd, frankly any of us can do it. There's a way to bring and draw and attract a crowd. . . . Let us never mistake a crowd for a church [or] think our business is to draw a crowd.[4]

How then does one strike a proper balance? More impor-tantly could Broadus, considering his context, experience, and thought, bring anything useful to the discussion? Notice the similarity between Broadus's words and those of Mohler:

> It is then to be feared that some sermons, and numer-ous parts of sermons, that are attractive, entertaining, perhaps even in some respects impressive, yet do no real good, and may actually lessen the total spiritual effect of the speaker's ministry. "But anything is bet-ter than empty pews." Is that certainly so? Pews may be crowded with people who are drawn and held by some quite irreligious interests, and are sent away more completely out of sympathy with spiritual things than when they came. A crowded church may thus do little or no good, may even do positive harm. People say "that's the sort of preacher—I tell you, he draws a

---

[4] R. Albert Mohler (Shepherds' Conference audio recording, March, 6, 2003), https://www.gracechurch.org/sc/default.asp.

large congregation." But how does he draw them, and what does he do for them?[5]

In Broadus's day, this subject was debated under the name of "sensation" preaching and while the term is no longer routinely applied in the contemporary context, the principles remain the same. This essay will look at the benefits, dangers, and safeguards suggested by Broadus (and some of his contemporaries) in regard to the subject of sensation preaching. It is believed that much can be learned from his recommended approach to attracting and maintaining hearers for the gospel.

So how far should a preacher go in attempting to gain attention and response from a congregation? What means are appropriate in order to bring an audience in and entice them to return? How can a preacher capture the ear of the listener without being irreverent toward God and the things of God? These and similar questions surrounded the concept of sensation preaching in the late nineteenth and early twentieth centuries. The subject attracted considerable attention among pulpit orators of the day. So much so in fact, that Broadus dedicated an entire message to the topic in his Lyman Beecher lectures at Yale University in January and February 1889.

What Is Sensation Preaching?

Preachers of the era were careful to differentiate between the creation of a sensation (as in an appeal to the emotions) and the abuses of sensationalism. Taylor wrote: "Plainly, therefore, we must admit that the production of a sensation is not, in itself, an evil thing in eloquence, and cannot be regarded as that which we designate sensationalism."[6] More precisely, Tucker viewed sensationalism as robbing truth of its reality by employing "unfit, exaggerated, and unscrupulous methods" in order to

---

[5] John A. Broadus. "On Sensation Preaching" (Lecture presented as one of the Lyman Beecher Lectures on Preaching at Yale University, January–February 1889), The John A. Broadus Collection, Southern Seminary Library Archives, Louisville, KY.

[6] William Taylor, "Sensationalism in Preaching," *The North American Review* 128:201 (February 1879): 203.

"gain a hearing."[7] Taylor went on to suggest that it was "the deliberate production by the preacher of an immediate effect which is not subordinated to the great purpose of his office, and is out of harmony with the sacred associations of the house of God."[8] In Dargan's revision of Broadus's *A Treatise on the Preparation and Delivery of Sermons*,[9] sensationalism was described in opposition to a legitimate pursuit of freshness. The revision stated:

> There is, however, a marked difference between fresh-ness and *sensation* in preaching. In trying to be fresh, preachers sometimes succeed only in being sensa-tio*nal*. Pertinency and timeliness in the application of Christian truth to the real present life and its grave problems are supremely important, but ministering to the prurient curiosity of the excited crowd, assailing men and measures with cheap and unseemly invec-tive, spending valuable time and strength in discussing mere side issues which have been unduly exaggerated for the time being into momentous concerns,—this is sensationalism.[10] (Editor italics added)

Taken together, a composite description of sensational preach-ing may be suggested as *using any means to gain the ear of, or have an effect on, the audience that does not honor the sacred nature of God and the things of God or ensure singular focus on the spiritual and theological message of God in the text.*

Sensation as a Positive Element in Preaching

Those who warned of the abuses of sensationalism, how-ever, did not suggest that appeals to the senses should be utterly

---

[7] William Jewett Tucker, *The Making and the Unmaking of the Preacher* (Boston: Houghton, Mifflin, and Company, 1898), 65.

[8] Taylor, "Sensationalism," 203.

[9] Hereafter, *A Treatise on the Preparation and Delivery of Sermons* will be referred to simply as *Treatise*.

[10] John A. Broadus, *A Treatise on the Preparation and Delivery of Sermons*, rev. ed. by Edwin C. Dargan (New York: Harper & Brothers, 1926), 149–51.

avoided. They understood sensation's potential, rightly applied, for arresting the attention of the congregation. In the course of his lecture on sensation preaching, Broadus stated: "Preachers must do all they can with propriety do, to make preaching attract attention—wake men up—compel them to listen, think, remember."[11] DeWitt Talmadge, of the Brooklyn Tabernacle, whose name was often associated with sensationalism, spoke of its potential merits when he declared:

> If a man, stands in his pulpit with the dominant idea of giving entertainment—mere intellectual entertainment or the stirring of the risibilities of his congregation—he is committing blasphemy; but if he proposes to make a sensation by introducing gospel principles in preference to worldly principles and bringing men to repentance for their sins and to faith in God, then the more sensationalism he has (with such ends in view) the better.[12]

Broadus also noted regarding the use of "startling statements and extreme cases," that the fact that sensational methods may be misunderstood was no proof that they should never be used.[13] Sensational methods, made subject to the sacredness of God and His purpose of transforming lives, could be employed with great effect to gain the ear of the listener. It was, however, the abuse of sensationalism that garnered the most attention. Baxter discovered that "ten of the Lyman Beecher lectures condemned

---

[11] Broadus, *Lecture.* Additionally Spurgeon in his *Lectures to My Students* wrote concerning the congregation that "their attention must be gained, or nothing can be done with them: and it must be retained, or we may go on word-spinning, but no good will come of it." *Lectures to My Students,* reprint (Grand Rapids: Baker, 1980), 137. David Burrell near the turn of the twentieth century wrote, "The preacher must have the attention of his audience or his preaching will be as unprofitable as baying at the moon or sowing sand. . . . In order to gain attention he must literally produce a 'sensation.' . . . It is for the preacher to make his auditors open their eyes and prick up their ears." *The Sermon: Its Construction and Delivery* (New York: Fleming H. Revell, 1913), 271.

[12] DeWitt Talmadge, quoted in Burrell, *The Sermon,* 271–72. No citation was given for Talmage's quote.

[13] Broadus, *Lecture.*

sensational preaching" adding that, "while only four of the speakers were found to indicate the need for interestingness in the sermon, ten pointed out the danger of too great a striving for interest and attention."[14]

Forms in Which Sensationalism Appears

Sensationalism may appear at many points in the preaching process. The majority of its manifestations, however, are found in three basic forms: (1) the advertising of sermons and/or sermon themes, (2) the theme or subject matter of the message, and (3) the use of language within the message.[15]

The Advertising of Sermons or Sermon Themes

Broadus warned that, in advertising subjects, there was a constant temptation to select topics (and deliver sermons), that appealed to interests that were not "really spiritual."[16] He and many others recognized the trap that many preachers had fallen into in which they had begun to rely more on the phraseology of their themes than on the theology of the Word.[17] It was not

---

[14] Batsell B. Baxter, *The Heart of the Yale Lectures* (New York: MacMillan, 1947), 138.

[15] Burrell summarized the categories as "Sensationalism of the Manifesto," "Sensationalism of the Theme," and "Sensationalism of Treatment" (*The Sermon*, 272–74). His works serve as an apt reflection of the writings of Broadus and his contemporaries. The reader is also referred to Baxter's Yale *Lectures* (as well as the individual writings of the homileticians he cites) and Taylor's article "Sensationalism in Preaching."

[16] Broadus, *Lecture*.

[17] Taylor wrote, "So when subjects are announced beforehand of such a character as the following: A Man getting out of a Ship; How Jonah lost his Umbrella; The Speckled Bird; A Little Man up a Tree; The Run-away Knock, we can not but recognize in such advertisements so many deliberate baits to catch a crowd, and it is impossible that the sermons should not be constructed with a view to pander to the multitudes when they come. All this is beginning at the wrong end, and is a mistaking of the expectation of curious hearers for that genuine acceptance which sooner or later always follows excellence. But worse it is a deliberate letting down of the great aim of the Christian ministry, and makes the gather of a large assemblage the primary object of the preacher; while the spiritual instruction of the people is treated as secondary and subordinate. We do not find fault with advertising the services. . . . But this hunting for taking sermonic titles, much as the author of a new romance cudgels his brain for a

advertisement of the services themselves that created an issue, but the promoting of tantalizing topics that compromised the goal of spiritual instruction and passionate proclamation.[18]

The Theme or Subject Matter of the Message

Broadus had much to say regarding the theme and subject matter of the sermon. In his lecture on sensation preaching, he also warned of the divisiveness of preaching on politics, the evil of promoting heresy to draw a crowd, and the shallow spiritual environment that too strong a focus on secular themes fostered.[19] This was not to say that Broadus condemned "Subject sermons" altogether. On the contrary, he noted in his *Treatise* that the address can be instructive and beneficial to both the preacher and the congregation. He stipulated, however, that in order for them to be truly fruitful, they must be derived from "precisely that which the text most naturally presents."[20] Specific topics reflecting secular themes were powerful tools for illustration and application but were not to be considered as legitimate material for the primary theme of a sermon.[21]

The Use of Language within the Message

Broadus also addressed the use of language within the sermon. During the Yale lectures he focused specifically on the pitfalls of humor and inordinate displays of learning. Broadus saw humor as an acceptable mode of communication. He did so,

---

fancy name to it, is out of all taste. Thus the subjects are chosen, not because the minister feels that there is something existing among his hearers that he can not keep silence about, or because there is something in his own heart which is as a burning fire shut up in his bones which he is weary with forbearing and he can not stay, but because he wishes to outrival others who have gone into the same line with himself." Taylor, "Sensationalism in Preaching," 205.

[18] Some preachers of the day, it was said, always advertised their topics hoping to draw people "by the quaintness of eccentricity of their titles." Matthew Simpson, *Lectures on Preaching* (New York: Philip & Hunt, 1879), 136.

[19] Broadus, *Lecture.*

[20] John A. Broadus, *A Treatise on the Preparation and Delivery of Sermons*, 10th ed. (New York: A. C. Armstrong & Son, 1887), 289–93. All subsequent references to "*A Treatise*" refer to this volume.

[21] Broadus, *Lecture.*

however, with the qualifications that it was natural to the situation and the preacher, the minister had the ability to "completely carry the congregation back with him" to the serious propositions of the gospel, and it was never accomplished through irreverence.[22] The preacher must be aware, Broadus warned, of the fact that many listeners were not able to pass from "grave to gay" and back again as easily as the speaker might.

The attempt to demonstrate great learning in preaching, where it clouds the communication of truth, was to be utterly avoided. Broadus wrote, "The most important property of style is perspicuity."[23] He displayed his disdain for affected approaches by stating, "Pretentious obscurity may excite a poor admiration, unmeaning prettiness may give a certain pleasure . . . but only truth, and truth that is understood, can bring real benefit."[24] He suggested that this can be accomplished by using words that are familiar to the listener and express the thought being communicated as precisely as possible.[25] This was eloquence to him. Broadus defined *eloquence* as "so speaking as not merely to convince the judgment, kindle the imagination, and move the feelings, but to give a powerful impulse to the will."[26] He sternly rebuked "vain pretenders who care only to please" and who regularly substituted "vain and worthless stuff" for genuine eloquence.[27] Having one's "fancy charmed" by a sermon as one might be moved by a poem or novel could never produce the powerful impulse on the will that true eloquence demands.[28]

---

[22] Ibid.

[23] Broadus, *Treatise*, 339. Broadus demonstrated the degree of importance which he placed on this subject matter by devoting nearly 19 pages to its discussion (339–357). Burrell quipped, "Pedants affect profundity; simplicity is the fashion of true scholarship; and the people can be trusted to distinguish between a fog and a sunrise."

[24] Ibid., 341.

[25] Ibid., 343–47.

[26] Ibid., 20.

[27] Ibid., 21. This is diametrically opposed to certain voices within the emergent church movement who not only use vulgarity but amazingly defend it as legitimate means of cultural communication. http://www.worldviewweekend. com/secure/cwnetwork/article.php?ArticleID=1742.

[28] Ibid., 20.

Major Criticisms of Sensation Preaching

It would be cumbersome to attempt an engagement of each of the arguments against sensationalistic preaching on a case-by-case basis. But the bulk of the objections, however, can be summarized into three basic categories the difficulty of maintaining any "gains" that might be made through sensational methods, the demeaning nature of the practice, and the harm that such preaching causes for both the preacher and the congregation.

Sensationalism as a Means to Gain and Keep Attention Is Difficult to Maintain

Broadus and other writers of the period warned against the precedent that sensational preaching sets. Once employed, sensational methods must become increasingly sensational if the preacher hopes to keep the audience he has gained. The strain and pressure to surmount past "performances" can become great.[29] To Broadus, preaching was a spiritual activity, and ministry focused on feeding the souls of the listener to draw

---

[29] Kelman remarked on the downward spiral that sensationalism brings, saying, "There are but few preachers so unfortunate as to be able to keep it up." John Kelman, *The War and Preaching* (London: Hodder & Stoughton, 1919), 161, quoted from Baxter, *Yale Lectures*, 139. Faunce wrote that "any man can secure attention for a few Sundays—but can he hold it for twenty years? Any man can secure absorbing interest by sensationalism in speech or garb or action; but the penalty of using strong spices is that the quantity of spice must be constantly increased to stir the jaded palate. Mere exhortation soon becomes wearisome to him that gives and him that takes. Physical fervor will not long serve as substitute for ideas. Pulmonary eloquence soon exhausts itself and its audience." William H. P. Faunce, *The Educational Ideal in the Ministry* (New York: MacMillan, 1911), 138. Taylor warned that the temptation among churches to seek ministers who could fill the pews (and subsequently they hoped the offering plates) by sensational antics would create only a momentary rush that would pass away as quickly as it came. Taylor, "Sensationalism," 210–11. John Hall declared, "Gains made by appealing to the 'risible faculties' of man tend to be dissipated in other directions," suggesting therefore that "our attractiveness, then, had better depend on clearness of enunciation and style, on natural grace of expression, on manliness, force, and sufficient rapidity of movement, and on vehemence not out of proportion to the temper and tone of the matter we utter." John Hall, *God's Word through Preaching* (New York: Dodd & Mead, 1875), 169.

people in and encourage them to invite others.[30] Such a path was preferred over an indulgent dependence on sensationalism. According to Broadus, "to make sermons such as the daily paper will . . . foster a growing appetite," and will make you "commit yourself to a downward movement, which must go faster, and lower every year."[31]

Sensationalism Is Demeaning to the Sacred Act of Preaching

Taylor was mentioned by Broadus as one whose ministry proved that sensationalism was not necessary to draw large crowds to hear the gospel.[32] He vehemently declared that the preacher was to rely on the cross of Christ as his only draw rather than the questionable attraction of sensationalism. The preaching of the cross, he held, was the only thing that in the end would prove to be sufficient in leading men to Christ, transforming them, and keeping them in the faith.[33] The passion of Broadus, Taylor, and others was borne out largely by their view that cheap tricks employed through advertising, shocking language, and pulpit performance were demeaning to the office and commission of the preacher. The subject matter was too grave and the costs too high to trifle with faddish appeals to human curiosity.[34] The pulpit was, to Broadus and those who shared his convictions, no place for cuteness. The opponents of sensationalism tended to have no problem with advertis-

---

[30] Taylor, "Sensationalism," 210–11.

[31] Broadus, *Lecture*.

[32] Ibid.

[33] Taylor, "Sensationalism," 211.

[34] Hall aptly summarized the prevailing mood of the opponents of sensation preaching in regard to reverence when he stated: "Men feel that while we are handling grave and most serious matters we ought to be serious. Did you ever see the pilot take a ship through a perilous passage? He is grave. I have seen the surgeon's knife drawn round the limb where an error of an inch would have been a terrible mistake. He was grave. I have heard a conscientious judge weigh and set out in the utmost fullness the evidence in a murder case, as earnestly bent on putting everything fairly as if his own life depended on the issue. Any levity here would be out of place; and, on the same principle, by the average of mankind, gravity will be looked for in us who deal with matters of life and death, and speak for God." Hall, *Preaching*, 170.

ing titles and topics but rather with the tendency in those who used such means toward "smartness" in the wording of them.[35] Taylor asserted: "We have heard fears expressed lest the pulpit should die of dignity; but that is no reason why it should be murdered by irreverence."[36] Broadus too lamented that preachers often spoke of sacred things, and even of God Himself, in far too familiar terms. Therefore he exhorted his listeners at the Beecher Lectures to "abjure and abhor all real irreverence in the pulpit."[37]

Sensationalism Is Harmful to Both the Preacher and the Listener

Broadus noted that sometimes great harm could be directly attributed to sensation preaching.[38] In his *Lectures on the History of Preaching* he wrote:

> It is scarcely necessary to caution you against the love of *sensation* which marks our excitable age. We see this in many writers of history and romance, even in some writers on science, to say nothing of numerous politicians and periodicals. A few preachers, some of them weak, but some really strong men, have fallen in with this tendency of the time. Where they have done much real good, it has been rather in spite of this practice than by means of it, and they should be instructive as a warning.[39]

Sensation preaching was seen as detrimental to the spiritual well-being of both the preacher and the audience.

---

[35] Men like Kelman saw this as a cheap ploy that made the preacher appear to be a peddler of "cheap wares." Kelman, *War and Preaching,* 161. Burrell noted that the advertising of such "outlandish" subjects as "Love and Courtship" and the "Snuffers of Divine Grace" would ultimately cause a "loss of self-respect" and a sacrificing of the "general esteem" of the listener. The practice, to him, recalled the midway barker who stood outside the doorway of the freak-show tent. Burrell, *The Sermon,* 273.

[36] Taylor, "Sensationalism," 207.

[37] Broadus, *Lecture.*

[38] Ibid.

[39] Broadus, *History,* 234.

Harm Brought to the Preacher

Sensation preaching can prove to be a snare for the preacher. Conscious exaggeration and the desire to say something "smart" (i.e., catchy) can become greater in the preacher's mind than his commission to preach the truth. Irreverent handling of the truth created a process of moral decline.[40] This happened when the preacher who "deals in the sensational method" came to no longer be able to take truth seriously because he had grown into the habit of using it for "mere effect."[41] Beyond that, Broadus remarked that it could tempt the preacher to begin to aim for the applause of the audience rather than a meaningful and respectful connection with them.[42] Finally, habitually basing sermons on popular vices created a danger of seeming to be too familiar with them and, again, would lower the preacher's worthiness in the eyes of the people.[43] Sensation preaching did not just harm the minister, however; it was also damaging to the congregation.

Harm Brought to the Listener

Sensationalism, the critics charged, distracted the congregation from vital truth and trained them to seek thrilling rhetoric more than solid biblical preaching. By making subjects such as major events, popular sins, or politics, the central focus of the message, the preacher actually distracted the listener. This diversion effectively kept the minister from communicating the spiritual truths of Scripture, which he had been called of God to deliver. Broadus wrote that it was

---

[40] Taylor remarked that "every time he (the preacher) deviates from or adds to the real state of the case he makes himself a worse man. Truth is the girdle of character, and he who loosens that is on the way to looseness in other departments of morality. He is on an inclined plane, and may some day produce the biggest sensation of his life by a terrible fiasco." Another danger in sensation preaching is that "such trifling" weakens the listener's confidence in the preacher and creates doubt that he "has a message for them from God." Taylor, "Sensationalism," 209–10.

[41] Tucker, *Making and Unmaking*, 65.

[42] Broadus, *Lecture*.

[43] Ibid.

perfectly proper to make references to recent events that specially interest[ed] the congregation, by way of illustration or of particular application. But remember this, illustration, application, and allusions must not be of such a nature, or so presented, as to distract attention from properly religious truth and duty.[44]

Sensation preaching built around earthly subject matter jaded the spiritual palate of the hearer and numbed their spiritual sensitivities. This led invariably to a diminished ability on their part to discern between sermons that only please the ear and excite the emotions and those which are truly spiritual. Once trained on a diet of sensational preaching, the listener lost his ability to distinguish between feeling and faith, divine truth, and duty.[45]

The question remained, given the tenets of the discussion thus far, what was the preacher to do? It has been said that in order to gain and hold attention some level of sensation must be used. It has also been argued that there was a great potential for harm. If that was indeed the case, how was the preacher to properly utilize sensation in the context of preaching?

The Example of Jesus: An Answer to the Problem of Sensation Preaching

Broadus provided a compelling answer. In his *Lectures on the History of Preaching,* he declared that "the notion of our 'sensation preachers' contain an element of truth. And to find that

---

[44] Ibid.

[45] Taylor's words in this regard are exceedingly revealing and must be shared at length to avoid losing the force of his displeasure at what he had observed. "One can see at a glance that it is hurtful to the hearers. It not only depraves their tastes, but it blunts their sensibilities. It renders them largely impervious to the ordinary presentation of truth. The pampered appetite disdains everything that is not gamey; and he who peppers the highest is surest to please. They have confounded the intoxication created in them by the gratification of their perverted tastes with that totally different thing which the apostle describes when he says, Be ye filled with the Spirit. It makes little difference whether intoxication be produced by the vulgar absinthe or the aristocratic champagne; the thing is always bad, and is not to be mistaken for the enthusiasm of a sober man. And the misfortune is that, in the case of those of whom we speak, a sensuous effect is regarded as a spiritual result to the detriment both of the self-deceiver and of the church at large." Taylor, "Sensationalism," 209.

true and good and mighty something which they grope after in darkness and do not reach, we have but to study the preaching of Jesus Christ."[46] He further asserted: "Jesus did not go out as 'a boy preacher,' and he wrought no miracles merely to gather crowds. . . . No thoughtful person would think of saying that Jesus was a sensation preacher."[47] Taylor's views effectively mirrored those of Broadus in challenging preachers to look to Christ who, when faced with multitudes seeking miracles and self-gratification, did not submit to them but rather preached a "deeply spiritual" message that resulted in the idly curious being driven away.[48] Broadus recognized the difficulty in attempting to speak exhaustively in regard to the preaching of Jesus and so stated: "Our Lord as a Preacher is a topic that has waited through all the ages for thorough treatment, and is waiting still."[49] However, he offered several aspects of the preaching of Christ that could be employed to guard the minister against the practice of inappropriately sensational preaching. He described how the preaching of Jesus demonstrated *authority, originality, appeal to the common mind, controversy, repetition, variety of method*, and a particular *tone and spirit*.

The Authority in the Preaching of Jesus

Jesus did not preach from a position of reliance on the rabbinical teachings handed down through the generations. To the Jew of the day, truth was best settled by reference to the

---

[46] Broadus, *History*, 35.

[47] Broadus, *Lecture*.

[48] Taylor, "Sensationalism," 211. His full quote is poignant and states, "Let him not forget that, when the sensation-loving multitude sought Him (Jesus) that they might see his miracles, he declined to gratify their curiosity, and gave them instead that deeply spiritual sermon which drove them largely away. But it was with the winnowed men that remained that he laid the foundations of his church. The call of the age for the exciting is a temptation to be resisted, rather than an influence to be yielded to, and if in resisting it the multitudes should be offended, then let them be offended, for in that case the discipline is only what they need. But they will not be offended, for, wherever the gospel is faithfully and earnestly proclaimed, the common people hear it gladly."

[49] Broadus, *"History,"* 22.

accumulated opinions of the respected teachers of the past.[50] In contrast, Jesus spoke from a personal prerogative that exceeded that of the rabbis. He spoke in a "tone of conscious and true authority."[51] No man can assume to be Christ's equal in this respect. One can, nevertheless, proclaim the Word of God with authority. Broadus remarked that "in truth every preacher who is to accomplish much must, in his manner and degree, speak with authority."[52] In light of that, he suggested means by which the preacher could attain a rightful authority to preach.[53]

1. *Personal study of Scripture*—What is gained by diligent personal study will be "unconsciously state[d] with a tone of authority."[54] This point cannot be overemphasized in the theory and convictions of Broadus and therefore warrants more thorough development than those that follow. He strongly emphasized this element of a preacher's life and ministry in his *Treatise* declaring that:

> the Scriptures themselves should at every period of his life be a preacher's chief study. . . . In the originals if possible, in the English version at any rate; by the rapid reading of large portions, by the thorough study of a given book, by the minute examination of particular passages, and sometimes even by looking at a sentence here and there as we turn over the leaves; by reading in company with others, for discussion or for sympathy, by reading when alone with our beating hearts and our God; by adopting new methods for variety, and by steadily maintaining old methods until they become habitual; by reading when we enjoy it, as a pleasure, and when at the beginning we do not enjoy it, as a duty,—every way, and continually, let us keep

---

50 Ibid.
51 Ibid.
52 Ibid., 23.
53 Ibid.
54 Ibid.

up, freshen, extend our acquaintance with the precious Word of God.[55]

Additionally, in the Yale Lectures, Broadus dedicated an entire session to the discussion of the "Minister and His Bible" in which, among other salient points, he presented various reasons the minister ought to read the Word. These include his personal benefit, to gain materials for preaching and teaching, to ease the search for texts on which to preach, to be able to quote Scripture "freely and felicitously," to be able to read the text aloud in an "interesting and impressive manner," and to gain a thorough knowledge of the Bible in order to preach expository messages.[56]

2. *Personal systematizing of the truths of Scripture*—examining every aspect of a proposed truth in light of the authentic teachings of Scripture. If the preacher was adequately to teach and exert lasting influence on the hearer, he must develop skill in systematic theology. This ability would allow him to "speak with the boldness of assured conviction," and to unfold and apply one text "without fear of offending another."[57]

3. *Personal experience of the power of the truth.*

4. *Personal character*—Personal piety was a "prime requisite to efficiency in preaching," and would gain for the preacher the sympathy of the listeners and entitle him to their respect.[58]

5. *Personal growth* as manifested through usefulness achieved by the practice of the sources listed above.[59]

---

[55] Broadus, *Treatise,* 121–22.

[56] John A. Broadus, "The Minister and His Bible" (lecture presented as one of the Lyman Beecher Lectures on Preaching at Yale University, January–February 1889), The John A. Broadus Collection, Southern Seminary Library Archives, Louisville, KY. Broadus continues here by explaining that one reason for this is a growing acceptance in the time of certain English and Scottish preachers evidently known for exposition. Further, he noted that weak and wearisome examples, offered by poor practitioners, were no reason to avoid preaching expositorily.

[57] Broadus, *Treatise,* 122.

[58] Ibid., 23.

[59] Broadus, *History,* 23.

In the *Treatise* Broadus delineated the primary role of Scripture in relation to authoritative proclamation stating:

> The Scriptures themselves are an authority indeed. All that they testify to be fact is thereby fully proven, all that they teach as true and right is thereby established and made obligatory. . . . The Christian reasoner should seek fully to appreciate this unparalleled authority, and should heedfully observe its proper relation to all other means of proof.[60]

The minister must be diligently aware of the danger of beginning to approach Scripture as merely "a professional duty," and instead foster a spirit of reverence before it that God would bless both himself and those he would strive to teach.[61] While the preacher can never equal the authoritative stance of Christ, he can, nonetheless speak with authority by intimate knowledge with, and faithful proclamation of the Word of God.

Originality in the Preaching of Jesus

Broadus noted Jesus' originality but chose not to dwell on the subject in his lectures stating that it had been sufficiently covered, and perhaps even overemphasized by popular writers of the day.[62] One could, however, glean his views on the subject from his writings in the *Treatise*. He held that "in the world of ideas it is very difficult to be absolutely original . . . but relatively, any man may be original, and to some extent every man is so."[63] Men may think thoughts original to themselves, even though they may have been thought in times past by others. Broadus referred to this as *relative* originality and explained that such thinking invigorates and motivates the preacher. He cautioned, however, that "the basis of preaching cannot be original, because it must come from Scripture."[64] While no one can

---

[60] Broadus, *Treatise*, 185.
[61] Ibid., 122.
[62] Broadus, *History*, 23.
[63] Broadus, *Treatise*, 128.
[64] Ibid., 128–29.

be original in the manner of Christ, it was possible to stimulate relative originality through a deepening understanding of the Bible and astute application of it to the human condition.[65] A final warning from the *Treatise* on the subject held that "he who runs after material for discourse that shall be absolutely new, may get credit for originality, and be amply admired, but he will not exert the living power that belongs to eloquence."[66]

Relation to the Common Mind in the Preaching of Jesus

Broadus did not want thinking about the originality of Christ's preaching to overshadow the fact that Jesus used plain language and familiar terms in order to make the truth available to common men. Speaking of Jesus' preaching, Broadus declared: "He did not startle His hearers with His originality, but employed current modes of thought and expressions."[67] His illustrations were drawn from familiar aspects of everyday life and employed parables to express difficult ideas so that they could be "remembered for future reflection."[68] Jesus' originality was built upon truth already understood by the ordinary mind of His listeners. In his *Treatise*, Broadus developed this idea under the subject of perspicuity.[69] There he emphasized the necessity of preaching that used "words and phrases that will be intelligible to our audience" and terms that "exactly express our thought."[70]

Controversy in the Preaching of Jesus

Broadus wrote that Jesus "was constantly aiming at some error or evil practice existing among His hearers" and that "there are very few of His utterances that have not a distinc-

---

[65] Ibid.
[66] Ibid., 22. Broadus defines eloquence as "so speaking as not merely to convince the judgment, kindle the imagination, and move the feelings, but to give a powerful impulse to the will." *Treatise*, 20.
[67] Broadus, *History*, 24.
[68] Ibid., 24–25.
[69] Broadus, *Treatise*, 339.
[70] Ibid., 343–46.

tively polemical character."[71] In fact, he went so far as to say that to forget this aspect of His preaching was to risk failing "to make a just interpretation of His teachings."[72] Broadus's own words best revealed the force of his argument:

> Truth, in this world oppressed with error, cannot hope, has no right, to keep the peace. Christ came not to cast peace upon the earth but a sword. We must not shrink from antagonism and conflict in proclaiming the gospel, publicly or privately; though in fearlessly maintaining this conflict we must not sacrifice courtesy, or true Christian charity.[73]

In applying this concept to the human preacher, Broadus once again cautioned that the minister should examine his own tendencies (either to be pugnacious or fearful) and seek a "golden mean" that neither sought controversy nor attempted to hide from it. One should not avoid following the example of the preaching of Jesus, which at times used terms of "terrible severity" in opposing those who were in error.[74] It was virtually impossible, he held, to declare some aspects of truth without actively opposing that which was false. He wrote: "The idea that a man can always 'talk about what he himself believes, and let other people's opinions alone,' is impracticable, if it were not improper. In many cases we cannot clearly define truth, save by contrasting it with error."[75] He also noted that "since errors held and taught by good men are only the more likely to be hurtful to others, we are surely not less bound to refute them in such cases as when advocated by bad men."[76] In conclusion, he advised that some controversies are perhaps best ignored

---

[71] Broadus, *History*, 25–26.
[72] Ibid., 26.
[73] Ibid., 26–27.
[74] Broadus, *Treatise*, 96. That is the preaching specifically of Paul and Peter as it was modeled after the "Master" (i.e., Jesus Christ).
[75] Ibid.
[76] Ibid. Broadus would prove true to this view in the dismissal of C. H. Toy, whom he dearly loved, from the seminary faculty for embracing the tenets of higher criticism.

because to oppose them only gives them more publicity and strength than they might have ever mustered on their own.[77]

Repetition in the Preaching of Jesus

In the New Testament Jesus (apart from simply looking at parallel accounts of the same incident) made great use of repetition. Broadus reported that "our Lord's frequent repetitions are remarkable and instructive."[78] Many examples exist throughout the New Testament of Jesus repeating the fundamental tenets of His teachings such as His mission, servanthood, humility, etc.[79] Jesus was not limited in His knowledge or in His ability to communicate. Yet He chose to use repetition as a rhetorical device. Since this was the case, Broadus concluded that "he repeated because it was best to repeat."[80]

Broadus disdained the clamoring of his age for all things novel. He felt that preachers were chasing after numerous worldly things to avoid being repetitious. He cautioned that "freshness and variety are very desirable, no doubt; but the fundamental truths of Christianity are not numerous, and men really need to have them often repeated."[81] Preachers should work diligently at understanding the audience to which they preach but "nearly all of the good that preachers do is done not by new truths but by old truths, with fresh combination, illustration, application, experience, but old truths, yea, and often repeated in similar phrase, without apology and without fear."[82] In the *Treatise* Broadus wrote: "A just rhetoric, if there were no higher consideration, would require that a preacher shall preach the gospel—shall hold on to old truths, and labor to clothe them with new interest and power."[83] The preacher should avoid the impulse continually to seek new things to stimulate the audience. Rather, in following the example of Jesus, the

---

[77] Ibid., 97.

[78] Broadus, *History,* 27.

[79] Ibid., 27–29. In this section Broadus provides numerous specific examples of phrases and teachings, with their textual reference, that are repeated.

[80] Ibid.

[81] Ibid.

[82] Ibid.

[83] Broadus, *Treatise,* 22.

pulpit orator must strive to teach the foundational truths of the Word in fresh ways and as often as possible.

Variety of Methods Observed in the Preaching of Jesus

While maintaining focus on several foundational truths, Jesus, nonetheless, delivered them with great variety. Broadus named three areas in which Jesus employed variety in His proclamation.[84] These included: *variety of place* (Jesus spoke at numerous venues including the synagogue, mountains, deserts, homes, crowds, one-on-one, "anywhere, everywhere"); *variety of occasion* (sometimes He spoke at occasions reflecting significant junctures of His ministry, others times he shared during seemingly isolated events); and v*ariety of modes of stating truth* (Jesus used assertions, illustrations, explanation, argumentation, appeal, warning, and "pithy, and paradoxical hyperbolic statements," to deliver truth to an audience that was sometimes indifferent and often hostile).[85] The truths that Jesus delivered using striking terminology were sometimes perplexing and often misunderstood, but they were rarely forgotten.[86] Again in the *Treatise,* Broadus instructed the preacher to vary the energy and passion of his delivery. This was to allow the listener to recover from highly impassioned moments in the message and, therefore, facilitate more effective communication.[87] Jesus' example demonstrated that monotony was not the aim in attempting to avoid sensational preaching.

The Tone and Spirit in the Preaching of Jesus

Because, without the luxury of being actually present as He taught, it is impossible exhaustively to analyze Jesus' tone and spirit. One is limited to seeking to develop a pattern to emulate based on what is described in Scripture. Broadus wrote that

---

[84] Broadus, *History*, 31.
[85] Ibid., 31–33.
[86] Ibid., 32–33.
[87] Broadus, *Treatise*, 378–79.

we must meditate on His perfect fidelity to truth, and yet perfect courtesy and kindliness; His severity in rebuking without any tinge of bitterness; His directness and simplicity, and yet His tact—wise as the serpent, with the simplicity of the dove; His complete sympathy with man, and also sympathy with God.[88]

Broadus's idea of "sympathy" can best be described by one of his most often quoted passages in his *Treatise*.

When a man who is apt in teaching, whose soul is on fire with the truth, which he trusts,

> has saved him and hopes will save others, speaks to his fellow-men, face to face, eye to eye, and electric sympathies flash to and fro between him and his hearers, till they lift each other up, higher and higher, into the intensest thought, and the most impassioned emotion—higher and yet higher, till they are borne as on chariots of fire above the world,—there is a power to move men, to influence character, life, destiny.[89]

In fact, so important was this aspect to Broadus that he felt that "if I were asked what is the first thing in effective preaching, I should say sympathy; and what is the second thing, I should say sympathy; and what is the third thing, sympathy."[90] Jesus' manner of preaching allowed Him to demonstrate great authority without sacrificing His approachability and connection with the listener.

Broadus argued that by following the example of Jesus the preacher could avoid being sensationalistic in his preaching. Christ never struggled to attract a crowd. He did so, however, not by appealing to the carnal cravings of the populace but by demonstrating authority, originality, sympathetic tone and spirit, and the proper use of originality, controversy, variety, and repetition.

---

[88] Broadus, *History*, 35.
[89] Broadus, *Treatise*, 18.
[90] V. L. Stanfield, "Elements of Strength in the Preaching of John Albert Broadus," *The Review and Expositor* 48, no. 4 (October 1951): 395.

Conclusion

John Albert Broadus was an extraordinary man born in an extraordinary age. As is true in this current era, his was a day of rapid change and shifting culture in nearly every avenue of life. Such developments created an atmosphere that compelled men to chase after increasingly new and exciting things. Preaching was, and is, not immune to the effects of such an environment. In fact, many ministers of the day had fallen prey to the temptation of sensation preaching. Catchy sermon titles advertised before the messages, trite subject matter focused on physical pursuits, and speech ranging from adorned to pedantic had become all too common for the tastes of preaching purists like Broadus. It was noted that the trend was creating a downward slope of degrading spirituality in both the ministers that practiced such preaching and the congregations that heard it. The habit of sensationalism was also found to lower the estimation of both the minister and God in the eyes of the listener. Sensation was necessary, in some degree, to attract and maintain attention, but it was never to replace deeply spiritual pursuits as the primary draw for the gospel.

What was Broadus's solution? He said simply to look to the model of Jesus. He challenged the preacher to emulate the Master rather than the faddish movements of the day. He called the minister to uphold the dignity of his office by shunning the temptation to follow the easier and more popular route of indulging the often worldly tastes of the crowd and instead follow the example of Christ. In short, Broadus exhorted the minister to subject every aspect of the preaching act to the spiritual purposes for which God created it. He wrote that the sermon and minister should exhibit, "1) An absorbing spirit, aim, and purpose, 2) A profound reverence for sacred things, and 3) A whole souled earnestness."[91]

This essay has served to shed a bit of light on Broadus's views of the nineteenth-century practice of sensation preaching.

---

[91] Broadus, *Lecture.*

It is hoped that the information gathered here regarding the benefits, evils, and safeguards against sensationalism will inform and invigorate the discussion regarding some of the current practices being observed in preaching today. Are contemporary trends involving multimedia, "seeker sensitive" practices, and "less is more" philosophies merely displays of modern sensationalism? Is the emergent movement simply a twenty-first-century version of the spiritual downgrade that Broadus and others spoke against? Has the form of preaching in question tended toward the omission of vital truths of the gospel in order to appeal to the most people possible? Mohler stated:

> The approach of many churches—and preachers—has been to present helpful and practical messages, often with generalized Christian content, but without any clear presentation of the Gospel or call to decision and accountability to the text or to the claims of Christ. The apostles should be our model here, consistently preaching the death, burial and resurrection of Jesus Christ. Of course, in order for the Gospel to make sense, authentic preaching must also deal honestly with the reality of human sin and must do so with a candor equal to that of the biblical text. All this presents the preacher with some significant challenges in our age of "sensitivities." But, in the end, preaching devoid of this content—preaching that evades the biblical text and biblical truth—falls short of anything we can rightly call Christian preaching.[92]

Alarming trends are continuing to develop in some circles of the contemporary church. Pulpits and "platforms" are out;

---

[92] R. Albert Mohler Jr., "The State of Preaching Today," *Commentary by R. Albert Mohler Jr.,* http://almohler.com/commentary_print.php?cdate=2006-08-28. Likewise MacArthur warned that "sinners will be intolerant of the uncomfortable truths. That is to be expected. On the other hand, they will want to hear comfortable lies. They may seek what is sensational, entertaining, ego-building, non-threatening, and popular. But what we preach is dictated by God, not the crowds we face." John MacArthur and the faculty at Master's Seminary. *Rediscovering Expository Preaching* (Dallas: Word, 1992), xvi.

theatrically lit stages are in vogue. Suits and dress casual are out; the skateboarder look complete with untucked shirt, baggy jeans, and strategically placed facial hair is in. Prophetic and authoritative proclamation of the theological and spiritual demands of the text is out; relevant "talks" offering suggestions on the practical details of living with a biblical spin are in. Expository journeys through books of the Bible are out; topically themed and temporally focused sermon series promoted with slick marketing campaigns are in. All of this is carried out under the auspices of gaining hearers.

Is asking individuals to come to a church under the pretense of improving their sex lives, savings accounts, or self-esteem really the best strategy to create an opportunity to share with them their desperate need for the Savior? Is it realistic to believe that the preacher who indulges worldly pursuits in order to attract the listener will then be able to tell him that too much concern for such things is sinful without sounding ironic or hypocritical? Does such an emphasis on temporal things facilitate an environment that encourages people to "seek first the kingdom of heaven," and "set their minds on things above"? If an audience gathers for less than spiritual reasons, and is fed from spiritually diluted subject matter and content, is it then reasonable to hope that the result will be self-sacrificing and spiritually vibrant disciples? Such practices, at best, inadvertently downgrade the message of Scripture to the level of life enhancement and the role of Christ to that of "life coach."

What was Broadus's solution? Look to Jesus as a model for preaching. Broadus warned that the attractions many saw as acceptable means by which to draw a crowd might actually be doing real spiritual harm. He was not impressed by those who spent entire sermons on subjects which he saw as fitting only as points of illustration or application. He even conjectured that when spiritual good came from such an approach it was probably in spite of it rather than because of it. What was his solution? Look to Jesus.

Jesus' example challenges the preacher to speak with authority from the Word, corral overactive yearnings for originality with the beauty of plain speech, refuse to avoid or seek controversy but forthrightly to oppose error by the unapologetic proclamation of truth, and continually to repeat the foundational teachings of the gospel whenever and wherever the opportunity arises in heart-level sympathy with both God and man. How would Broadus advise today's preachers to avoid *gaining attention by means that do not honor the sacred nature of God and the things of God or ensure singular focus on the spiritual and theological message of God in the text*? Perhaps he would say "take up your cross and follow Christ."

The results revealed here suggest the need for a careful evaluation of the present age. For now Broadus's concluding words from his lecture "On Sensation Preaching" will provide a good starting point for those who wish to avoid the dangers of sensation preaching. He stated his convictions firmly and with a rhetorically poignant statement:

> What then shall be the conclusion of this whole matter? If you are naturally inclined to what others regard as sensational preaching, carefully word everything that would be really objectionable. Avoid also such frequently as might repel. Cultivate reverence, spirituality, earnestness, and good taste, and you can to some extent act out your bent. Consider the great importance of cultivating good taste, a delicate perception of aesthetic propriety—as to literary style—elocution—and appearance and demeanor—and so as to the matter we have been discussing. If, on the other hand, sensitively afraid of being sensational, or of being so regarded, yet when something swells within you, give it utterance. Be not fastidious or over sensitive. And be sure to reflect afterwards upon every impulsive saying, and learn from your mistakes.[93]

---

[93] Broadus, *Lecture.*

Chapter X

Broadus's Living Legacy

James Patterson

T he preceding chapters amply testify to the extraordinary impact of John A. Broadus as a preacher and homiletician; indeed, his exemplary accomplishments in those venues could stand by themselves in verifying the eminence of the man. At the same time Broadus embodied a rare combination of gifts that allowed him to excel on many fronts. Thomas McKibbens, who focused primarily on Broadus's preaching, nonetheless pointed to a bigger picture when he remarked that the nineteenth-century divine "possessed a gracious spirit, a love for truth, and a breadth of learning which made him one of the greatest Baptist leaders of all time."[1] Although Broadus battled health issues throughout most of his career, his impressive list of achievements in a wide range of contexts gives credence to McKibbens's assessment.

---

[1] Thomas R. McKibbens Jr., "John A. Broadus: Shaper of Baptist Preaching," *Baptist History & Heritage* 40 (Spring 2005): 21. This article is a revision of a section in McKibbens's book, *The Forgotten Heritage: A Lineage of Great Baptist Preaching* (Macon, GA: Mercer University Press, 1986), 187–97. The author gratefully acknowledges the research assistance rendered by Bill Sumners, director of the Southern Baptist Historical Library and Archives in Nashville, Tennessee. He also is indebted to the SBHLA for a Lynn May Study Grant, which defrayed some of the costs of doing research in Nashville.

The Broadus legacy was forged most notably in the emergent denominational life of Southern Baptists during the second half of the nineteenth century. In that setting Broadus functioned as one of the strategic pioneers or patriarchs who helped to shape the institutions, culture, and theological ethos of his denomination. W. O. Carver, who studied under Broadus and then served for almost 50 years on the faculty at The Southern Baptist Theological Seminary, measured his professor's broader attainments with this glowing tribute: "No Baptist of his generation surpassed Broadus in his influence among Southern Baptists."[2] Broadus's preaching undoubtedly constituted a weighty component of his fame; even so, as some earlier chapters have illustrated, his pulpit exploits overlapped considerably with several of his lesser-known credentials.

Apart from the obvious homiletical insights and skills, Broadus's crucial place in the Baptist—and wider evangelical—tradition is secure for three major reasons. First, he consistently defended and exemplified a vibrant biblical orthodoxy in a way that was both scholarly and respectful to the text of Scripture. Second, Broadus excelled in the roles of denominational servant and statesman at a time when Southern Baptists sorely needed unassuming and wise leadership. Finally, the Virginia-bred preacher established himself as one of the foremost Protestant theological educators of the nineteenth century during his many years of service at Southern Seminary. While these contributions do not fully explain the multifaceted Broadus heritage, they do represent the vital core of his enduring significance for Baptist life and thought today.

Advocate of Biblical Orthodoxy

In his seminary classroom, pulpit, and published writings, John Broadus vigorously articulated a biblical theology that upheld scriptural authority and preserved the historic orthodoxy of the Christian faith. A. T. Robertson, who built on the exegeti-

---

[2] W. O. Carver, quoted in William A. Mueller, *A History of Southern Baptist Theological Seminary* (Nashville: Broadman Press, 1959), 61.

cal tradition that Broadus had launched at Southern Seminary, once attempted to characterize his father-in-law's approach to the Bible and doctrine as "progressive conservatism."[3] Broadus himself, while acknowledging the progressive nature of divine revelation, nevertheless cautioned against a cavalier attitude toward "the faith once delivered." In his most definitive statement on biblical authority, for example, he warned that "a 'progressive orthodoxy' that forsakes or adds to the teaching of Christ becomes heterodoxy."[4] For Broadus, biblical and theological fidelity required some clear boundary markers as safeguards against heresy; he would not have supported the doctrinal pluralism that began to find a home in some Southern Baptist institutions by the mid-twentieth century. In fact, he confronted some issues in this regard quite early in the history of Southern Seminary when his colleague and former student Crawford Toy crossed the acceptable borders of orthodoxy in his views on the Pentateuch and Darwinism. Following Toy's resignation, Broadus and faculty chair James Boyce regretfully saw the Old Testament scholar off from the Louisville train station, both wishing that Toy's earlier evangelical beliefs had not been so substantially altered.[5]

Broadus's understanding of the inspiration and authority of Scripture reflected his basic conservatism. Unlike later neo-orthodox thinkers, he averred that the Bible was the "word of God" and did not merely "contain" it. In the same context he contended that the Baptists of his day remained essentially unified because they elevated the Bible over any other authority,

---

[3] A. T. Robertson, "As a Teacher" in "Broadus Memorial," *Seminary Magazine* 8 (April 1895): 360. This term was picked up by James Roland Barron in "The Contributions of John A. Broadus to Southern Baptists" (Th.D. diss., Southern Baptist Theological Seminary, 1972), 231. On the continuities between Broadus and Robertson, see David S. Dockery, "The Broadus-Robertson Tradition," in *Theologians of the Baptist Tradition*, ed. Timothy George and David S. Dockery (Nashville: Broadman & Holman, 2001), 90–114.

[4] John A. Broadus, *Paramount and Permanent Authority of the Bible* (Philadelphia: American Baptist Publication Society, 1887), 8. This is also available in a PDF format from http://www.BaptistTheology.org.

[5] Broadus, *Memoir of James Petigru Boyce, D.D., LL.D.* (New York: A. C. Armstrong and Son, 1893), 263–64.

whether it was reason, Christian "consciousness," the spirit of the age, the church, or subjective "inspiration." His *Catechism of Bible Teaching*, which was the first publication of the new Sunday School Board, likewise exhibited a high view of Scripture. Broadus did not commonly use the term *inerrancy*, but his sermon at the Southern Baptist Convention in 1883 indicated that he was unsympathetic with "attempts to show that the Bible contains errors."[6] Overall, his position meshed well with that of his Baptist forbearers; in addition, it generally accords with the three versions of the Baptist Faith and Message, all of which affirm Scripture as "the supreme standard by which all human conduct, creeds, and religious opinions should be tried."[7]

Broadus's biblical conservatism, however, was not simply a blind fideism but was entirely compatible with rigorous scholarship. In his faculty post at Southern Seminary, he taught New Testament interpretation as well as homiletics; his typically thorough pedagogy mandated extensive use of the Greek text and standard scholarly resources. J. Estill Jones, a Southern Seminary professor in a later era, aptly described the methods that Broadus employed in teaching and research:

> He treated textual considerations extensively and exercised some independence from recognized textual critics. He utilized church fathers, rabbis, reformers, and contemporary scholars. He dealt fairly with problems of chronology and revealed great ability in historical details.[8]

[6] See respectively Broadus, *Paramount and Permanent Authority of the Bible*, 1–8; idem, *A Catechism of Bible Teaching* (1892) in *Baptist Confessions, Covenants, and Catechisms*, ed. Timothy and Denise George (Nashville: Broadman & Holman, 1996), 261–63; and idem, *Three Questions as to the Bible* (Philadelphia: American Baptist Publication Society, 1883), 26–34. For comments made in the context of the conservative-moderate conflict in the SBC that linked Broadus's commitment to biblical authority with evangelism, see Lewis Drummond, "Theological Views on the Nature of the Bible and the Subsequent Impact on Evangelism and Missions," in *Proceedings of the Conference on Biblical Inerrancy, 1987* (Nashville: Broadman Press, 1987), 517–20.

[7] See a comparative listing in *Report of the Baptist Faith and Message Study Committee to the Southern Baptist Convention*, 14 June 2000, 2.

[8] J. Estill Jones, "The New Testament and Southern," *Review and Expositor* 82

In other words, Broadus fully realized that declaring biblical authority and inspiration did not exempt the Bible student from interpretive challenges. For him the truths of Scripture remained unchanged, but interpretations often varied from one cultural context to another.

At the same time Broadus encouraged the cause of responsible interpretation, particularly stressing the value of grammatical-historical exegesis. His *Commentary on the Gospel of Matthew* perhaps best displayed his careful interpretive procedures, as well as his commitment both to explicate and applied biblical truth. As Union University president David S. Dockery has commented, "Broadus's work on Matthew is a model commentary, and in many ways ushered in a new era of commentary writing within evangelical scholarship."[9] Broadus's stature as a biblical exegete thus underlines another notable feature of his legacy.

Besides his manifest passion for the Bible, Broadus drew on a keen historical sensitivity as he engaged in the hermeneutical task. Robertson, who knew something about the value of historical insight, remarked at Broadus's memorial service that his father-in-law "was fond of saying that history was the noblest of all human studies."[10] Broadus, for instance, especially treasured church history; he included it among the subjects that he pursued on his own after he received his M.A. from the University of Virginia in 1850, and then lectured on it at his church in Charlottesville. His historical work in turn enriched his perspective on interpretive developments through the ages.[11] To be sure, many of his publications in both biblical studies

(Winter 1985): 22.

[9] Dockery, "The Broadus-Robertson Tradition," 107. See Broadus, *Commentary on the Gospel of Matthew*, An American Commentary on the New Testament Series, ed. Alvah Hovey (Philadelphia: American Baptist Publication Society, 1886). For more on his significance for New Testament studies, see Barron, "The Contributions," 89–149.

[10] Robertson, "As a Teacher," 360.

[11] See, for example, Broadus, *Paramount and Permanent*, 12ff. On his personal study of Christian history and ensuing lectures, see Robertson, *Life and Letters of John Albert Broadus* (Philadelphia: American Baptist Publication Society, 1901), 77 and 118–19.

and other areas included references to historical figures like the church fathers, Bernard of Clairvaux, Thomas Aquinas, Martin Luther, and John Calvin. His deep appreciation for history also enhanced his proficiency in homiletics, as is seen unmistakably in his 1876 lectures at the Newton Theological Institute, which were published as *Lectures on the History of Preaching*.[12] For Baptists and other evangelicals in the early twenty-first century who frequently appear to suffer from historical amnesia, Broadus's grasp of and applications from history suggest an effective antidote.

In contrast to the liberal Protestantism that was expanding in late nineteenth-century America, Broadus unflinchingly granted miracles an honored status in his philosophy of history, theology, and attitude toward Scripture. In his 1890 lectures to the Young Men's Christian Association at John Hopkins University in Baltimore, he devoted an entire address to the miracles of Jesus. For Broadus, there was no way to separate the miraculous from Christ's personal character or ethical teachings: "Tear out the supernatural elements from the gospels, and the remainder will be no history at all, but a mass of shattered and broken matters worse than the ruins of so many noble buildings which the other day I left shapely and useful in the city where I dwell."[13] In what became an obvious sticking point between modernists and conservatives, Broadus unequivocally took the biblically orthodox position. It was not Broadus's style to engage in harsh and sustained polemics like some early twentieth-century fundamentalists; nevertheless, he refused to compromise on what he considered to be Christian essentials. In particular, he showed no sympathy for those who effectively gutted the Bible of its supernatural content. He assured the Baptists of his day

---

[12] Broadus, *Lectures on the History of Preaching* (New York: Sheldon & Company, 1876). Apparently this volume was the first account of the history of preaching in English. See E. C. Dargan, "As an Author" in "Broadus Memorial," 365.

[13] Broadus, *Jesus of Nazareth* (New York: A. C. Armstrong and Son, 1890), 72.

that it was a legitimate endeavor to reinvestigate and reinterpret Scripture but not to set aside its divine authority.[14]

Finally, Broadus's Reformed doctrines denote a feature of his conservative orthodoxy that sheds light on a relatively recent controversy in the Southern Baptist Convention. Broadus and his early colleagues at Southern Seminary openly identified themselves as Calvinists. In fact, they all signed off on an Abstract of Principles, which was principally prepared by Basil Manly Jr. and which upheld a robust view of divine providence, single predestination, a "corrupt" Adamic sin nature, monogeristic salvation, and perseverance of the saints.[15] While the Abstract diverges from Dordtian five-point Calvinism, it is well within the orbit of the classical Reformed tradition.

Even though Broadus never really donned the mantle of a systematic theologian, he postulated a distinct line of continuity that ran from Paul through Augustine to Calvin. The Southern Seminary professor, moreover, often expressed genuine admiration for the Geneva Reformer's preaching and commentaries: "Calvin gave the ablest, soundest, clearest expositions of Scripture that had been seen for a thousand years, and most of the other great Reformers worked in the same direction."[16] During an 1891 trip to Europe, which included a stop in Geneva, Broadus paid homage to Calvin's historical stature in a piece for the *Western Recorder*: "The people who sneer at what is called Calvinism might as well sneer at Mont Blanc."[17] Broadus's words of praise did not preclude criticism of some of Calvin's thought and actions, but his overall assessment certainly flowed in an affirmative direction.

What Broadus and the other original faculty at Southern Seminary in essence bequeathed to later generations of Baptists was an evangelical Calvinism that suitably balanced God's controlling hand in human history with an urgent sense of proclaiming

---

[14] Broadus, *Paramount and Permanent*, 13.
[15] "Abstract of Principles," [1858] in Mueller, *A History*, 238–41. On Manly's role, see ibid., 14.
[16] See Broadus, *Lectures*, 81 and 115.
[17] Broadus, quoted in Robertson, *Life and Letters*, 396.

the gospel to the lost. In one of Broadus's transcribed messages, he maintained that "concern for the salvation of others is not prevented by a belief in what we call the doctrines of grace; it is not prevented by believing in divine sovereignty, and predestination and election."[18] The preacher went on to connect these doctrines to the apostle Paul, who ardently held to election yet also uttered the jarring offer that he might be accursed if such an act would lead to the salvation of his fellow Jews (Rom 9:3).

Broadus, without necessarily endorsing a full-fledged Calvinism, still defended against the charge that a Reformed viewpoint caused complacency toward the lost: "Now, I say that whatever be true, for or against the apostle's doctrines of predestination and divine sovereignty in salvation, it is not true that they will make a man careless as to his own salvation or that of others."[19] Since the contemporary debate over Calvinism in the Southern Baptist Convention rarely invokes historical depth or nuance, a fresh glance at the outlook of denominational pioneers like Broadus might help to diffuse some of the tension surrounding this theological battleground.[20] It could also serve as a reminder that Broadus and his colleagues stood in continuity with the evangelical Calvinism of English Baptists like Andrew Fuller, William Carey, and Charles Spurgeon.

Overall, Broadus's conservative orthodoxy encompassed a full acceptance of the inspiration and authority of Scripture, a sharp awareness of the interpretive issues in biblical studies, a seasoned historical intuition, a thorough supernaturalism, and a moderately Reformed theological perspective. While all these elements did not constitute a tidy package of systematic

[18] Broadus, "Intense Concern for the Salvation of Others," in *Sermons and Addresses* (Baltimore: H. M. Wharton, 1886; reprint, Nashville: Sunday School Board of the Southern Baptist Convention, n.d.), 116–18. The precise context for this message is not indicated in this collection.

[19] Ibid.

[20] The dialogue between seminary presidents Albert Mohler (Southern) and Paige Patterson (Southwestern) at the 2006 SBC meeting in Greensboro, NC, represents a more encouraging turn in this controversy. See Michael Foust, "Patterson, Mohler: Calvinism Shouldn't Divide Southern Baptists," SBC.NET press release posted 13 June 2006; available from http://www.sbcannualmeeting.net/sbc/newsroom/newspage.asp?ID=21; Internet; accessed 13 June 2006.

theology, it might be too much to demand from a scholarly practitioner whose main fields were homiletics and New Testament interpretation. Even so, his resolute commitment to the apostolic faith and its historic expressions provided the indispensable resources that he needed for his roles as denominational leader and theological educator.

Denominational Servant and Statesman

John Broadus adeptly complemented his service to Southern Seminary, which is discussed in the next section of this essay, with several other noteworthy denominational undertakings. During the period from the commencement of his public ministry in the early 1850s until his death in 1895, it is unlikely that any other figure in Southern Baptist life compiled as lengthy a register of denominational activity as Broadus. In all his endeavors, he toiled diligently to bring vitality, peace, and stability to his beloved Southern Baptist Convention, which was experiencing the normal growing pains of a youthful entity.

In 1851, Broadus launched his ministerial career in the shadows of his college alma mater, the University of Virginia, when he assumed the pastorate of Charlottesville Baptist Church. The young preacher continued to lead this congregation—with a two-year leave of absence when he served the university as chaplain—until Southern Seminary opened in 1859. His parishioners included future missionary Lottie Moon and eventual colleague Crawford Toy, both of whom Broadus baptized. Overall, the Charlottesville church enjoyed revival and marked growth during Broadus's tenure. The busy pastor, however, was not satisfied to confine his ministry to one locale. In addition, he (1) helped to establish the Albemarle Female Institute, where he also sat as a trustee; (2) became heavily involved with committee work in the Albemarle Baptist Association and chaired its Board of Colportage; (3) participated in the work of several boards of the Baptist General Association of Virginia, including a stint as president of the state Foreign Mission Board;

and (4) initially started his relationship with what became The Southern Baptist Theological Seminary through his service on the Board of Education of Virginia Baptists.[21] Clearly the rising preacher put a high premium on involvement in Baptist work beyond the level of the local church.

While Broadus joined the original Southern Seminary faculty in 1859, the outbreak of the Civil War in 1861 brought disruption and made it impossible to hold normal academic sessions by 1862. Professor Broadus found additional denominational outlets with which to occupy his time during the war years. Although he was not technically a chaplain in the Confederate army, Broadus consented—at the request of General Stonewall Jackson—to preach to the troops on several occasions. In particular, he joined an interdenominational camp ministry effort in the summer of 1863 that evangelized the soldiers and led to what William Earl Brown has referred to as a "church in exile" for those separated from their home churches by the hostilities.[22] Furthermore, Broadus and Basil Manly Jr. organized the first Sunday School Board for Southern Baptists in 1863, and the former was the only paid (part-time) officer between 1863 and 1866. Broadus also penned many articles for the Board's publication known as *Kind Words for Sunday School Children*.[23] Throughout the war era Broadus continued to model a sacrificial approach to denominational activity; he likewise helped to chart new territory for Southern Baptists in matters relating to both the military chaplaincy and Christian education.

---

[21] For good overview of the Charlottesville years, see Barron, "The Contributions," 26–41.

[22] William Earl Brown, "Pastoral Evangelism: A Model for Effective Evangelism as Demonstrated by the Ministries of John Albert Broadus, Alfred Elijah Dickinson, and John William Jones in the Revival of the Army of Northern Virginia in 1863" (Ph.D. diss., Southeastern Baptist Theological Seminary, 1999), chap. 2, 4, and 5 passim.

[23] See Barron, "The Contributions," 189–96; and Mueller, *A History*, 66. What eventually became "Broadman" Press under the second Sunday School Board represented a conflation of the names Broadus and Manly, the early pioneers. The moniker continues today as "Broadman & Holman" (a.k.a. B&H Publishing Group) under LifeWay Christian Resources.

After the Civil War, when he returned to full-time duties at Southern Seminary, Broadus constantly maintained a high degree of participation in denominational life. At the state level he served a one-year term as president of the South Carolina Baptist Convention; and, after Southern Seminary moved from Greenville to Louisville in 1877, he was actively engaged with the General Association of Baptists in Kentucky. In the Southern Baptist Convention, Broadus sought to reduce conflict between the denomination's Home Mission Board and the American Baptist Home Mission Society, which was primarily a northern agency. In 1879, the seminary professor introduced a resolution at the annual meeting of Southern Baptists in Atlanta that encouraged cooperation with Baptists in the North yet clearly declared that Southern Baptists would retain separate denominational organizations. In essence, this action saved the Home Mission Board, which at that point was not doing well in direct competition with the American Baptist Home Mission Society. Apparently Broadus's goal was not to antagonize Northern Baptists—he often did supply preaching in their churches—but to strengthen Southern Baptists at a time when war and reconstruction had taken its toll.[24]

Unlike his seminary collaborator James Boyce, Broadus never attained the presidency of the Southern Baptist Convention. At the same time he capably assisted the young denomination in establishing its identity and institutions during a formative period of its history. The immense respect that Broadus had earned in Southern Baptist circles perhaps became most evident at the Birmingham convention in 1891. In that context the Convention deliberated on a recommendation to establish a new Sunday School Board; previous efforts in this strategic area had not survived much beyond the Civil War, and the Home Mission Board had subsequently assumed a limited role in publishing educational materials. J. M. Frost of Virginia enthusiastically promoted the notion of a new Sunday School Board but faced

---

[24] On these state convention and SBC activities, see Barron, "The Contributions," 197–212.

a major opponent in the person of J. B. Gambrell of Mississippi. Gambrell, editor of the *Baptist Record*, was a paid agent of the American Baptist Publication Society, a largely northern body. At a tense moment in the debate, Broadus took the floor on behalf of the proposed board. One admiring observer painted the scene in dramatic terms: "It was a brief but passionate appeal for peace. The great throng bowed to his will. The spirit of controversy was muzzled. . . . He had saved the South."[25] Hyperbole aside, Broadus certainly was a major contributor to the birth of one of the SBC's foremost agencies. In this case, he combined his oratorical expertise with a great love for the denomination to help bring about a favorable outcome.

John R. Sampey, a Southern Seminary faculty member who also served as president from 1929 to 1942, once set forth a perceptive analysis of Broadus's success as a denominational statesman: "Plain and uneducated men could understand him, and they came to trust him as a safe leader. He was aware of the weaknesses in our ultra-democratic denominational life, but he believed in our Baptist doctrines and polity."[26] In other words, Broadus could communicate skillfully, but he also had something substantive to say that was rooted in an unwavering commitment to Baptist distinctives. This provided a steady foundation for his denominational service.

At the Indianapolis meeting of the American Baptist Publication Society in 1881, Broadus reminded the delegates of their solemn responsibility to teach the principles and beliefs that set Baptists apart from other Christian groups. He began by enumerating his understanding of the distinctive views of Baptists, including (1) biblical authority, (2) regenerate church membership, (3) believer's baptism and a memorial view of

---

[25] J. H. Farmer, quoted in Robertson, *Life and Letters*, 394. On Broadus and the second SSB, see also Barron, "The Contributions," 202–7.

[26] John R. Sampey, "John A. Broadus: The Representative Baptist," *Florida Baptist Witness* (24 August 1933): 5. Even a prominent Landmarker commended Broadus for teaching "sound Baptist doctrine" to his students. See Ben M. Bogard, *Pillars of Orthodoxy, or Defenders of the Faith* (Louisville: Baptist Book Concern, 1900), 313.

the Lord's Supper, (4) and the independency and autonomy of local churches.[27] He then proceeded to detail reasons Baptists needed to teach their distinctives as he emphasized duties to themselves, other Christian believers, an unbelieving world, and Christ.[28] Finally, the professor-preacher addressed the issue of *how* Baptists should teach their distinctives; he counseled, among other things, godly living, an irenic approach to non-Baptists, and a unity among Baptists that would be marked by freedom, forbearance, and patience.[29] In a foreshadowing of Sampey's judgment, Broadus also stressed the need for Baptist preachers to communicate effectively about controversial subjects: "The highest function of scholarship in preaching is to take assured results and make them plain to the general understanding, and certain thorough evidence which the unlearned can appreciate."[30] Above all, Broadus's Indianapolis message strongly assumed that a charitable spirit and firm convictions were fully compatible.

In the early twenty-first century, many ecclesiastical pundits have surmised that we live in a postdenominational age. We do not hear much about Baptist distinctives in our churches, and it is likely that many Baptists would have a difficult time articulating how their views on doctrine and polity differ from those of other traditions. If this is indeed the case, the Broadus legacy may well point to some needed correctives if Baptist identity is to claim any meaningful space in the postmodern religious landscape. John Broadus functioned as an esteemed denominational servant and statesman in large measure because he understood and appreciated what made Baptists unique. His beliefs,

---

[27] Broadus, *The Duty of Baptists to Teach Their Distinctive Views* (Philadelphia: American Baptist Publication Society, 1881), 2–5. This and succeeding page citations are from the PDF format of this booklet available from http://www.BaptistTheology.org; Internet. In this address, Broadus appears to be somewhat indifferent regarding the proper mode of baptism. See Broadus, *Immersion Essential to Christian Baptism* (Philadelphia: American Baptist Publication Society, 1892), 66, where he stated that "there is no baptism where there is not an immersion."

[28] Broadus, *The Duty*, 5–8.

[29] Ibid., 8–13.

[30] Ibid., 11.

in fact, profoundly energized his broad-ranging involvement in Southern Baptist life.

Theological Educator

Over three decades of service as professor and administrator at The Southern Baptist Theological Seminary encompassed the real heart of Broadus's contributions to Baptist life, thought, and identity. His relationship with the school actually began, as noted above, through his membership on the Education Board of the Baptist state convention in Virginia during the 1850s. As early as 1854, this board reopened the question of theological education in the Southern Baptist Convention, which had been investigated on a limited scale before by leaders like Basil Manly Sr. and his namesake son. In turn, Virginia Baptists received a report from its Education Board in 1855. In the meantime, a series of educational conventions in other parts of the South and James P. Boyce's lobbying efforts in South Carolina indicated that seminary training was a Southern Baptist Convention-wide interest. By 1857 an educational convention in Louisville approved the establishment of a theological institution in South Carolina, and Boyce was requested to commence raising money for the project. Later that year the Committee on Plan of Organization for the Southern Baptist Convention, which consisted of Boyce, Broadus, and Manly Jr., developed a curriculum design and doctrinal standards that were approved in 1858 by an educational convention in Greenville, South Carolina.[31]

While Manly Jr. bore primary responsibility for the Abstract of Principles, Broadus prepared the curricular plan for the new seminary. Three key factors exercised considerable influence on Broadus as he organized the curriculum and a plan of instruction. First, he knew well that most Southern Baptist preachers were unlearned and that many of their constituents shared deep suspicions about theological—or even general—education.

---

[31] For background information on the founding of SBTS, see Barron, "The Contributions," 42–51; and Mueller, *A History*, 6–14.

Since he comprehended the pressing leadership needs of Southern Baptist churches, he shared Boyce's aspiration to provide theological training for those who had not completed or even attended college. Boyce, who closely followed Francis Wayland of Brown University in this regard, formally expressed his vision for expanded educational opportunities while a professor at Furman University in 1856.[32]

Second, the elective system at the University of Virginia had made a tremendously favorable impression on Broadus during his student days, and he convinced Boyce and Manly about its virtues. In a letter that he wrote in 1857, Broadus obviously saw a program based on electives as a way to avoid the uniformity that stamped Protestant theological education in the mid-nineteenth century: "In this way too, we may in some measure counteract the tendency to formalism, to making men all on one pattern, which has so commonly characterized the theological seminaries of the country."[33] He later voiced his ongoing concerns about educational homogeneity in an 1881 address to the Missouri Baptist Educational Society, where he protested "artificial" notions of education and "mechanical" processes that worked against "a process of growth and the training of a living thing."[34]

Finally, Broadus realized that the elective system had to be coupled with comprehensive instruction in the English Bible, especially if the needs of students with weaker educational backgrounds were to be met. Hence, students who were not ready or inclined to pursue Greek and Hebrew would still receive biblical training to support their preaching. The core requirements in English Bible, moreover, meant that there was some curricular consistency because all students who sought a diploma had to fulfill them. The emphasis on English Bible represented, as

---

[32] Mueller, *A History*, 21–26. On the broader context of Baptists and education, see ibid., 3–4.

[33] Broadus to Cornelia Taliaferro, 28 July 1857, quoted in Robertson, *Life and Letters*, 145.

[34] Broadus, "Ministerial Education," in *Sermons and Addresses*, 208–9.

University of Chicago president William Rainey Harper noted, an innovative turn in theological education.[35]

In his dissertation on Broadus, James Barron fittingly suggested that the original plan of instruction for The Southern Baptist Theological Seminary served "the democratic individualism of the Baptist ministry" of that day.[36] After it had been in place for several years, Broadus himself seemed to extol that very feature of the curriculum:

> Men do that for which they have preparation, turn of mind, and time or patience; and get credit for exactly what they do. Every year some men come for a single session, and are led to complete an English [course] or a full course. . . . Here, as in the New Testament form of Church Government, the benefits of freedom far outweigh its inconveniences. The free choice of studies, provided for by James P. Boyce and his associates, has shown itself thoroughly adequate to furnish theological education for students of very diverse grades as to preparation, all in the same institution, and for the most part in the same classes.[37]

At the same time this flexible plan seemingly made it difficult to finish a degree, encouraged excessively long examinations, and created other logistical problems that eventually forced the seminary to make curricular changes.[38] All the same Broadus gained appropriate recognition as the primary architect of Southern Seminary's program of study.

The Southern Baptist Theological Seminary was ready to open in 1859 with a curriculum, doctrinal statement, and the appointment of Professor William Williams to join Boyce, Broadus, and Manly Jr. as the initial faculty members. War and financial shortfalls first brought interruption of classes between

---

[35] Mueller, *A History*, 114. Harper was still a professor at Yale Divinity School when he made his comments.

[36] Barron, "The Contributions," 228.

[37] Broadus, *Memoir of James Petigru Boyce*, 160–61.

[38] Mueller, *A History*, 115–18.

1862 and 1865, and then a move from Greenville, South Carolina, to Louisville, Kentucky, in 1877. In both locations Broadus honed his classroom and administrative skills to such an extent that his impact during the institution's early period was equaled only by Boyce. In fact, despite their differences on governance issues, they fashioned a formidable team that seminary historian Mueller described by labeling Boyce as "the head" and Broadus as "the heart."[39] It is startling to consider that both men were 32 when the school held its first classes.

The ministry of Broadus in the classroom arguably constitutes the greatest part of his legacy in theological education. Teaching a range of New Testament and homiletics courses, many of which had sizable enrollments, he conscientiously mentored a host of students who in due course pastored churches or took faculty positions in Baptist institutions of higher learning. In particular, he directly influenced several soon-to-be professors at the seminary, including son-in-law and biblical scholar, A. T. Robertson, church historian William Whitsitt, Old Testament specialist and future president John Sampey, and missiologist W. O. Carver. Then, of course, he touched many through his classic text *A Treatise on the Preparation and Delivery of Sermons*, which had its origins in an unusual classroom setting—Broadus and one blind homiletics student.[40]

Numerous testimonials speak to Broadus's diligent class preparation, inspiring lectures, and ability to blend scholarship with spiritual admonition. At the Southern Seminary's Founder's Day program in 1930, W. J. McGlothlin proclaimed that his former professor and colleague was "without peer" as an instructor. The Furman University president then captured some of the energy and charismatic presence that typified a Broadus classroom: "Electric with intellectual power and alertness, filled

---

[39] Ibid., 61. On their tensions over the role of the faculty in governance, see ibid., 50.

[40] Dockery, "The Broadus-Robertson Tradition," 96. See Broadus, *A Treatise on the Preparation and Delivery of Sermons* (Philadelphia: Smith, English, 1870) for the original edition. On students that Broadus affected, see Mueller, *A History*, see chap. 4–7 and 9 passim.

with a profound practical wisdom that was Socratic in its reach and penetration, often glowing with an ardent devoutness that moved students to tears."[41]

Broadus also sought to cultivate high standards in his students and often expressed impatience at those whom he felt did not measure up in terms of work ethic or quality of performance. Mueller acknowledged that the revered teacher "could be stern in his reproofs and sometimes even cruelly sarcastic" although he was just as likely to offer an apology when that happened.[42] So the human dimension of Broadus no doubt enhanced his value as a classroom communicator. Furthermore, he never expected any more of his students than he was unable to shoulder himself. In short, Broadus offered a worthy model for several generations of college and seminary professors.

In light of all his other achievements at Southern Seminary, it is easy to forget that Broadus served as president from early 1889, shortly after the death of Boyce, until his own death in 1895. The loss of Boyce, his "true yokefellow," deeply grieved him.[43] The seminary's second president, however, brought to the helm a greater disposition than his predecessor to implement the "faculty method" of administration. Broadus's managerial style and approach consequently appeared to be collegial and even low key. F. H. Kerfoot, who was seminary treasurer and also a professor under Broadus's leadership, described it this way: "It is safe to say that no president ever protruded his presidency less than did Dr. Broadus."[44]

Although Broadus was the president of Southern Seminary during his twilight years, he still directed the school's progress in meaningful ways. Before he became president, when institutional survival was in doubt, he had already gained experience in fund-raising; thus it is not surprising that during his presidency the seminary became debt-free and the first Norton Hall

---

[41] W. J. McGlothlin, "John Albert Broadus," *Review and Expositor* 27 (April 1930): 162 and 164.

[42] Mueller, *A History*, 83.

[43] Broadus, *Memoir of James Petigru Boyce*, 371.

[44] F. H. Kerfoot, "As Seminary President" in "Broadus Memorial," 385.

was constructed. Enrollment grew to 267 students, whereas in the 1889–90 academic year it had been 164. Broadus, who earlier had worked on a curriculum for graduate studies, helped to launch a Doctor of Theology program in 1892; the first Th.D. recipients graduated in 1894.[45] In many ways, his death the following year closed off a distinct and exhilarating era in the history of Southern Seminary.

Broadus's career at the seminary revealed a professor, curriculum designer, and institutional leader who understood his calling and resolutely persevered in it. Offers to become president at other schools failed to distract him from his chosen path of service.[46] Just as he contributed to the identity of the Southern Baptist Convention and Baptists in general, he helped to shape the culture of The Southern Baptist Theological Seminary with its unique traditions. Along with James Boyce, Broadus best personified what Southern Seminary was all about for the last four decades of the nineteenth century.

Conclusion

Thomas Armitage, a nineteenth-century Baptist historian and pastor, published *A History of the Baptists* in 1887 that featured an embossed image of John Broadus on the cover.[47] Evidently Broadus had come to symbolize the Baptists of his time in a way that transcended the boundaries of the Southern Baptist Convention (or even of Baptists in America). In addition to his pulpit ministry, he distinguished himself through his staunch defense of biblical orthodoxy, his many areas of denominational service in the Southern Baptist Convention, and his devoted

---

[45] Barron, "The Contributions," 81–88. For the 1889–90 enrollment figure, see Mueller, *A History*, 47.

[46] For examples of such invitations, see Robertson, *Life and Letters*, 282.

[47] Thomas Armitage, *A History of Baptists: Traced by Their Vital Principles and Practices: From the Time of Our Lord and Saviour Jesus Christ to the Year 1886* (New York: Bryan, Taylor, 1887). I learned of the cover from the anonymous "A Baptist Page Portrait John A. Broadus"; available from http://www.siteone.com/religion/baptist/baptistpage/Portraits/broadus.htm; Internet; accessed 3 May 2006. This information was confirmed for me by Bill Sumners of the SBHLA.

labors at The Southern Baptist Theological Seminary. Indeed Broadus was one of the most visible and well-known Baptists of the nineteenth century, and his life deserves a modern, critical biography.

While historians rightly caution against using history to discover "lessons" or to crown "heroes," the achievements of Broadus point to a rightful legacy that speaks of many of the issues in Baptist life and thought today. As long as it is recognized that Broadus's historical context differed significantly from ours, and that he was a real man who displayed both strengths and weaknesses, then it is legitimate to assess his continuing relevance. Baptists of the twenty-first century need to know about a pivotal leader who so consistently represented some of the best characteristics of their denominational tradition.

Name Index